The Gospel according to Harry Potter

Revised and Expanded Edition

The Spiritual Journey
of the World's Greatest Seeker

Connie Neal

Westminster John Knox Press
LOUISVILLE • LONDON

Book design by Sharon Adams
Cover design by designpointinc.com

First edition
Published by Westminster John Knox Press
Louisville, Kentucky

This book is printed on acid-free paper that meets the American National Standards Institute Z39.48 standard. ∞

PRINTED IN THE UNITED STATES OF AMERICA

08 09 10 11 12 13 14 15 16 17 — 10 9 8 7 6 5 4 3 2 1

Library of Congress Cataloging-in-Publication Data

Neal, C. W. (Connie W.)
        The Gospel according to Harry Potter : the spiritual journey of the world's greatest seeker / Connie Neal.— Rev. and expanded ed.
        p. cm.
        ISBN 978-0-664-23123-1 (alk. paper)
    1. Rowling, J. K.—Religion. 2. Children—Books and reading—English-speaking countries. 3. Christian fiction, English—History and criticism. 4. Children's stories, English—History and criticism. 5. Fantasy fiction, English—History and criticism. 6. Rowling, J. K.—Characters—Harry Potter. 7. Potter, Harry (Fictitious character) 8. Spirituality in literature. 9. Religion in literature. I. Title.

        PR6068.O93Z78 2008
        823.914—dc22

                                                                2007050330

For those who have eyes to see

Contents

Introduction to the Revised and Expanded Edition

I write as one privileged to be among those to whom J. K. Rowling addressed the seventh part of the dedication of the seventh book. She wrote, "to you, if you have stuck with Harry until the very end." This describes those of us who had the privilege of experiencing a unique literary journey shared around the globe. We had to read and wait, and think and discuss—and sometimes argue in Harry's defense—and read and wait, book by book by book. We are the only generation who will have experienced each novel as mystery after mystery, unfolding ever so slowly. The final revelations at the conclusion of Book Seven vindicated Harry's defenders with obvious parallels to the Christian gospel, while the vehement and volatile attackers dropped their stones—one by one—and quietly withdrew.

Never before in the history of the world and literary experience have so many been united as a human family—despite differences in age, gender, ethnicity, culture, politics, nationality, or religion—by a series of books read globally and simultaneously in 65 languages. Yet, as often before in literary history, these books have also been maligned and misunderstood, banned and burned. In this experience and the world's unprecedented response to Harry Potter we have learned much, even apart from what we learned in the stories themselves. Those who go back to the stories and let them speak for themselves will find that there is still much to learn.

However, some refused to let the books speak for themselves, insisting on imposing a sinister (and supposed) intentional scheme to lead readers into real-world witchcraft and occult practices. In my attempt to remove the stories from the shadows cast over them by those who slandered and superimposed a dark purpose, I used a curious tool. The tool I chose—after reasoned argument seemed not to work—was to align the stories with allegorical meanings drawn from the Bible and Christianity (the basis from which most who assailed the stories took their stand). My original intent was to demonstrate that one could find as much of Christianity as witchcraft in the novels if one had eyes to see, and was determined to do so. This is in keeping with something noted by C. S. Lewis in his 1958 book *Reflections on the Psalms:*

> As we know, almost anything can be read into any book if you are determined enough. This will be impressed on anyone who has written fantastic fiction. He will find reviewers, both favourable and hostile, reading into his stories all manner of allegorical meanings which he never intended. (Some of the allegories thus imposed on my own books have been so ingenious and interesting that I have often wished I had thought of them myself.) Apparently it is impossible for the wit of man to devise a narrative that the wit of some other man cannot, and with some plausibility, find a hidden sense.[1]

From the start, I stated clearly that I did *not* think the author was setting out to cleverly disguise Christian evangelism amid tales set in a school of witchcraft and wizardry. She confirmed this in a 2007 *Time* magazine interview:

> "At least as much as they've been attacked from a theological point of view," she says, the books "have been lauded and taken into pulpit, and most interesting and satisfying for me, it's been by several different faiths." The values in the books, she observes, are by no means exclusively Christian, and she is wary of appearing to promote one faith over another rather than inviting people to explore and struggle with the hard questions.
>   Rowling's religious agenda is very clear: she does not have one. "I did not set out to convert anyone to Christianity. I wasn't trying to do what C. S. Lewis did."[2]

However, it was still necessary when I began writing this book to quell the condemnation from some Christians. I chose to do so by pointing out Christian themes in the stories along with universal themes of goodness. There were clear traces of biblical story lines and character development, so much so that my early published conjecture about the direction the stories would take—based on my understanding of Judeo-Christian themes—turned out to be strikingly accurate. This may be because the author's own Christian faith infused the stories even though that was not her intention or because, being set within historic British mythology and folklore, the symbols resonated with Judeo-Christian imagery. Or it may just be that in my determination to defend Harry against what I considered ill-founded attacks by my fellow Christians I was able to—as C. S. Lewis wrote—"with some plausibility, find a hidden sense" therein.

Something wonderful happened as we "stuck with Harry until the very end"—over the better part of a decade. With changing attitudes there was less of a need to be defensive; therefore, this book took on a different purpose, and I discovered greater value in the exercise than anticipated. I finished the first half of this book in 2003, after Book Four had been published but before Book Five. The conclusion of Book Four left readers hanging on the verge of war, with Voldemort having returned to human form and all wondering how the wizarding world would bear the threat and recover from the seeming triumph of darkness. I wrote the concluding half of this book in 2007, after the series was complete and all the mysteries revealed. I chose to leave the first half as it was originally published because it will let generations to come capture the tension, controversy, and suspenseful progression we in the original audience experienced along our unique literary journey. I was relieved to find that my projections, based on Christian themes, held up in the end and did not need to be changed.

The changing literary climate caused a shift in my perceived audience and my relationship to them (and to you). The value of the themes of the Harry Potter stories themselves took on greater credence, and the need to defend against anti–Harry Potter arguments diminished. You may detect this in the tone of the writing as it changes from the first half to the concluding half of this book.

Something else wonderful happened among those of us "who stuck with Harry to the very end." We became united by our shared love of the stories and the values espoused. As Harry brought us together, we experienced the joys of overcoming bigotry even among ourselves and our various factions. I spoke at *Prophecy 2007: From Hero to Legend,* an academic Harry Potter symposium that brought together over 1,500 devotees of Harry Potter from around the world. I was part of a keynote panel on the canon of Harry Potter and gave an address on "Harry's Hero's Journey within His Stories and in Our World." In that address I depicted some of the vitriol hurled at the books early on and related some of the Christian themes I delineate in this book, especially those found in the finale. Afterward, during the question and answer session, the first woman to the microphone introduced herself as an atheist. She asked, "Do you think someone like me—who has never had any interest in the Bible or Christianity—needs to know something of the Bible and Christian themes in order to fully grasp the depth of the Harry Potter canon?" "Yes, perhaps," I replied. "At least having a Christian perspective would enrich one's grasp of the stories and stimulate depth of conversation." To my own surprise, what began as one kind of literary exercise developed into another. In sharing a distinctly Christian perspective, as it can be aligned with the stories, I found much to offer those who come from other faiths or no faith at all—this in addition to proving my original point.

So I hope this volume is of value to several audiences: those who love the Harry Potter stories (of any faith or no faith) who want to look at them again from another perspective and in light of the Bible; Christians who were told to beware of these stories, in the hope that they may find themselves enriched spiritually; those who are called upon to defend Harry against attacks from those who deem these stories evil—librarians, preachers, and laypeople alike. I hope this last part of the audience dwindles as more and more people find that which is truly good in these modern-day mythic fairy tales. To all, I hope the power of the biblical themes enriches your understanding of the Harry Potter stories, of the battle of good against evil, and of the idea that love among all people is the most powerful force for good. Just love? Yes, just love.

Introduction to the First Edition

As I write this, I am in my yard on a bright spring day. Overhead, a host of white clouds decorate a brilliant blue sky. On days like this I long to let my gaze linger to see if I can make out shapes in the clouds. This was one of my most pleasant childhood pastimes, as I suppose it has been for children throughout the ages, regardless of their culture. When my children were little, watching clouds together was a fun way to get them to stay still and hear what was on their minds. Even now that they are in their tween and teen stages, we enjoy looking at clouds on days like this, calling out to each other, "Oh look, can you see the horse?" or, "Yeah, and if you wait a minute it may have a chariot. See those clouds moving in behind it?" or, "I see a castle over there." Actually, those are comments typical of my daughters and me; my son will usually add something like, "Look! A frog with a Popsicle!" Sometimes we go on to form a narrative to tie the cloud pictures together.

This is a simple way of using our God-given imagination. I consider the irresistible urge to do so, and the joy such exercises give us, a unique stamp of being human, made in the image of God—the ultimate Creator and Storyteller. Of course, these flights of fantasy don't mean that my children and I don't know what clouds really are; in first grade, each of my children learned about the water cycle. Our power to see what the clouds might represent to us doesn't deny reality, it takes us higher. Our ability to find a cloud horse and chariot and have it carry us on to the telling of a story is one of the joys of being human and an indication that we are unique in all of creation.

On a more sophisticated level, reading and discussing fantasy, fairy tales, folklore, mythology, and legends holds similar enjoyment. Not only can we enjoy the story itself, we can go on to share what it means to us, what it reminds us of, and what that makes us think about in other stories and in real life. Such has been a treasured part of my family life. My husband and I have spent much time reading aloud with our children and discussing the stories we read. The outcome has been that we are raising avid readers and youngsters who can think both creatively and critically.

As Christians who take passing on our faith very seriously, our reading is always built on the foundation of the Bible as our standard of absolute truth; stories are discussed in relation to what the Bible teaches. However, we do not discourage reading fantasy just because it is fantasy, as long as we make sure our children have made the proper distinctions between fantasy and reality. We often use discussions that began with a fantasy story to lead into themes in the Bible, but our children are not confused into thinking that the Bible is to be treated as fantasy.

Then along came Harry Potter, and the Christian community became embroiled in heated debate between those asserting that the Harry Potter books were a veiled attempt to popularize occult practices, and those Christians (along with most of the rest of the world) who saw the stories as fantasy, following the age-old traditions of classic children's literature. I see how both sides can see it as they do, and I have tried to help both sides understand and be respectful of those with opposing convictions. This book is not meant to delve into that argument. (For more on this, see my previous book, *What's a Christian to Do with Harry Potter?* [Waterbrook Press, 2001].)

This book began as a counterpoint to one idea being put forward by anti-Potter critics, that just because they can look into the Harry Potter books in an attempt to find things they can correlate to real-world occult practices—and find some—that proves the Harry Potter books are about witchcraft. I disagree with that idea. This book is the friendliest way I could think of to ask people to stop and think about that again.

Let me give you an example. While publicly discussing my previous book, I encountered several people voicing beliefs along these lines: *I know all about the occult and real witchcraft. I went into Harry Potter looking to see if that is in these books and I found it.* One man counted sixty-four specific aspects of real-world witchcraft that correlate to something he found in Harry Potter. Since he was very familiar with real occult practices and knew far more about that than I know—or care to know—I take him at his word. I don't dispute what he saw there or the meaning it has come to carry for him.

However, it is the conclusion to such findings I want people to think about a little further. The conclusions are like this: *Since I have seen for myself that there are occult aspects to Harry Potter, I believe that Harry Potter popularizes, promotes, or perhaps intentionally hides real witchcraft and occult rituals. And I will not be dissuaded from this belief, regardless of what you show me to the contrary.* These conclusions take precedence over repeated denials by the author, because *they have seen it for themselves.*

To enter such an argument from this starting point usually results in hearing a laundry list of real occult practices that bear some resemblance to those referred to in Harry Potter, or more in-depth explanations of real-world witchcraft (which I am opposed to myself on biblical grounds, but don't care to be schooled in), or in simple name-calling. My response has been not to enter such arguments. Since the parties use different definitions, different forms of literary criticism, and different sources, the arguments are futile even when both parties believe the Bible. This book was prompted and shaped by this debate, although its content has far more to offer the reader.

My premise raises this question: What if I can use the same techniques of interpretation and selective reading, but look for the Christian gospel in the Harry Potter books? If I am able to find numerous parallels, would that prove that is what Harry Potter is about? (No.) Or might that reveal that the author has secretly hidden the gospel in her stories and is using witchcraft and wizardry as a disguise so unsuspecting children will not catch on? (No.) If, by using the same techniques, groups can find both the occult and Christian teachings in a fantasy story, what does that prove? I think it proves a point J. K. Rowling made.

When *Today* show host Katie Couric asked J. K. Rowling about accusations that she was using Harry Potter to lure children into Satanism, she flatly denied it. She said, "People tend to find in books what they look to find." That is my point. Some people go looking for the occult, and if they are well informed with regard to real-world witchcraft and occult rituals they may see that in the books. There are indeed points of similarity for readers who do not make a clear distinction between these fantasy stories and real life. They can then go on to fill that cloudy chariot with meaning and then to share that meaning with others. Indeed, they can point to specific parts of the books and say, "See!" and people can make out those shapes with their help. Such things are there to see and are worthy of discussion, but that does not mean that they are the only clouds in the sky.

Some may want to know my motivation. Given the divisive nature of this controversy, I have been misunderstood and denounced by all sides, Christians and non-Christians. Harry Potter fans assume that I am against Harry because I am a Christian, and Christian critics object to my using Harry Potter to spark spiritual discussions relating to the Bible. If you are not interested in this controversy, please skip ahead, but for those who care to know, here is a brief reply to the question *How could you?* Or for some, *Why bother?*

My most basic motivation is one I have held since January 31, 1973, when the story of God's love revealed in Jesus Christ suddenly became real to me. Since then, I have endeavored to communicate the Bible message in fresh ways so that those who have never really heard it can apprehend it. These motives are not ulterior. I ran across a mention of me and my previous book at the Wicca and Witchcraft News Web site. I was relieved to see that the article was titled, "Harry Potter Perverted to Preach Christ," and I took it as a backhanded compliment. I would have been troubled if they endorsed my Christian book. However, I took issue with their comment that I have "ulterior motives" in seeking to preach the gospel. Anyone who knows me knows that my life has been devoted to sharing the gospel, and I am not ashamed of that. So my motives are out in the open. The stunning story told in the Gospels has as much and more to offer than Harry's story, so I hope you will be open to hear it, perhaps for the first time.

The method of using something familiar to the culture to relate unfamiliar spiritual truth has been used by Christians back to the time of Christ, and by Jesus himself, even though it is guaranteed to cause raised eyebrows among some religious folks. Martin Luther did it when he used the familiar tunes of beer hall ballads to compose hymns. Jesus did it when he dared to make the hated Samaritan sinner the hero of one of his stories. The term "Good Samaritan" was an oxymoron to his audience. Therefore, I can confidently use this technique to communicate effectively with my culture too.

This technique is not something I devised when Harry Potter came along. I practiced this when I was a youth pastor and made a game of it with my own children. Once I had taught them the basic tenets from the Bible, I would have my kids (those in my youth group and later my own children) look at everything in our culture to see if they could find "glimmers of the gospel" by relating one to the other. Surprisingly, Harry Potter has more useful parallels to the gospel than almost any other piece of popular literature I have seen in decades.

I am alarmed that anti-Harry Potter sentiment has sparked book burnings by Christians. These have attracted media attention, and rightfully so, since the works being burned have expanded to include even Shakespeare, and many of those burning them have never read what they are burning. Even though this is an extreme and unusual occurrence, it has become almost the only mention of Christians with relation to Harry Potter. Almost no attention has been given to the many Christian leaders and educators who take a different view of Harry Potter, see both sides, enjoy, and/or recommend the Harry Potter books. I hope the media will use the discussion sparked by this book to counter some of the commotion and heightened emotion stirred up when they selectively report book burnings to the neglect of an alternative point of view that many Christians are trying to interject into this important public discourse.

Dubious distinctions are being made between the works of C. S. Lewis and J. R. R. Tolkein, as opposed to those of J. K. Rowling. The most basic is the suggestion that since Tolkein and Lewis were openly Christian and admitted that their faith worked its way into their fantasy—indeed, that it was an integral part—their fantasy is okay. However, since J. K. Rowling has been reserved in announcing her religious beliefs (although she openly declares her belief in God and attends the Church of Scotland), critics treat her fantasy as different in kind and inherently dangerous.

Do we really want to start determining what we will or will not read on the basis of whether the author shares our religious faith? If so, does it matter that Tolkein was a Catholic and Lewis was from the Anglican stream of Protestantism? Would those making such distinctions go on to read only that which is written by those of their own sect? Not only are Christians making such choices for themselves, some are seeking to ban such work in the public arena, thus threatening our cherished freedoms. Christians followed a similar path into the Dark Ages.

Is our own faith so fragile that we dare not know what those of a different sect of Christianity, or those of undisclosed religious persuasions, or those of different religious backgrounds are thinking? As a freedom-loving Christian and American, I hope and pray we never come to that. Perhaps this book can help us think this through again.

The kind of literary criticism being used by some Christians to discredit Harry Potter while touting Tolkein's and Lewis's fantasy writings is certainly not what Tolkein and Lewis taught their students. On this point I refer you to Thomas L. Martin, an expert far more knowledgeable than I. See his book *Reading the Classics with C. S. Lewis,* particularly the chapter "Lewis: A Critical Perspective." The essays on mythology and children's literature also touch on this subject.

In the epilogue to *Finding God in The Lord of the Rings,* Christian authors Kurt Bruner and Jim Ware say of Tolkein, "Fantasy, as he understood it, is, in its highest and purest form, a place where art, theology, and primal human desire meet and intersect." They conclude, "For the Christian this can mean only one thing: Fantasy is a place where we can come face to face with Christ."[3] I agree! So, to those who ask *How could you?* or *Why bother?* I answer: With all the uproar over Harry Potter in Christian circles, with all the wonderful parallels to the gospel waiting to be pointed out, with my desire to interest people who have been turned off by traditional ways of communicating the message, and with fantasy being a place where one may be able to "see Christ face to face," I could hardly resist.

I hope that you will enjoy thinking through the Harry Potter stories again and seeing new aspects of the story that may spark fresh thoughts and (hopefully) respectful discussions. Whatever our personal convictions or stance on the issues related to Harry Potter, I hope we can be guided by this biblical advice:

> But let everyone be quick to hear, slow to speak *and* slow to anger; for the anger of man does not achieve the righteousness of God. (Jas. 1:19b–20 NASB)

Notes to the Reader

1. This book is written primarily for those who have read the Harry Potter books already. My brief summary points are made for comparison to focus on the point at hand, not to give a literary overview of these books. If you have not read the books you can still enjoy the parallels, but I do not recommend substituting my summary, or anyone's, for the books themselves.

2. Since I am replicating the techniques used by anti-Potter critics to look for the opposite of what they were looking for, you can expect this work to be extremely selective. I admit that I went in with a metaphorical magnifying glass to look for "glimmers of the gospel" while at the same time I disregarded the other elements of the story that were not my focus of attention. I too object to this technique as a mode of serious literary criticism (what J. R. R. Tolkein and C. S. Lewis eschewed as reductionism). I am using it to cause readers to question how reliable such techniques are to literary criticism if the same can be used to "prove" two opposite conclusions.

3. I will be drawing parallels between the *fantasy* story told in the Harry Potter books and spiritual teachings and happenings in the Bible, declared to be true with regard to the *real world*. Since there are many similarities, we need to clearly distinguish between the fantasy world of Harry Potter and the real world.

4. For the sake of clarity, when paralleling spiritual insights and teachings of the Bible with elements of the Harry Potter stories, I will call the fantasy world in the Harry Potter books either "Harry's world" or "the wizarding world"; I will refer to the parallel (including supernatural aspects of our world revealed in the Bible) as "our

world" or "the real world," even though I do understand that some readers may not believe that the invisible realms and miraculous events described in the Bible are literally or factually real.

5. You do not have to be a Christian or even believe the Bible to enjoy drawing such parallels. I am hoping, however, that many will find their interest in the Bible sparked by looking at it in relation to things in the Harry Potter stories. For the record, I do believe the Bible to be God's word, a supernatural revelation from God to us. Even though it has happenings similar to some described in Harry's world, I do not read the Bible as fantasy. I believe our desire for the real (although veiled and miraculous) supernatural realm causes us to love fantasy stories that hint of worlds beyond our own. I view Harry's world as the fantasy subcreation of J. K. Rowling, who uses "magic" as a literary device to tell a story. I view our world as it is revealed to be in the Bible. This includes accepting God's revelation about life in the material realm and spiritual realms that are invisible or only seen by those who have eyes to see. However, I hope that all readers—whether or not they hold the exact same view of Scripture that I do—will be able to find in this book glimpses of the gospel that will pique their interest and make them take another look at both the Harry Potter books and the Bible.

6. Given that I respect the author's stated intent and the work itself as a fantasy, I do not equate the "witchcraft" or "magic" of Harry's world with occult practices or witchcraft forbidden in the Bible, nor do I equate it with the Wiccan religion in our world. (If you want to understand how a Bible-believing Christian who rejects occult practices forbidden in the Bible can enjoy Harry Potter with a clean conscience, I refer you to my previous book, *What's a Christian to Do with Harry Potter?*)

7. Since I approach Harry Potter as fantasy, I will not stop to draw or refute any possible claims of a correlation between the literary "magic" of Harry's world with occult practices in our world. This book, in part, is a response to such claims and a counterpoint to that approach.

8. I laid out this book along the story lines of the four Harry Potter books published at the time of this writing. I did so to help

readers refresh their memories. I have been careful to keep each section focused on the book at hand, so as not to give away plot points in subsequent books. If you have not read all the books and do not want the plots revealed, only read the sections covering the books you have already read.

9. The page numbers in this book refer to the original hardcover editions of the Harry Potter books, published in North America by Arthur A. Levine/Scholastic and in the United Kingdom by Bloomsbury Children's Books.

Glimmers of the Gospel in Book One

Harry Potter and the Sorcerer's Stone

Introduction to Book One

I have had more opportunities than most to discuss Harry Potter with my fellow Christians. While conducting interviews for my previous book, *What's a Christian to Do with Harry Potter?* I found it disconcerting that more often than not the interviewer on a Christian radio broadcast had never read a Harry Potter book, but held views adamantly against the series. One host introduced me like this: "Next we'll be discussing the Harry Potter books. The first book, about to become a major motion picture, has this theme—and I quote—'There is no good or evil, only power and those too weak to seek it.' Our guest is a Christian who approves of the Harry Potter books. Mrs. Neal, please explain how you can support a book with such a theme."

I replied, "I'm afraid you're mistaken about that theme. The line you quoted is stated by one of the villains. The book clearly shows him to be evil and that believing the philosophy you quoted led to his downfall, indeed, to his death. The theme of the book is the opposite of what you concluded. It's a story about the necessity of resisting and defeating those who live by such a philosophy."

The host quickly asked another guest, opposed to Harry Potter but who had actually read the books, "Is what she said true?" He replied, "Well, . . . yes, but that's not really the point."

The host missed the theme of the story because she had been convinced it promoted evil. She had been shown only select items that related to occult practices so her concluding assumptions were upside down.

A magnifying glass does a fine job if you use it to examine something in detail. It is designed to exaggerate small areas and magnify that small part for closer consideration. However, if you lift up a magnifying glass and try to view the entire room or landscape, the entire image flips upside down. This explains what happened above. As critics examine Harry Potter microscopically by looking specifically for any offending similarities to occult practices—or by

listening to hearsay from those who have, as with this radio host—
they run the risk of turning the theme of each book upside down. In
literary terms, this approach is called reductionism. Such a practice
of literary criticism was rejected by both C. S. Lewis and J. R. R.
Tolkein. Reductionism was summed up nicely in the essay "Lewis:
A Critical Perspective" in *Reading the Classics with C. S. Lewis*.
There, Thomas L. Martin says this of those who practice reductionism: "Yet for their one slice of reality they should not think they
have the whole pie."

I do not deny that those who have carefully examined the Harry
Potter books to look specifically for elements that correlate to real
world occult practices—which they are very familiar with—find
some. However, I agree with Lewis and Tolkein's aversion to
reductionism as a primary way of viewing literature—especially
fantasy. I chose to use the reductionist approach myself in this
book to show that such techniques could find the gospel as readily
as the occult in Harry Potter.

There is a danger to this literary exercise I want to avoid. In taking up my literary magnifying glass to look for glimmers of the
gospel in each book, I do not want to overlook the larger story and
theme of the books in their entirety, nor do I want to give the impression that I believe the parts I magnify sum up the whole picture. To
make sure my use of reductionism does not miss or misconstrue the
real point, I have added a brief commentary on the general themes
of each book in its entirety at the beginning of the section for that
book. I hope these brief interludes between books will let you put
down the magnifying glass I have raised for the purpose of one kind
of instruction, so that you may think more broadly about the worthy themes the Harry Potter stories raise for us.

Even in considering the broader themes of each story, I look at
these from a Judeo-Christian perspective. Perhaps of great surprise to many who have heard only negative things against Harry
Potter, I believe that the general themes of each book uphold and
promote foundational beliefs and Judeo-Christian values empha-
sized throughout the Bible. I had considered including specific
Bible verses but found that the themes were so pervasive through-

out the Bible that that would not be necessary. Even those not well versed in the Bible will be able to recognize that these themes are indeed biblical.

The major themes of Book One are the triumph of good over evil and the power of love. We meet a boy who enters a realm where the villain and his servant are seeking immortality so that the evil villain can seize power and rule over those who hold firmly to that which is good. The villain's philosophy, adopted by his servant, is "there is no good or evil, only power and those too weak to seek it." In order to thwart the destructive aims of the villain, Harry and his friends must understand that there is a fundamental difference between good and evil, and that to let evil prevail is to accept murderous and destructive oppression in their world. To resist evil and keep evil from overpowering good, Harry and his friends must do their part, alongside the adults.

Throughout the story, courage and self-sacrifice are required to overcome evil with good. The greatest example of this is how Harry's mother sacrifices herself to protect her baby, thus causing the curse of death to rebound on the evil villain. That destroyed his power partially, but the story shows that unless evil is destroyed utterly, it will always seek to regain power. Therefore, those on the side of good must persist in their resistance to the forces of evil.

The Curse of Death
and the Boy Who Lived

"That's what yeh get when a powerful, evil curse touches yeh—took care of yer mum an' dad an' yer house, even— but it didn't work on you, an' that's why yer famous,

Harry. No one ever lived after he decided ter kill 'em, no one except you."

           —Hagrid to Harry, Book One, p. 55

*B*efore Harry was born, a wizard "went . . . bad. As bad as you could go. Worse. Worse than worse." He terrorized the wizarding world with a deadly curse. The Dark Lord Voldemort murdered Harry's father, then threw the curse of death at Harry, but Harry's mother loved him so much that she threw herself in front of the curse to shield him. With Harry's parents both dead, baby Harry seemed helpless. Voldemort hit him with the curse again. But, instead of killing Harry, the curse rebounded on Voldemort. His power was mysteriously broken. He disappeared, and his reign of terror came to an abrupt end.

This "great myst'ry"—as Hagrid calls it—is the mystery of love. Lily Potter loved her son so much that she laid down her life for his. Hagrid said there was something going on that night that Voldemort had not counted on. Something about Harry stumped him, and Harry became famous as "the boy who lived."

This is where the story begins, with the whole wizarding world rejoicing, sending owls and shooting stars across the sky in an unrestrained outburst of joy. Their celebration was so great, it was even sighted in the Muggle world. Showers of shooting stars all over Britain, indeed! Owls flying in daylight!

The Bible says that before the world began, an angel went bad. Worse. Worse than worse. He rebelled, turning from light to darkness. God cast him out of heaven, and he began looking for ways to bring death and destruction on the people God had made in his image. This fallen angel lured the first man and woman to disobey God. When they did, they were hit with a deadly curse—which God had warned them against. From that time on the whole world lived in fear of the curse of death.

The love Lily Potter demonstrated for her infant son—to the point of being willing to lay down her life for him—can remind us of the love of Jesus Christ: "For while we were still helpless, at the right time Christ died for the ungodly. For one will hardly die for a righteous man; though perhaps for the good man someone would dare even to die. But God demonstrates His own love toward us, in that while we were yet sinners, Christ died for us" (Rom. 5:6–8 NASB).

Apparently this was not something the evil one in our world had counted on either. The curse of death was broken and rebounded in life, not only for Jesus but for everyone who believes in him: "For God so loved the world that he gave his only Son, so that everyone who believes in him may not perish but may have eternal life" (John 3:16).

The opening scene of Harry Potter's story is reminiscent of another story we all know, when a baby slept out in the cold night air while the residents of another realm broke through the skies to proclaim their unrestrained joy to the world.

A Lightning Bolt Scar

Under a tuft of jet-black hair over his forehead they could see a curiously shaped cut, like a bolt of lightning.
—Book One, p. 15

*T*he Dark Lord wielded such destructive power that most people in the wizarding world were afraid even to speak his name. Instead, they called him "He-Who-Must-Not-Be-Named" or "You-Know-Who." He killed without remorse, inflicted torturous pain on his victims, and made them do whatever he decreed, usually to their own harm. No wonder people were terrified of him. No wonder those who were not followers of the Dark Lord celebrated when he was brought down.

The Bible reveals that "the evil one" in our world has control over fallen angels, also known as demons. These evil spirits at times torment, even take control of people, forcing them to do terrible things against their will and to their own harm. The force of evil can also be seen when oppressive regimes hold control over nations. Evil is real, it is loose in the world, and the Bible tells us that "the Son of God was revealed for this purpose, to destroy the works of the devil" (1 John 3:8).

Throughout the accounts given in the four Gospels, we see that whenever Jesus came into an area, people would bring to him those who were possessed by or under the influence of demons. Jesus commanded these spirits to leave the people they afflicted. At his word, these evil spirits had to go. When this happened, some people who had been paralyzed could walk, some who had been deaf could hear, some who had been unable to speak could speak again, some who were suffering from lingering illnesses were freed from the bondage of their diseases.

At one point, Jesus gave seventy of his disciples the power to cast out demons in his name. They were sent out to preach about the kingdom of God. As they preached, they validated their claims that the kingdom of God was more powerful than the kingdom of darkness by casting out demons. Even the disciples were amazed that the demons were subject to them in Jesus' name. Jesus told them, "I watched Satan fall from heaven like a flash of lightning. See, I have given you authority to tread on snakes and scorpions, and over all the power of the enemy; and nothing will hurt you" (Luke 10:18–19). Because God was more powerful than Satan, God cast him out *like lightning*.

So the lightning bolt scar on Harry's forehead can serve as a reminder that the curse of death was broken (which is what happened when Harry got his scar) and that good is more powerful than evil. Jesus gave his disciples the power to "trample on snakes and scorpions"—demonic influences—"and to overcome all the power of the enemy" (Luke 10:19 NIV). Therefore, although they are real and dangerous, we need not cower in fear of evil spirits. Like Harry and friends, we can learn to practice Defense Against the Dark Arts, trusting that there is a greater power at work that we may not yet fully understand.

Scars Can Come in Handy

"Is that where—?" whispered Professor McGonagall.
"Yes," said Dumbledore. "He'll have that scar forever."
"Couldn't you do something about it, Dumbledore?"
"Even if I could, I wouldn't. Scars can come in handy."
—Book One, p. 15

*H*arry was hit with the death curse by the evil Lord Voldemort. The cut was still fresh when Hagrid, Dumbledore, and Professor McGonagall first saw it. He had been hit, yet, astonishingly, he was alive! That cut would become a famous scar, standing silent witness to the facts of history in Harry's life and the wizarding world. As Dumbledore pointed out, "Scars can come in handy," like the one on his knee that is a perfect map of the London Underground. Harry's scar would remind all who saw it that there is something more powerful than the curse of death.

The Christian gospel makes the startling assertion that God entered history by becoming incarnate in human flesh. With that, "Myth became fact," as C. S. Lewis put it.[4] God became a baby, who grew up to lay down his life as a sacrifice for us. That is how he received the wounds and cuts as the curse of death hit him. He was nailed to a cross, hands and feet, before many witnesses. To prove he was truly dead, the Roman executioner pierced his side with a spear. The flow of blood and water proved his heart had ruptured and that he was verifiably dead. His enemies feared his disciples would steal the body and then say he had risen from the dead. So, at their request, his tomb was guarded by soldiers. A crucified man, rising from the dead! Who would believe such a story? But they dared not leave that to chance.

On the third day after the crucifixion, wild stories began to circulate. Most of Jesus' closest disciples were convinced, except for Thomas. He was far too logical to accept such emotionally charged rumors as truth. He said to the other disciples, "Unless I see the mark of the nails in his hands, and put my finger in the mark of the nails and my hand in his side, I will not believe" (John 20:25).

That would be arranged. A week later, Jesus' disciples were all together, and Thomas was with them:

> Although the doors were shut, Jesus came and stood among them and said, "Peace be with you." Then he said to Thomas, "Put your finger here and see my hands. Reach out your hand and put it in my side. Do not doubt but believe." Thomas answered him, "My Lord and my God!" Jesus said to him, "Have you believed because you have seen me? Blessed are those who have not seen and yet have come to believe." (John 20:26–29)

The wounds were still fresh for Thomas; the rest of us will have to make do with scars.

I dare say those scars will be as famous in our world as Harry's scar is in the wizarding world. The Bible predicts a day when those scars will be seen by all—those who believe and those who remain in doubt: "Look! He is coming with the clouds; every eye will see him, even those who pierced him" (Rev. 1:7). People stare at Harry's scar when they see it for themselves for the first time. Before, it had just been something they had read or heard about. What a day that will be when everyone sees the scars Jesus bears and comes to realize that the stories they heard were true accounts of something remarkable that actually happened, leaving a lasting reminder in the form of a scar etched in human flesh.

The Unstoppable Invitation

Uncle Vernon stayed at home again. After burning all the letters, he got out a hammer and nails and boarded up the cracks around the front and back doors.

—Book One, p. 40

*P*oor Harry! Never in all his life had he received a letter addressed personally to him. So when a letter arrived for him, he was amazed. Whoever sent it treated him with respect, addressing him as "Mr. H. Potter." Someone out there knew where he lived, but beyond that, knew that his "bedroom" was the cupboard under the stairs.

Who wouldn't be eager for Harry to open such a letter? The answer is Uncle Vernon. He made it his highest priority to keep Harry from receiving his letter, despite Harry's best efforts to lay hold of one. I say one, because the first—and many subsequent—letters were intercepted and destroyed by Uncle Vernon. When he found it impossible to stop the letters from arriving at 4 Privet Drive, Uncle Vernon made a mad dash to escape. But every time, whoever was sending the letters knew precisely where to find Harry. This had to be maddening to Uncle Vernon, but comforting to Harry. When Harry finally received his hand-delivered invitation, it was addressed as follows:

Mr. H. Potter
The Floor
Hut-on-the-Rock
The Sea

God would not be deterred in getting his invitation delivered to humanity. Even though some people act like Uncle Vernon and try to escape, there is no way to successfully run away from God, who is by nature omniscient and omnipresent. King David recorded these truths in one of his psalms:

> O LORD, you have searched me
> and you know me.
> You know when I sit and when I rise;
> you perceive my thoughts from afar.
> You discern my going out and my lying down;
> you are familiar with all my ways.
> Before a word is on my tongue
> you know it completely, O LORD.

You hem me in—behind and before;
　　you have laid your hand upon me.
Such knowledge is too wonderful for me,
　　too lofty for me to attain.
Where can I go from your Spirit?
　　Where can I flee from your presence?
If I go up to the heavens, you are there;
　　if I make my bed in the depths, you are there.
If I rise on the wings of the dawn,
　　if I settle on the far side of the sea,
even there your hand will guide me,
　　your right hand will hold me fast.
　　　　　　　　　　　(Psalm 139:1–10 NIV)

There is Someone out there who knows each of us, loves us, cares about our situation, and calls us each by name. His message has been sent out through prophets who wrote it down, read it aloud, and delivered it to kings and peasants, religious and irreligious, young and old alike. God's message, compiled in the Bible, holds an invitation to enter a supernatural realm where we can learn his ways and take an active part in the battle between good and evil.

God's message has also encountered great opposition and interference, at times quite similar to Uncle Vernon's burning Harry's letters. Once God sent a particularly unwelcome message through his prophet Jeremiah to a king who did not want anyone to receive the message. In those days, the message was dictated to a scribe who painstakingly wrote it by hand on a scroll. As the scroll with Jeremiah's prophecy was read to the king, he cut it off, piece by piece, and burned it in the fire. He assumed that would be the end of that. But the message could not be deterred. God repeated the message to Jeremiah, who delivered it to the king again, with a few choice words added to it (see Jer. 36:23–32).

As it became necessary to have Harry's letter delivered in person, a time likewise came for God to send his message in person: "In the beginning was the Word, and the Word was with God, and the Word was God. He was in the beginning with God" (John 1:1). "The Word became flesh and lived among us, and we have seen his glory, the glory as of a father's only son, full of grace and truth" (John 1:14).

Jesus came on a mission to seek out and save those who are lost. Harry may have thought he was lost out on that rock in the middle of the sea, but he was not lost to Hagrid. Hagrid would not stop until he had fulfilled the mission given him by Dumbledore to deliver Harry's invitation to attend Hogwarts. Likewise, God's Holy Spirit continues to seek out those who are lost and to urge them to accept God's invitation to come into his kingdom and learn of him.

The Leaky Cauldron:
A Door to an Unseen World

The people hurrying by didn't glance at it. Their eyes slid from the big book shop on one side to the record shop on the other as if they couldn't see the Leaky Cauldron at all. In fact, Harry had the most peculiar feeling that only he and Hagrid could see it.

—Book One, p. 68

*H*agrid and Harry took the train to London on their way to buy Harry's school supplies. Harry was a bit astonished that one could buy such things in London. According to Hagrid, you just had to know where to go. Hagrid led Harry to the Leaky Cauldron, but it seemed to Harry that the people passing by did not even see the entrance. It proved real enough—a doorway from our world into the magical one for those who could see it and knew which bricks to tap to get into Diagon Alley.

Spiritual things are funny that way. Some people have eyes to see them and others don't. It seems that prophets and children are more likely than others to be able to see what some cannot. There is an account in the Bible when Elisha the prophet of Israel was not only able to see what others could not see, but hear what others could not hear—such as what the king was saying in private. So the king sent his armies to arrest the prophet. Elisha was not worried, but his servant was quite upset at seeing a sizable force coming for them. Elisha urged calm: "'Do not be afraid, for there are more with us than there are with them.' Then Elisha prayed: 'O LORD, please open his eyes that he may see.' So the LORD opened the eyes of the servant, and he saw; the mountain was full of horses and chariots of fire all around Elisha" (2 Kgs. 6:15–17).

The state of someone's heart can affect his or her ability to see things in the spiritual realm. Jesus told his disciples that the reason he taught people in parables was because the lessons were for some to see and others not to see. He explained by relating this to a prophecy by Isaiah that states, "For this people's heart has become calloused; they hardly hear with their ears, and they have closed their eyes. Otherwise they might see with their eyes, hear with their ears, understand with their hearts and turn, and I would heal them" (Matt. 13:15 NIV).

Those who "have eyes to see" such things are counted as blessed, but there is an element of revelation that must take place. Even Jesus' own disciples seemed to be unable to see what Jesus was getting at or to recognize the way into the kingdom they were seeking. (And this was after three years of following him.) Shortly before Jesus' departure back to heaven, he consoled his disciples:

> "Do not let your hearts be troubled. Believe in God, believe also in me. In my Father's house there are many dwelling places. If it were not so, would I have told you that I go to prepare a place for you? And if I go and prepare a place for you, I will come again and will take you to myself, so that where I am, there you may be also. And you know the way to the place where I am going." Thomas said to him, "Lord, we do not know where you are going. How can we know the way?" Jesus said to him, "I am the way, and the truth, and the life. No one comes to the Father except through me." (John 14:1–6)

The crowds that hurry by the Leaky Cauldron without seeing that doorway into another realm can remind us that many have eyes but do not see either the supernatural battles taking place around them or the doorway into the kingdom of God. Those things are invisible to them, or perhaps are just a blur among all the other attractions of the world.

Diagon Alley: First Stop, Gringotts

"D'yeh think yer parents didn't leave yeh anything?"
—Hagrid to Harry, Book One, p. 63

*B*efore setting out for Hogwarts, Hagrid took Harry to Diagon Alley to get his school supplies. Harry was concerned that he would not be able to get what he needed because the Dursleys had never given him spending money. Harry soon learned that his parents had set aside a small fortune for him, kept safely in the vault at Gringotts, the wizards' bank. Of course, the currency of the wizarding world is different from that in the world where Harry had grown up, but it would get him everything he needed in the wizarding world.

Similarly, there are riches available to us in the kingdom of God that are not recognized in the world in which we live. Harry arrived at Gringotts technically poor, but left with enough to buy goodies from the cart to share with Ron; so too Paul was able to rightly describe himself and his fellow servants of God as "poor, yet making many rich; as having nothing, and yet possessing everything" (2 Cor. 6:10). The Bible promises that "God will meet all your needs according to his glorious riches in Christ Jesus" (Phil. 4:19 NIV). This covers a simple assurance that our basic physical and material needs will be met but also includes "the full riches of complete understanding, in order that they may know the mystery of God, namely, Christ, in whom are hidden all the treasures of wisdom and knowledge" (Col. 2:2).

The riches set aside for Harry by his loving parents will give him everything he needs for life and for his education at Hogwarts so he can grow to be completely equipped to operate well in the magical world, particularly by defending against the Dark Arts. Likewise, God's "divine power has given us everything we need for life and godliness through our knowledge of him who called us by his own glory and goodness. Through these he has given us his very great and precious promises, so that through them you may participate in the divine nature and escape the corruption in the world caused by evil desires" (2 Pet. 1:3–5 NIV).

Having previously known financial deprivation and the shame that comes with it, Harry is sensitive to those who have less than he. So, too, Christians are commanded to be sensitive to those who are poor in this world's goods, to not look down on those who have less but, rather, to treat them with respect (see Jas. 2:5).

Getting onto Platform Nine and Three-Quarters

"All you have to do is walk straight at the barrier between platforms nine and ten. . . . Best do it at a bit of a run if you're nervous."
—Mrs. Weasley to Harry, Book One, p. 93

After receiving his invitation to Hogwarts, Harry still had to get there. Hagrid had given him a ticket for the Hogwarts Express, but Harry had to get onto the right platform. Uncle Vernon laughed derisively when he left Harry at King's Cross Station standing between platforms nine and ten, with his trunk and Hedwig's cage. There had to be a way to get onto platform nine and three-quarters, but Harry didn't know how until the Weasleys showed up. It did seem a bit odd—just walk straight into the barrier.

The process for getting onto platform nine and three-quarters was something anyone *could* do, but no reasonable person *would* do unless he or she believed that was the way—however strange it might seem to onlookers—to find the platform. Harry watched the Weasleys go through, one by one. Mrs. Weasley offered her encouragement, and Harry followed her instructions. He reached the platform and was able to see the Hogwarts Express and experience what others could not. He came out onto platform nine and three-quarters the same person, but he had stepped into a whole new world of possibilities and was now on his way to learning how to function in the supernatural world.

The Uncle Vernons of the world say, "Seeing is believing." Faith says, "Believing is seeing." Or as the Letter to the Hebrews puts it, "Now faith is the assurance of things hoped for, the conviction of things not seen" (Heb. 11:1). Therefore, *if* you believe, you are willing to act on what you believe, which is why real faith leads to decisive actions. There is also merit to being guided by those who have already entered the spiritual realm. Mrs. Weasley's advice is reminiscent of the Nike slogan, "Just do it!" In athletic and spiritual terms, the way to begin moving toward power, greater prowess, and victory is to "just do it." But do what? What is the spiritual act called for in order to enter the invisible kingdom of God?

Strange as it might seem to onlookers, the point of entry given in the Bible is baptism. John the Baptist came to prepare the way for the Lord. He told people to come down to the Jordan River, repent of their sins, go under the water, then come up to a new life. Even though Jesus was born without sin, he came to John and asked to be baptized "to fulfill all righteousness" (Matt. 3:15). He led so his followers would see the prescribed way to enter the kingdom of God. When Jesus came up out of the water, we know it "worked" because of what happened—even the "Muggles" of his day could see. Matthew describes it this way: "And when Jesus had been baptized, just as he came up from the water, suddenly the heavens were opened to him and he saw the Spirit of God descending like a dove and alighting on him. And a voice from heaven said, 'This is my Son, the Beloved, with whom I am well pleased'" (Matt. 3:16–17).

Jesus invited everyone to come, even common people. Many of them obeyed the instructions of John the Baptist and Jesus by getting baptized. However, many of the religious leaders scoffed and refused; therefore, they did not get into the kingdom of God (see Luke 7:30). Here is the ticket we have been handed: "The one who believes and is baptized will be saved; but the one who does not believe will be condemned" (Mark 16:16).

Later, after the disciples received power from heaven, Peter addressed a crowd. They wanted to know how to get in. He said, "Repent, and be baptized every one of you in the name of Jesus Christ so that your sins may be forgiven; and you will receive the gift of the Holy Spirit. For the promise is for you, for your children, and for all who are far away, everyone whom the Lord our God calls to him" (Acts 2:38). Here we see the connection between obeying the instructions in this natural world and entering into a realm where supernatural power becomes suddenly available.

Just as Harry believed in what he could not see, and was prompted to obey even odd-sounding instructions, likewise those who believe God's word will obey it and will follow the path of those who went before us into God's kingdom.

The Sorting

Harry gripped the edges of the stool and thought, Not Slytherin, not Slytherin.

"Not Slytherin, eh?" said the small voice. "Are you sure? . . . Well, if you're sure—better be GRYFFINDOR!"

—Book One, p. 121

*E*ven before Harry arrived at Hogwarts he began to wonder where he would fit in. He had met Draco Malfoy while getting his robes fitted and heard more than he cared to about Malfoy's preference for Slytherin House. He met the Weasleys and recognized how different they were from Malfoy, and they were all in Gryffindor. His parents had been in Gryffindor too. (Hufflepuffs were just, loyal, true, and hard working. Ravenclaws were known for their wit, learning, and ready mind.) Then there was that important bit of history: Every wizard known to have gone over to the evil side had been in Slytherin.

Harry and the other first years were worried that they would have to pass some kind of test or wrestle a troll to get to be chosen. Harry even worried that he might not be chosen at all. But soon the sorting was underway and they were all sorted into the houses that would become like their family while at Hogwarts. With Harry's turn we learn a bit more of what goes on under the hat. Harry thought, *"Not Slytherin!"* and that came into play as the hat decided where to place him. Once the hat shouted out "GRYFFINDOR!" Harry was relieved just to have been chosen and not put in Slytherin.

The mystery of the sorting ceremony brings up some interesting thoughts. Harry resisted evil, and was sorted into Gryffindor. He was "chosen" to be a Gryffindor, but also exercised free will. He wanted to follow in his parents' footsteps, and did not yield to the hat's suggestion that he could be great in Slytherin. Perhaps the hat was only testing him. Perhaps he was destined for Gryffindor all along, chosen before he ever sat on the stool, but the hat wanted to give him the chance to exercise his own will by choosing to resist evil.

This parallels one of the paradoxes of Christianity that theologians have debated for centuries. We are "chosen" by God's grace, but we are also created with free will, so our allegiance to God and opposition to evil will not be robotic. There is an interplay between predestination, alluded to in Ephesians 4:1 (NASB),

"He chose us in Him before the foundation of the world," and free will, as in "And let everyone who hears say, 'Come.' And let everyone who is thirsty come. Let anyone who wishes take the water of life as a gift" (Rev. 22:17). This interplay holds a perplexing mystery.

We see the same kind of perplexity at Harry's sorting. There is a growing sense throughout the books that Harry is predestined to some great calling, and yet we see him going through the process of *choosing* to resist evil and *being chosen* to go into the house of the lion, Gryffindor House. It was founded by Godric Gryffindor, and includes a long line of those who have bravely fought evil, James and Lily Potter among them. In biblical terms, Jesus is referred to as the "Lion of the tribe of Judah" (Rev. 5:5), acknowledging his human ancestry from Judah, one of the twelve sons of Israel. Revelation shows Jesus pitted against "that ancient serpent, who is called the Devil and Satan, the deceiver of the whole world—he was thrown down to the earth, and his angels were thrown down with him" (Rev. 12:9). This reminds us of Slytherins, whose symbol is the serpent and whose nature reveals a cunning and willingness to use any means to achieve their ends. The cunning and deceptive nature of the serpent was witnessed in the temptation of Adam and Eve in the garden and is referred to in the New Testament (see 2 Cor. 11:3).

So the basic imagery of the rivalry and conflict between Gryffindor and Slytherin parallels the basic imagery of the Bible's description of the battle between those on God's side and Satan. But please note: It is important to remember that the Harry Potter stories are fantasy, and *never mention Satan*. Any parallels in that regard are drawn in the mind of the reader by making a correlation between the wizarding world of Harry Potter and the supernatural world the Bible reveals in the real world.

Dumbledore's Dire Warning

"I must tell you that this year, the third-floor corridor on the right-hand side is out of bounds to everyone who does not wish to die a very painful death."
—Dumbledore to students, Book One, p. 127

*H*arry didn't quite know what to make of Dumbledore's dire warning, given at the start-of-school banquet his first year. At first he thought the headmaster couldn't be serious, but Percy put that idea to rest. What kind of headmaster makes such a pronouncement to students? Was he joking? Apparently not. Was he being cruel? Not Dumbledore. From the start, his kindness, care for the students, calmness, and good humor were apparent. So how does this make sense?

Dumbledore was simply telling the truth. He knew that there was a real danger in that corridor. Fluffy, the three-headed dog, could indeed cause a very painful death to any students who went where they were warned not to go. Dumbledore, as headmaster, knew things the students were not supposed to know. He was under no obligation to explain himself to them—not even to the prefects, to Percy's chagrin.

Some who did not understand what was going on behind the scenes might think Dumbledore was being mean. *How could he scare them so? They're only children.* But he was not being mean. On the contrary, his dire warning was meant to spare them pain. Granted, Harry, Ron, Neville, and Hermione did not heed his warning closely enough and got the scare of their lives. Once they realized what was in that corridor and why, Dumbledore's warning made sense. It also reinforced their growing understanding that Dumbledore was a refuge for them, one who would do everything in his power—which was considerable—to keep them safe.

In the opening pages of the Bible, at the very beginning of the relationship between God and humanity, God gives a dire warning: "You are free to eat from any tree in the garden; but you must not eat from the tree of the knowledge of good and evil, for when you eat of it you will surely die" (Gen. 2:16–17). Was God just trying to scare the man? Was God being cruel? No. God simply understood what would happen if anyone ate from that particular tree. It was because God did not want people to experience death that he gave that warning.

We know that the man and woman in the garden of Eden did not heed the warning. They paid far more heavily than Harry and company. When they disobeyed, precisely what God warned would happen did happen. Death came into their lives. They did not die on the spot, but they began to die. Those whom God intended to live eternally without death and corruption became corrupt. They immediately fell under the penalty of death spiritually (separated from God with a disposition toward sin) and subject to mortality and physical death. Eventually, one of the sons of Adam and Eve killed his brother, and they experienced a kind of death in their own souls too (see Gen. 3 and 4).

God's warnings simply tell us what he knows to be true so that we can avoid the pain, danger, and death he wants to spare us. When God warns us away from sin, it is because he knows therein lies danger. When God warns of hell, he is not being cruel. He is not trying to scare us unnecessarily. Hell is scary, but since God knows that hell is a terrible reality, he would be cruel not to warn us. The older students who knew Dumbledore well trusted that he was serious in his warning but also kind. Likewise, those who have been close to God for a while will be the first to tell others that God's warnings are to be taken seriously, but that they are in keeping with his nature, which is love.

Hagrid's Temptation

"Hagrid's always wanted a dragon, he told me so the first time I ever met him," said Harry.
"But it's against our laws," said Ron.

—Book One, p. 230

*H*agrid has a fondness for dangerous magical creatures, even illegal ones like dragons. As a boy, he even tried raising werewolf cubs. So when the opportunity arose to have a dragon's egg, how could Hagrid refuse? He was at a pub down in the village when a friendly stranger struck up a conversation, bought him a few drinks—another of Hagrid's weaknesses—and showed Hagrid a dragon's egg. He suggested playing cards for it. It never dawned on Hagrid that there might be more at stake than an egg.

Hagrid knew it was wrong to keep the dragon; that is why he pulled his curtains closed. But Harry, Ron, and Hermione were much more concerned about the illegality of having the egg than Hagrid. He was too taken with his lifelong desire to have a dragon. Hagrid lovingly stoked the fire to keep the egg hot, waiting with anticipation for it to hatch. From the moment it hatched, the baby dragon was sneezing sparks and snapping at Hagrid's fingers, but Hagrid was as protective of his pet as if it were his child.

The increasing dangers were apparent to Hagrid's friends. Norbert the dragon grew at an alarming rate, which made hiding the dragon more of a challenge. Malfoy had caught sight of it and could report Hagrid to the authorities. Hagrid became derelict in his duties because Norbert demanded so much of his time and attention: feeding him, hiding him, keeping others from discovering his secret. Besides, as Hermione pointed out, dragons breathe fire and Hagrid lives in a wooden house!

Hagrid kept making excuses for Norbert. Even when the dragon bit Ron with its poisonous fangs, Hagrid told Ron off and went on singing "baby Norbert" a lullaby. Even when Norbert took to biting Hagrid's leg, Hagrid passed it off as "jus' playin'." Eventually,

Hermione, Harry, and Ron helped Hagrid realize that he simply could not manage the situation. They convinced him to let them send Norbert off to Charlie Weasley, who was legally studying wild dragons in Romania.

This is a striking image of the process by which one is tempted and progresses into a life dominated by sin. The Bible teaches that whenever we are tempted, "no one should say, 'God is tempting me.' For God cannot be tempted by evil, nor does he tempt anyone; but each one is tempted when, by his own evil desire, he is dragged away and enticed" (Jas. 1:13–14 NIV).

Just as there was a personality behind the temptation Hagrid experienced, one with ulterior motives, so too behind all sin there is an evil one who generally is up to no good. However, we are tempted by those things each one of us desires. Hagrid just happened to have a hankering for a dragon. Each person is attracted to some things that are against God's law, but these differ according to the person. When the opportunity arises for us to have what we have always wanted or fantasized about having—even though we know it is wrong—and we are enticed by our own desire, that is where temptation begins.

The progress from temptation to sin to the consequences goes like this: After desire has conceived, it gives birth to sin; sin, when it is full grown, gives birth to death (see Jas. 1:15). Just as it is the nature of the dragon to grow up to breathe fire and use its poisonous fangs, so it is the nature of sin to progress to deadly proportions. Sometimes this means death to good relationships or self-respect; sometimes it means death to the one who is caught up in a delusion over sin, or in trying to cover up the shame of it.

When people become protective of their sins, the first thing that happens is that they close the curtains of their lives, hiding in shame and trying to keep out the prying eyes of those who might force them to give up what they know is wrong but dearly want to keep. From the very first sin, we see this to be true. Adam and Eve were *hiding* in the garden after they disobeyed God. To this day, the desire to conceal that which we know is wrong is a hallmark of living with sin. Jesus described it this way: "For all who do evil hate the light and do not come to the light, so that their deeds may not be exposed" (John 3:20).

When someone is caught up in sin—even a nice person—that person needs friends who will confront the problem and help get rid of the sin. This is not to be done in a condemning way, but gently, since all of us are prone to temptation and sin. These are the instructions found in the Letter to the Galatians: "If someone is caught in a sin, you who are spiritual should restore him gently. But watch yourself, or you also may be tempted. Carry each other's burdens, and in this way you will fulfill the law of Christ" (Gal. 6:1–3 NIV). At the heart of the gospel is the promise that there is a way we can get rid of our guilt for sin (in general), but it goes on to show us how to help each other get rid of particular sins that threaten our own well-being as well as the lives of others.

Hagrid's temptation gives us a good model of the destructive, dangerous, and potentially deadly consequences of giving in to our sinful desires. Harry, Ron, and Hermione model a biblical way of helping someone caught up in the delusions and dangers of sin. We see this in their concern, the way they spoke the truth in love and eventually carried their friend's burden—this time in the shape of a Norwegian Ridgeback dragon—up to the tower to be taken away so Hagrid could be free of it.

Note: Some may be troubled that Harry and Hermione broke school rules in getting rid of Norbert. For those attuned to such details, it might be noted that they were willing to break a lesser rule to accomplish the greater good of protecting the whole school from a dangerous dragon. However, they did risk punishment to do so, were caught, and willingly accepted their punishment as fitting because they did break a rule.

Dangerous Designs of the Dragon-Egg Dealer

"Don't you think it's a bit odd," said Harry, . . . "that what Hagrid wants more than anything else is a dragon, and a stranger turns up who just happens to have an egg in his pocket?"
—Harry to Ron and Hermione, Book One, p. 265

*T*he stranger Hagrid met in the pub was not simply looking for a friendly game of cards. He came in with the intention of getting Hagrid drunk and seeing if he could find out how to get past Fluffy, the three-headed dog Dumbledore had borrowed to help guard the Sorcerer's Stone. After a few drinks, Hagrid volunteered that he had always really wanted a dragon. Funny, that's just what the hooded stranger managed to pull out of his pocket. But before he would let Hagrid have the dragon's egg, Hagrid would have to convince him that he could handle it. What experience did he have with other dangerous magical creatures? Indeed, the hooded stranger seemed very interested in Fluffy.

Hagrid hadn't given the stranger's intentions much thought. That was a mistake. It took Harry a while, but eventually it dawned on Harry that it was strange that Hagrid was offered what he had always wanted but the stranger sought nothing in return—or did he? Indeed, he got what he was scheming to get all along: the secret of how to get past Fluffy.

But that was not the extent of the scheming that went on under that hood! Later, when Professor Quirrell revealed that he was the one hiding under that cloak, we learned that his real aim was to steal the Sorcerer's Stone, kill Harry, and give the stone to his master, Lord Voldemort. That would give Voldemort the wealth and immortality he sought so that he could regain power and dominate the wizarding world again. Would Hagrid have ever thought a game of cards with a stranger—albeit one who held the fulfillment to an illicit desire in his pocket—could contribute to the destruction of Hogwarts or lead to Harry's death? Perhaps, but only in retrospect. Unfortunately, Hagrid was outwitted by the deceptive schemes of one working on the side of evil.

What appeared to be a chance encounter was later revealed to be much more. There was an intelligent force working toward evil aims hiding under a cloak of secrecy. When the Bible warns against "the evil one" or Satan, it does not describe a general force of evil, but rather an evil personality with evil intentions. We are warned to be aware of his schemes, alert to the danger of being outwitted, and that we should not be "ignorant of his designs" (2 Cor. 2:11; see also Eph. 6:11). The word *schemes* denotes a pattern of thought, a plan that is in keeping with the nature and intentions of the one doing the planning.

Therefore, if we know the overall intentions of those on the side of evil—both people and the spiritual forces of evil motivating them—we can think more critically when we face decisions. This understanding of the nature of the evil one (hateful, deceptive, and murderous) along with a general understanding of his aims (coming to steal, kill, and destroy) can inform us so that we are not outwitted.

The upside of this understanding of our struggle against evil is that we can learn to make more intelligent decisions to fend off dangerous deceptions. We must stop and back up a little whenever we are in a situation where sin is handed to us.

I cannot help but think of publicly disgraced ministers who must not have been thinking straight when they gave in to temptations to engage in sexual sin or to mishandle funds or power. Surely they should have anticipated that "the evil one" was working behind the scenes with dangerous designs to discredit and destroy their reputation, family, and ministry. Surely, if they had foreseen the related consequences, they would not have given in. No doubt, Hagrid later wished he had stopped to think more clearly about what might have been going on behind the scenes and what might be at stake. His lapse left Harry's life in danger, his reputation and the continuance of Hogwarts at risk. Indeed, all he held dear in his own life, in his community, and in the larger battle being waged between good and evil was impacted because he was outwitted by Professor Quirrell's scheme. We can learn a lot by reflecting on the dangerous designs of the dragon-egg dealer.

The Quest for the Sorcerer's Stone

"The Sorcerer's Stone [is] a legendary substance with astonishing powers. The stone will transform any metal into pure gold. It also produces the Elixir of Life, which will make the drinker immortal."

—Hermione reading from a library book, Book One, p. 220

On the first day Harry entered the magical world, someone tried to steal the Sorcerer's Stone from Gringotts. That stirred up Harry's curiosity. But Harry, Ron, and Hermione's interest became urgent once Harry realized who was trying to steal the stone and why.

While Harry was in the Forbidden Forest trying to find out what had been killing the unicorns, he was helped by Firenze the centaur. Firenze pointed out, "Only one who has nothing to lose, and everything to gain, would commit such a crime" (Book One, p. 258). After that conversation, Harry realized that Voldemort was trying to steal the Sorcerer's Stone. The wealth and immortality it could produce (through the Elixir of Life) would allow him to return to power. Then he could once again destroy all that was good and dominate the wizarding world.

Harry then correctly understood that this was a matter of life and death, good versus evil. Therefore, he determined to fight—to the death, if necessary—to keep those on Voldemort's side from getting the stone. When Hermione tried to dissuade him, he pointed out that he was not worried about being expelled. If he failed, there would not be a Hogwarts to get expelled from. The Dark Lord would destroy it or turn it into a school for the Dark Arts. Harry knew that letting evil prevail would leave those on the side of good in mortal danger. Whoever was trying to get the Stone for Voldemort must be stopped.

In the opening pages of the Bible we read about a tree of life, one that could grant immortality (similar to the Elixir of Life). When Adam and Eve were deceived by the serpent and ate from the forbidden tree of the knowledge of good and evil, they fell under the curse of death. Then God drove them out of the garden of Eden. He also stationed an angel with a flaming sword to keep anyone from eating of the tree of life. Why? Perhaps having immortality before one has a remedy for the curse of sin and death would be terrible. So God made sure people could not have that which would give them immortality until he had rid the world of evil (see Gen. 3).

God did not want to keep people from having immortality; he created us to share eternity with him. God had to make sure that immortality would be free of the corruption and living death that came as a result of the fall. Jesus came to Earth to solve that problem. He also knew that the evil one who showed up as the serpent in the garden of Eden had sent false teachers to keep people from recognizing him and his mission. Jesus said, "The thief comes only to steal and kill and destroy" (John 10:10a).

In both Harry Potter's story and the Christian story, the villain has the same aims. Professor Quirrell was a false teacher who came to steal the Sorcerer's Stone, kill Harry, and destroy all that was good when Voldemort returned to power. However, those on the side of good set themselves against these aims. Jesus went on to say, "I came that they may have life, and have it abundantly" (John 10:10b).

God is not trying to keep us from immortality, but to let us have it when we are ready for it. Even Dumbledore showed concern over people using the Stone to have as much life and money as they wanted. He saw to it that the Sorcerer's Stone was destroyed, but we get the idea that he is not opposed to immortality. He did make sure Harry understood that there was a way in which death was not the end, but "the next great adventure" (Book One, p. 297). We do not know the end of Harry's story yet, but we can read the end of our story in the Bible. Humanity will not be deprived of immortality. Once sin, death, and evil are out of the way, God says, "To everyone who conquers, I will give permission to eat from the tree of life that is in the paradise of God" (Rev. 2:7). Then we won't need the Sorcerer's Stone to live forever; the paradise God promises gives eternal life and everlasting riches.

Harry, Ron, and Hermione's Soft Landing

"I know what this is—it's Devil's Snare!"
—Hermione to Harry and Ron, Book One, p. 277

*H*arry, Ron, and Hermione were racing to reach the Sorcerer's Stone before someone on Voldemort's side could lay hold of it and use its powers for evil. They had to get past Fluffy, through the trap door, and past all the enchantments guarding the Stone. When they dropped into the darkness through the trap door, Harry and Ron were relieved to land on a soft, comfortable plant. They thought themselves lucky that it was there. Only Hermione recognized the danger they were in, and pulled free of the entangling plant immediately before it could get a hold on her.

Harry and Ron were not as attentive in Herbology class as Hermione, nor were they aware of what was really happening while they made themselves comfortable. The plant that promised comfort was entwining its tendrils around them, clinging dangerously to them, and entangling them so that they could not escape.

Only Hermione knew that it was Devil's Snare. A soft landing, a gradual entangling, a deadly end so that the race is never finished.

The Bible speaks of sin in the same way. Our lives are like a race, where the forces of evil are also on the move in our world. Even when we are endeavoring to do good or work against the larger evil, we can fall into "Devil's Snare." Think of the "little sins" we settle into ever so comfortably: the little lie that covers our shame or keeps us out of trouble, the way we slip right into gossip, the temporary exhilaration of alcohol and recreational drugs, or the sensual pleasures of sexual sin. The initial benefits or pleasures of sin are the devil's snare *because* they offer temporary comforts; otherwise, who would settle into such a thing? The Bible does not deny that sin indeed holds out temporary pleasures. Moses is commended for "choosing rather to share ill-treatment with the people of God than to enjoy the fleeting pleasures of sin" (Heb. 11:25).

As soon as Harry, Ron, and Hermione landed, Devil's Snare began immediately—although almost imperceptibly—to wrap its tendrils around them. So too with all of us who may fall into a situation we did not anticipate where sin is waiting with quickly entangling tendrils. Hermione made the right move—away from the Devil's Snare the instant she landed in it. The Letter to the Hebrews urges, "Let us throw off everything that hinders and the sin that so easily entangles, and let us run with perseverance the race marked out for us" (Heb. 12:1–2 NIV).

The race of life, toward the good ends God intends for us, is always hindered by and sometimes stopped whenever we settle into sin, whose nature is such that it easily entangles. Therefore, we need to throw it off quickly and repeatedly whenever we fall into it. If we settle down for too long, it eventually becomes deadly—to soul and spirit if not to life itself. Solomon wisely put it this way, "Sometimes there is a way that seems to be right, but in the end it is the way to death" (Prov. 16:25).

We can also take a lesson from Hermione's knowledge of the plant. Devil's Snare thrives in the dark. Therefore, Hermione was able to defeat it with light. God's remedy is similar for avoiding and defeating any snare of the devil: "God is light and in him there is no darkness at all. If we say that we have fellowship with him while we are walking in darkness, we lie and do not do what is true; but if we walk in the light as he himself is in the light, we have fellowship with one another, and the blood of Jesus his Son cleanses us from all sin" (1 John 1:5–7).

If Harry and Ron had remained comfortably resting in Devil's Snare, they would have died. They needed to get into the light, and to get out of that snare. Likewise, people need to become alert to the fact that their sins—perhaps especially the most comforting ones—may be a snare of the devil to lull them into a cozy place in the dark where no one will see their sins, but where they are destined to die if they do not break free. It is the light and truth of Jesus Christ that is able to set us free.

This Isn't Magic, It's Logic!

"Brilliant," said Hermione. "This isn't magic—it's logic—a puzzle. A lot of the greatest wizards haven't got an ounce of logic, they'd be stuck in here forever."
—Hermione to Harry, Book One, p. 285

*H*emione is the logical one of the group; she studies hard and uses her mind to benefit her friends. When she and Harry made their way past the living game of chess, they entered a room where seven bottles sat on a table. Each of the two doors was filled with flames they could not pass. A roll of paper next to the bottles explained that one would allow the drinker to move forward, one would transport the drinker back, two were harmless, and three held deadly poison. The riddle gave enough information for anyone who used logic to figure out which were which.

Hermione was relieved. Harry was afraid they would be stuck

in there forever. Hermione thought it through and was confident she knew which bottles they should choose. They decided that Harry would proceed while Hermione went back to get Ron and summon Dumbledore. Hermione discounted her contribution as "Books! And cleverness!" admiring Harry's friendship and bravery more, but her logic played a vital part in their quest.

A lawyer asked Jesus, "Teacher, which commandment in the law is the greatest?" Jesus replied, "'You shall love the Lord your God with all your heart, and with all your soul, and *with all your mind.*' This is the greatest and first commandment. And a second is like it: 'You shall love your neighbor as yourself'" (Matt. 22:36–39). Some people seem to think that loving God is something that requires one to leave logic and intellect out of the process. In his reply to the lawyer, Jesus indicated that this is not so.

On the other hand, just as Hermione's use of logic by itself was not enough to get them all the way through, neither can one fully comprehend God and the things of the spiritual realm by a purely rational evaluation. Other elements come into play, not the least of which is faith, but also a willingness to do God's will. However, for the one who puts a lot of stock in things making sense logically, God has provided enough to satisfy an intelligent examination of the claims of Christ and the Bible. For example, the book of Acts says that after Jesus' suffering "he presented himself alive to them by *many convincing proofs,* appearing to them during forty days and speaking about the kingdom of God" (Acts 1:3).

The four Gospels and the book of Acts are firsthand accounts of eyewitnesses or those who interviewed eyewitnesses. The details given are set in history, and are able to be considered logically as one would consider any other historical testimony. These things took place at specific places, at specific times, so the seeker can check to see how well the accounts of Jesus' life and ministry line up with history, archaeology, and with one's sense of reason. Those who have never considered Christianity to be logical would do well to read Josh McDowell's *The New Evidence That Demands a*

Verdict, Lee Strobel's *The Case for Christ*, William Lane Craig's *Reasonable Faith*, or J. P. Moreland's *Scaling the Secular City*.[5]

Hermione had taken time to study and to sharpen her skills in logic. This preparation enabled her to confidently choose the only bottles that would get her and Harry safely through the flames and free them from being trapped. Likewise, those who want to safely escape fiery spiritual dangers and not live their lives trapped in a spiritual quandry would do well to resort to using logic even in spiritual pursuits. Like Hermione, we will need to study and apply our minds to considering the many convincing proofs God has provided in the Bible and in the life, death, and resurrection of Jesus Christ.

Professor Quirrell's Defense against the Dark Arts Lessons

"Next to [Snape], who would suspect p-p-poor, st-stuttering, P-Professor Quirrell?"
—Professor Quirrell to Harry, Book One, p. 288

*E*very reader of Harry Potter quickly learns to be alert to deception. Not everyone is what he or she appears to be. The first stark realization of this comes at the end of Book One, with the unveiling of Professor Quirrell's true nature and aims. As the Defense Against the Dark Arts teacher at Hogwarts, Quirrell was supposed to teach students to defend themselves against evil. He feigned timidity and nervousness, supposedly having been frightened during his studies while fending off forces of darkness. However, his friendliness toward Harry and his skittishness were a cover for a ruthless determination to kill Harry and do whatever was necessary to return Lord Voldemort to power.

Harry, Ron, and Hermione knew someone was trying to hurt

Harry, steal the Stone, and restore Voldemort, but they targeted the "obvious" suspect, Professor Snape. His overt hatred of Harry, dark countenance, and ominous presence led to assumptions that caused them to totally misjudge the situation and people involved. This left them vulnerable to the real danger that was carefully disguised.

In the end, even though Professor Quirrell's classes did not teach much about really defending against the Dark Arts, his life became an object lesson of a warning in the Bible to protect oneself from evil. Jesus said, "Watch out for false prophets. They come to you in sheep's clothing, but inwardly they are ferocious wolves. By their fruit you will recognize them. Do people pick grapes from thornbushes, or figs from thistles? Likewise every good tree bears good fruit, but a bad tree bears bad fruit" (Matt. 7:15–17).

Professor Quirrell was not recognized immediately for what he was because fruit takes time to grow; thus, his evil plans remained concealed until they reached fruition. Down in the dungeons, when he thought he had Harry trapped and intended to kill him, Quirrell revealed that he had been the one to let the troll in during the Halloween feast. He had tried to knock Harry off his broom during the Quidditch match, while—astonishingly—Professor Snape was trying to protect Harry. Quirrell was the one who had broken into Gringotts in a vain attempt to steal the Sorcerer's Stone, and had continued trying to steal it so he could give his master the wealth, power, and immortality it promised. He was the one who had been killing the unicorns and drinking their blood. Why? Because *inwardly* he was a ferocious wolf, although he clothed himself in a sheepish, seemingly harmless manner. This is in keeping with the nature of evil; it sets out to accomplish dark deeds by way of deception. Therefore, to defend against the Dark Arts, one must remain alert to deception and understand that people are not always what they present themselves to be.

Hagrid's Remorse

"I told the evil git how ter get past Fluffy! I told him! . . .
Yeh could've died! All fer a dragon egg! I'll never drink
again!"
                                    —Hagrid to Harry, Book One, p. 303

*O*nce Hagrid realized that his lapse had put Harry in danger, he was distraught. He burst into tears when he came to see Harry in the hospital. He accepted full responsibility for what he had done wrong. He admitted that his drunkenness and giving in to his weaknesses and desire for an illegal dragon egg put him at fault. He declared that he would never drink again. He felt so guilty that he was harder on himself than others were. He was overcome with grief and remorse.

While the Bible does not forbid drinking, it says, "Wine is a mocker and beer a brawler; whoever is led astray by them is not wise" (Prov. 20:1 NIV). It says, in effect, "Do not get drunk," which is related then to making unwise decisions and to an awareness that we live in times when evil is at large (Eph. 5:15–18). The Bible also says, "Conduct yourselves wisely toward outsiders, making the most of the time. Let your speech always be gracious, seasoned with salt, so that you may know how you ought to answer everyone" (Col. 4:5–6). Hagrid came to realize that his drinking let the evil one get the advantage, that he did not conduct himself wisely toward the stranger, and that he was not careful about how he answered him.

Hagrid may not have handled himself well with the stranger, but he handled his sins in exactly the right way! He came to the ones he had hurt, and confessed with heartfelt remorse. He willingly repented and declared his determination never to do it again. The Bible says, "If we say that we have no sin, we deceive ourselves, and the truth is not in us. If we confess our sins, he who is faithful and just will forgive us our sins and cleanse us from all unrighteousness.

If we say that we have not sinned, we make him a liar, and his word is not in us" (1 John 1:8–10). Hagrid would be in good shape.

Some might argue that Hagrid does drink again in subsequent books. I have even heard one person say, "Hagrid is drunk in every scene." This is not true. Even though we see Hagrid drinking later, we see his heart in this scene. Moreover, we do not see a repeat of overt drunkenness. However, the Bible is very gracious to people who fall repeatedly into the same pattern of sin, as is recorded in the Psalms:

> The LORD is compassionate and gracious,
>   slow to anger, abounding in love.
> He will not always accuse,
>   nor will he harbor his anger forever;
> he does not treat us as our sins deserve
>   or repay us according to our iniquities.
> For as high as the heavens are above the earth,
>   so great is his love for those who fear him;
> as far as the east is from the west,
>   so far has he removed our transgressions from us.
> As a father has compassion on his children,
>   so the LORD has compassion on those who fear him;
> for he knows how we are formed,
>   he remembers that we are dust.
>
>   (Ps. 103:8–14 NIV)

When Peter came to Jesus to ask how many times he had to forgive someone who repeated the same offense, he thought he was being generous when he suggested, "Up to seven times?" No doubt he was staggered when Jesus replied, "Not seven times, but seventy-seven times" (Matt. 18:21–22).

Harry responded to Hagrid's remorse beautifully. He forgave him without a second thought, and even comforted him. For the Christian, such forgiveness may not come as easily as it came to Harry, but it is not optional. Jesus made it clear that his followers must forgive from their hearts (see Matt. 18:35). We also see that receiving forgiveness does not encourage further sin for one who is rightly corrected. No doubt, Hagrid would be less likely to fall into such behavior again because he was instructed by the consequences of his actions. (Still, although true biblical forgiveness can bring reconciliation, it does not remove the subsequent consequences of wrongdoing. One can be sorry and be forgiven, but one must still live with the consequences.)

Hagrid and Harry act as good models of how to repent of sin and to seek and extend forgiveness. The reconciliation, comfort, and restored relationship between Hagrid and Harry is a high point of Book One. These also highlight the new life God wants us to enjoy in his kingdom. The "gospel" is good news because it brings reconciliation, comfort, and restored relationship between people, but also in our relationship with God himself.

Harry's Battle with the Dark Lord

"See what I have become?" the face said. "Mere shadow and vapor . . . I have form only when I can share another's body . . . but there have always been those willing to let me into their hearts and minds."
—Voldemort to Harry, Book One, p. 293

When Harry came face to face with Voldemort, he learned that he had become a disembodied spirit, forced to work through others by taking up residence in them. Harry resisted the evil one, and after the battle—which left Harry unconscious and Quirrell mortally wounded—the evil spirit fled.

Later, when discussing the whole battle with Ron and Hermione, Harry contemplated how he had come to have the confrontation with Voldemort. He thought that Dumbledore wanted to give him a chance to face Voldemort himself. He recalled how he had learned to use the Mirror of Erised, with the help of the Invisibility Cloak provided by Dumbledore, and figured it was no accident. He said, "I think he knows more or less everything that goes on here, you know. I reckon he had a pretty good idea we were going to try, and instead of stopping us, he just taught us enough to help" (Book One, p. 302).

There are several similarities between Harry's encounter with Voldemort and things the Bible teaches about our interaction with the evil spiritual forces at work in this world. The Bible speaks of disembodied spirits that can come into a person and take over. Sometimes we see that these evil spirits were just filling a spiritual void, taking possession of that person without the person's consent. But there are also spiritual forces that are identified as being behind the destructive belief systems of false prophets. These take hold of persons when they willingly open their hearts and minds to a spirit other than the Holy Spirit of God. We guard against these by refusing to believe their false teachings. It was in the battle for the heart and mind that Harry won the battle, and Quirrell lost it.

The apostle John wrote a warning to early Christians that still applies today:

> Dear friends, do not believe every spirit, but test the spirits to see whether they are from God, because many false prophets have gone out into the world. This is how you can recognize the Spirit of God: Every spirit that acknowledges that Jesus Christ has come in the flesh is from God, but every spirit that does not acknowledge Jesus is not from God. This is the spirit of the antichrist, which you have heard is coming and even now is already in the world. (1 John 4:1–3 NIV)

Some may think it strange that God does not simply do away with the evil one, since he has the power and knows all that is going on, but for some reason God has chosen to give people the opportunity to fight the evil one and—hopefully—win. To this end he instructs us: "Submit yourselves therefore to God. Resist the devil, and he will flee from you" (Jas. 4:7). Seeing how the "shadow and vapor" that Voldemort had become fled from Harry after he resisted giving in to evil can serve to remind us of this promise.

Why the Evil One Could
Not Touch Harry

*"Love as powerful as your mother's for you leaves its own
mark. Not a scar, no visible sign . . . to have been loved so
deeply, even though the person who loved us is gone, will
give us some protection forever."*
—Dumbledore to Harry, Book One, p. 299

*H*arry was surprised to find that Quirrell could not bear to touch
him without great pain and injury to himself. When he asked
Dumbledore about it, the answer all came down to the power of
love. The love of Harry's mother when she gave her life for him
not only spared him from death, it left him with an invisible protection. The extent of this protection is still a mystery, but its
source is clear.

As Lily Potter's act of self-sacrificial love saved Harry from the
curse of death and made it so that the evil one could not touch him,
the Bible says that those who are born of God through faith in the
self-sacrificial death of Christ have a special protection. The reality that the "whole world lies under the power of the evil one" does
not negate this. The Bible promises those who are born of God that
"the one who was born of God protects them, and the evil one does
not touch them" (1 John 5:18). However, it also acknowledges that
we live in a world dominated by evil. That same passage goes on
to say, "We know that we are God's children, and that the whole
world lies under the power of the evil one" (1 John 5:19).

Harry's protection against his evil foe, received as a result of
his mother's love, can remind us of the protection God offers his
children in a world where we too come under the attack of our
evil foe.

A Last-Minute Change of Decorations

[Dumbledore] clapped his hands. In an instant, the green hangings became scarlet and the silver became gold; the huge Slytherin serpent vanished and a towering Gryffindor lion took its place.

—Book One, p. 306

*W*hile Harry and his friends were busy trying to save the wizarding world, Slytherin was still far ahead in points to win the house cup. As the students came together for the end-of-term awards banquet, it looked like Slytherin had won. The Great Hall was decorated with the silver and green banner of Slytherin, bearing the symbol of the snake. The Slytherins were celebrating, but there was to be a sudden turn of fortunes.

Professor Dumbledore awarded points to Ron, Hermione, Harry, and Neville for their respective demonstrations of intelligence and courage. At the last moment, the silver and green banners of Slytherin bearing the snake were replaced with the red and gold banners of Gryffindor bearing the lion. Slytherins who had been rejoicing a moment before fell silent; Gryffindors who had been subdued were suddenly cheering.

Sometimes it looks like evil is winning, but things can change suddenly. God is the only one who knows everything that is going on, and he keeps the score. Jesus tried to explain this to his disciples so they would not get discouraged:

> I tell you the truth, you will weep and mourn while the world rejoices. You will grieve, but your grief will turn to joy. A woman giving birth to a child has pain because her time has come; but when her baby is born she forgets the anguish because of her joy that a child is born into the world. So with you: Now is your time of grief, but I will see you again and you will rejoice, and no one will take away your joy. (John 16:20–22 NIV)

When Jesus was crucified, his disciples wept and the world rejoiced. Even though Jesus had forewarned them, they thought the contest was over and that evil had won. But Jesus had a few points to give them. When he did, it only took an instant for their grief to turn to joy as they realized their side was victorious. In Luke 24:13–35, two of Jesus' followers are walking along, discussing the recent events, when the risen Jesus begins to walk with them. They do not recognize him, however, and begin to tell him the story of the crucifixion. Then they stop to eat. "When he was at the table with them, he took bread, blessed and broke it, and gave it to them. Then their eyes were opened, and they recognized him; and he vanished from their sight. They said to each other, 'Were not our hearts burning within us while he was talking to us on the road, while he was opening the scriptures to us?'" (Luke 24:30–32).

Even now, with the terrorism, wars, and poverty in our world, it may seem that evil has the upper hand. However, we are called to act like Harry and his friends did and to keep focused on fighting evil, even if it seems like evil is winning. Things can change suddenly in such battles. When it comes down to the final battle and the final prizes are awarded, God says there will be an upset. The Bible says that the world will get worse and worse, but that an instant will come when Christ will return, evil will be put down, and all those on God's side will celebrate like never before.

Glimmers of the Gospel in Book Two

Harry Potter and the Chamber of Secrets

Introduction to Book Two

Book Two's predominant themes are freedom for those held captive or enslaved, and the rejection of prejudice and hatred on the basis of bloodline. Another prominent theme is that whatever you send out will come back on you in like kind. Book Two so richly weaves these themes throughout the book that I consider it very sad that many Christians who are working diligently to eradicate racial hatred and bigotry do not even know that these are primary themes throughout the series.

I was interviewed on the radio by a highly respected African-American woman who carries substantial influence within the Christian community. Before having me on to discuss Harry Potter, her staff spent several hours trying to track down a woman who had been quoted in a piece about Harry Potter leading children into Satanism. They were unable to locate her, so the host asked me if I knew her. I told them the article they had received was quoted from the satirical Web site *The Onion,* and that the "quotes" were from fictitious people.

We all laughed, but there was an undercurrent of discomfort that such a fabricated story had been passed along as fact and adapted in such a way that many otherwise credible Christians were believing it and persuading others to believe it. I followed this by asking the host if anyone had made her aware that the books carry a warning of the dangers and destructiveness of hatred and bigotry on the basis of bloodline, as well as strong themes about eradicating slavery and oppression. She had never heard any mention of those themes that were close to her heart as a Christian and as an African-American woman.

Let me summarize some of these themes from Book Two. First comes the theme of freedom for those who are enslaved and oppressed. The book starts with Harry being forced to pretend that he does not even exist, then being imprisoned in his own bedroom by the Dursleys. Harry is freed by Fred, George, and Ron. Throughout the book we see the suffering of Dobby the house-elf as a perpetual slave to the house of Malfoy from generation to generation, and how Dobby is finally freed by Harry's act of redemption. We also see how Ginny is taken captive by Tom Riddle. She becomes enslaved within that relationship, falls under his influence, and becomes a slave to her own sins and the secrecy created by trying to cover up what she has done. She ends up being taken captive by Tom down in the Chamber of Secrets. The climax of the story comes when Harry and Ron risk their lives to free her. In all these ways, we see the dangers and destructiveness of oppression countered with the efforts of others to set the captives free and eradicate oppression wherever it is imposed.

A secondary theme in Book Two is that it is not right to be prejudiced against others on the basis of their bloodline; one should discriminate—in the healthy sense of the word—on the basis of what a person has chosen to become. We see this in the hatred against those born of Muggle parents or of mixed heritage and in the outrage of good students against the use of the word "Mudblood" as a racial slur. The book also explores the history of such bigotry. Those on the good side rejected this belief promoted by Salazar Slytherin and split from him over it.

Another secondary theme in Book Two is that one must be careful what one dishes out to others because it could come right back at oneself (nicely contrived with a broken wand that sends the curse meant for another back on the sender). Gilderoy Lockhart made his reputation by using the Memory Charm to remove the memories of those whose knowledge and expertise he had appropriated as his own. When he tried to use the Memory Charm on Harry and Ron, it rebounded on him.

Ron was delighted to see this happen to Professor Lockhart because he saw through Lockhart from the beginning. But Ron had no room to gloat, for he also had an experience of getting back precisely what he aimed at someone else. When he tried to use his wand to make Draco Malfoy belch up slugs, he was hit with the curse instead, which left him belching the slugs he had intended for his enemy. This is a novel way of saying what Jesus said: "So in everything, do to others what you would have them do to you, for this sums up the Law and the Prophets" (Matt. 7:12 NIV).

Mr. Weasley's Loophole in Magical Law

"Yeah, Dad's crazy about everything to do with Muggles; our shed's full of Muggle stuff. He takes it apart, puts spells on it, and puts it back together again. If he raided our house he'd have to put himself under arrest."
—Fred Weasley to Harry, Book Two, p. 31

*B*ook Two begins with Dobby's warning and the incident with Aunt Petunia's pudding. As punishment, Harry was held captive in his bedroom at the Dursleys'. Ron was concerned because Harry had not responded to any of his letters. Then Fred, George, and Ron learned that Harry had received a warning from the Ministry of Magic for using magic in front of Muggles, so they came to check on him. They "borrowed" Mr. Weasley's flying car, although flying it violated wizarding law, but when they found Harry locked in his bedroom with bars on the window, they felt justified. After they rescued Harry, they chided him for doing magic in front of Muggles (missing the irony entirely), but he insisted that he had not done so. He also rightly pointed out that they had no place to talk, given that they were driving a flying car!

The fact that Mr. Weasley worked in the Misuse of Muggle Artifacts Office and had an enchanted car only heightened the irony. Given his enthusiasm for "Muggle stuff," it seems Mr. Weasley could not resist breaking the very laws he was committed to upholding. Even though the Weasley boys justified their behavior to themselves,

Mrs. Weasley did not share their view. They got in plenty of trouble when they arrived home and found her waiting for them. Mrs. Weasley also confronted Mr. Weasley about his flying car.

Mr. Weasley admitted that it was "very wrong indeed" for the boys to fly the car. When Mrs. Weasley pointed the finger at him, he pointed out that there was a loophole in the law so that he could *have* a flying car as long as he was not *intending* to fly it. Mrs. Weasley was obviously unimpressed by this technicality.

This episode is quite revealing, not only about how Fred, George, and even Mr. Weasley attempt to justify their misdeeds to themselves (as we all tend to do) but also how it relates to the universal human need to satisfy the law, while escaping the prescribed judgment against breaking God's law. In religious terms, this has to do with finding atonement for sin.

Before a person can look for a way to get out of deserved punishment, he must realize that he has been convicted. The Letter to the Romans leads up to this point in an inescapable way. It starts by convincing the reader that God's being is self-evident, except to those who choose to believe a lie (which conveniently releases them from any moral obligation to God in their own minds). Then it points to the more obvious and less socially acceptable sins (rightly presuming that those who are inclined toward more socially acceptable sins will condemn those they deem worse sinners than themselves). Then comes the twist that catches everyone in the net.

Addressing the teachers of the law, the apostle Paul asks, "You, then, that teach others, will you not teach yourself? While you preach against stealing, do you steal? You that forbid adultery, do you commit adultery? You that abhor idols, do you rob temples? You that boast in the law, do you dishonor God by breaking the law?" (Rom. 2:21–23). Surely any individual reading that passage would not have broken all these laws, but in going through a laundry list of the things we know are legally right, all of us will come to realize our own guilt on some point. As the Letter of James concludes, "For whoever keeps the whole law but fails in one point has become accountable for all of it" (Jas. 2:10).

What is the Bible getting at that is similar to what Mr. Weasley did? Those who prided themselves on teaching the law and holding others accountable were not better than those they looked down on as "sinners." Everyone is shown to be "under the power of sin" (Rom. 3:9) "so that every mouth may be silenced, and the whole world may be held accountable to God. For 'no human being will be justified in his sight' by deeds prescribed by the law, for through the law comes the knowledge of sin" (Rom. 3:19–20).

Once a person recognizes his or her own sin, that person must find a loophole or die. The Bible says the punishment for sin is death, followed by the wrath of God being unleashed against all who have sin held to their account. This is a disturbing thought because the Bible also says that God is love. How can a loving and holy God satisfy his love for people who break his law and maintain justice? The spiritual "loophole" Christians rely on is found in the doctrine of atonement.

Throughout the Old Testament, God made provision for sins to be covered with the shed blood of animal sacrifices. Each year the Jewish law allowed people to assign their sin to a scapegoat, which was set free to carry their sins away. Also, the high priest would offer the blood of animals to atone for his own sin and the sins of the people (see the instructions given to Moses in Lev. 16). The sacrifices for atonement of sin were taken into the temple in Jerusalem, into the Most Holy Place, where God's presence resided over the Ark of the Covenant (which held the Ten Commandments). If God accepted their sacrifice, their sins were covered for another year. In this way, the people could escape their due punishment for sin while still acknowledging that God is just and his law righteous (even though they were not).

I believe that God ingeniously planned all along to send Jesus, holy and sinless, to shed his blood on the cross to pay our penalty for sin once and for all. (The Letter to the Hebrews explains this in detail.) Therefore, the penalty is paid, and those who put their faith in the atoning power of the blood of Jesus can be spared the due punishment of death, God's wrath, and eternal separation from our righteous God.

The New Testament asserts that this "loophole" is the only one left open, and that there is no longer any need to go back year after year: "For it was fitting that we should have such a high priest, holy, blameless, undefiled, separated from sinners, and exalted above the heavens. Unlike the other high priests, he has no need to offer sacrifices day after day, first for his own sins, and then for those of the people; this he did once for all when he offered himself" (Heb. 7:26–27).

Consider also Paul's understanding of this new reality:

> But now, apart from law, the righteousness of God has been disclosed, and is attested by the law and the prophets, the righteousness of God through faith in Jesus Christ for all who believe. For there is no distinction, since all have sinned and fall short of the glory of God; they are now justified by his grace as a gift, through the redemption that is in Christ Jesus, whom God put forward as a sacrifice of atonement by his blood, effective through faith. He did this to show his righteousness, because in his divine forbearance he had passed over the sins previously committed; it was to prove at the present time that he himself is righteous and that he justifies the one who has faith in Jesus. (Rom. 3: 21–26)

In everyday terms, the discussion between Mr. and Mrs. Weasley can be seen as a model of the outworking of the spiritual implication that flows from the doctrine of atonement. In ancient Israel, the Day of Atonement was a day of solemn reflection, of sorrow over and repentance from sin—even though the people received God's covering for sin. Atonement was never meant to give them license to break God's law. Those who now trust in Christ's blood as their atoning sacrifice have remission of sins and forgiveness for their infractions of the law, but this should never be used as license to sin. Similarly, Mrs. Weasley's heartfelt conviction that the loophole in the law was not to be used as license to condone law-breaking is a necessary balance to Mr. Weasley's overreliance on it. The balance they strike in this conversation is at the heart of living out the gospel life.

The Mystery of the
Shrinking Door Keys

"Of course, it's very hard to convict anyone because no Muggle would admit their key keeps shrinking—they'll insist they just keep losing it. Bless them, they'll go to any lengths to ignore magic, even if it's staring them in the face."

—Mr. Weasley, Book Two, p. 38

*M*r. Weasley had been out all night on raids looking for Muggle artifacts that had been enchanted. Upon coming home, he told his family and Harry, "All I got were a few shrinking door keys and a biting kettle." Mr. Weasley complained that it was hard to get convictions because Muggles "go to any lengths to ignore magic, even if it's staring them in the face."

If one thinks of the kind of magic in Harry Potter's world as representing miracles in our own, this comment points to something of note about people's response to Jesus. Any cursory reading of the Gospels reveals that Jesus went about openly doing things that were clearly miraculous. In broad daylight, in front of large crowds, Jesus made blind people see, caused the deaf to hear, restored withered limbs, cleansed lepers of their dreaded skin disease, caused the lame to walk, even raised the dead—all right before their eyes!

Most people marveled and gave thanks to God. His enemies, however, seemed to be blind to what he was doing. Technically, they saw what he did. Sometimes they would even argue with him because he was doing these miracles on the Sabbath day, which—in their minds—constituted work and was a violation of religious interpretations of God's law. But they refused to admit that his miraculous power was a sign from God, even though it was staring them in the face!

One time a huge crowd saw Jesus feed thousands, themselves included, with a little boy's lunch. Soon after, they said, "What sign will you show us so that we may believe in you?" *What sign?* Jesus rightly answered that he would give them "the sign of Jonah." This meant that he would die and be resurrected three days later, similar to how Jonah went down into the depths and spent three days and three nights in the belly of a great fish. But even then Jesus knew they still would not believe.

Their spiritual blindness was astounding. On one occasion it was almost funny, if you think of what it must have been like among those discussing how to get rid of Jesus and his trouble-some miracles. Near the culmination of Jesus' ministry, his friend Lazarus became sick and died. Friends and foes of Jesus came for the funeral, wondering aloud how Jesus could have let Lazarus die when he had healed so many others. Jesus finally showed up, four days after Lazarus had been put in the tomb—without being embalmed. Jesus publicly put an end to the mourning when he called Lazarus to come out. And Lazarus came out, alive from the dead! This sign was a demonstration of Jesus' proclamation, "I am the resurrection and the life. Those who believe in me, even though they die, will live, and everyone who lives and believes in me will never die" (John 11:25). Not surprisingly, this was an effective object lesson, and many believed in Jesus because of this miracle.

How did this impact those who had set themselves against Jesus (mostly religious leaders who were jealous of his following)? Did they say, "Wow! He must be the Son of God!"? No! Instead, they accelerated their plans to have Jesus arrested and killed. Here is the funny part that shows how they would go to any lengths to ignore the miraculous even when it was staring them in the face: While they plotted to have Jesus arrested and put to death, they planned to kill Lazarus too, even though he didn't stay dead the first time! John's Gospel reports, "When the great crowd of the Jews learned that he was there, they came not only because of Jesus but also to see Lazarus, whom he had raised from the dead. So the chief priests planned to put Lazarus to death as well, since it was on account of him that many of the Jews were deserting and were believing in Jesus" (John 12:9–11).

After Jesus' crucifixion, the religious leaders were bombarded with inescapable miracles: The soldiers they had sent to guard Jesus' tomb came running back terrified because they had seen angels and Jesus' resurrection. The religious leaders had to pay them hush money. These leaders most likely felt the earthquake that occurred that morning. They could see that the curtain in the temple had been torn from top to bottom (signifying that the way was now open for people to come directly into God's presence). They may have seen or at least heard reports of saints of old who made appearances in Jerusalem at the time of the resurrection. With all of this staring them in the face, they somehow managed to ignore it all.

The Bible gives us an explanation for this: "In their case the god of this world has blinded the minds of the unbelievers, to keep them from seeing the light of the gospel of the glory of Christ, who is the image of God" (2 Cor. 4:4). In our world, the insistence on denying the miraculous has a more ominous source than what we see with the Muggles who refuse to admit that their door keys keep shrinking.

The Best Seeker Wins the Game

"This," said Wood, "is the Golden Snitch, and it's the most important ball of the lot."
—Oliver Wood to Harry, Book One, p. 169

When Oliver Wood explained Quidditch to Harry for the first time, he turned his attention to the Golden Snitch, stressing that it is very hard to catch because it is fast and difficult to see. But it was the Seeker's job to catch it. The Seeker had to keep seeking the Golden Snitch, even while weaving in and out of the Chasers, Beaters, Bludgers, and Quaffle to catch it before the other team's Seeker. Whichever Seeker caught the Snitch would win an extra hundred and fifty points for his or her team. Generally speaking, it is the team with the best Seeker that nearly always wins the game.

Let's consider a modern-day parable that relates to a Quidditch match in Harry's second year: The kingdom of heaven is like a Seeker (Harry) who goes out to play the most important game of the season—Gryffindor versus Slytherin, with Draco Malfoy playing Seeker for Slytherin. When he sees the Snitch he risks all to catch it, even though he has been hit by a rogue Bludger and one arm is broken. He darts after the Snitch, even taking both hands off his broom to catch it and win the game (see Matt. 13:45–46).

As a Seeker, Harry has a knack for spotting things other people do not, but he also devotes himself to training with all his heart and strength. God says, "When you search for me, you will find me; if you *seek me* with all your heart, I will let you find me, says the LORD" (Jer. 29:13). Such dedication is sure to pay off in spiritual and practical terms according to these promises made by Jesus: "But *seek* first [God's] kingdom and his righteousness, and all these things [food, clothing, etc.] will be given to you as well" (Matt. 6:33 NIV). "Ask and it will be given to you; *seek* and you will find; knock and the door will be opened to you. For everyone who asks receives; he who *seeks* finds; and to him who knocks, the door will be opened" (Matt. 7:7–8 NIV).

In life, as in a game of Quidditch, it is usually the best seekers who win the game.

You've Got to Make Some Sacrifices

"Harry Potter risks his own life for his friends!" moaned Dobby.

—Dobby the house-elf, Book Two, p. 179

*O*ne of the distinguishing characteristics of those in the house of Gryffindor in the Harry Potter stories is their willingness to make sacrifices for each other. This is certainly different from the Slytherins. As Book One begins, Lily Potter has just made the ultimate sacrifice by giving her life for Harry. Then when Harry, Ron, and Hermione reached the life-sized chess board in their search for the Sorcerer's Stone, Ron knew best how to play the game:

> "Yes . . ." said Ron softly, "it's the only way . . . I have got to be taken."
> "NO!" Harry and Hermione shouted.
> "That's chess!" snapped Ron. "You've got to make some sacrifices!" (Book One, p. 283)

As a knight, Ron let himself be taken by the white queen, not knowing if that would hurt, if it would knock him out, or if it would kill him. It certainly looked painful to be captured in a game of wizard's chess. He did know that it was the only way they could win, and therefore the only way his friends could proceed in their attempt to stop the thief and save the school.

In Book Two, Dobby the house-elf did all he could to get Harry to go home and avoid the mounting danger at Hogwarts. Dobby knew more than he could say, but there was a monster on the loose intent on killing Muggle-borns, which included Hermione. Harry ended up being hurt severely by a rogue Bludger—followed by having the bones in his arm regrown, thanks to Professor Lockhart's lame attempts to mend the broken bone. Nevertheless, Harry adamantly refused to go home when Dobby urged him to escape danger.

> [Dobby squealed,] "Go home, Harry Potter, go home!"
> "I'm not going anywhere!" said Harry fiercely. "One of my best friends is Muggle-born; she'll be first in line if the Chamber really has been opened—"
> "Harry Potter risks his own life for his friends!" moaned Dobby. (Book Two, p. 179)

All of these are beautiful examples of the kind of friendship Jesus wanted to characterize his followers. Jesus told his disciples, "This is my commandment, that you love one another as I have loved you. No one has greater love than this, to lay down one's life for one's friends" (John 15:12–13). Jesus proved his friendship for us when he lay down his life for us on the cross. He knew it was the only way the game could be won. So when we think of those in Gryffindor House who willingly sacrifice for each other, let us not forget the greatest sacrifice of all, and determine to make sacrifices for our friends.

Pure-Bloods, Muggles, and Mudbloods

> *"What's the new password again?"* he said to Harry.
> *"Er—"* said Harry.
> *"Oh, yeah—pure-blood!"* said Malfoy.
> —Book Two, p. 221

*B*ook Two reveals the history of the bigotry among some in the wizarding world against Muggles and those who are the children of Muggles. It dates all the way back to one of the founders of Hogwarts, Salazar Slytherin. He believed that only "pure-bloods," those of purely wizarding parentage, should be allowed to study at Hogwarts. This difference of opinion between Slytherin and the other three founders created quite a rift. This tradition of bigotry became more pronounced through time, so that fifty years before Harry's time at Hogwarts, a monster released by the Heir of Slytherin killed a girl. In Book Two, that same monster was once again set loose to target "Mudbloods," a vulgar term for anyone not of pure wizarding family heritage.

Those who align themselves with Salazar Slytherin share his bigotry toward those who are not "pure-bloods," but also any who accept Muggle-borns and those of mixed parentage. We see this in

Lucius Malfoy's comments to Mr. Weasley. The Weasleys have pure-wizarding ancestry, but they accept all students, regardless of their bloodline. Mr. Weasley's Muggle Protection Act seems to be the target of Mr. Malfoy's attempts to discredit the Weasley family. Some of the students in Slytherin House are openly bigoted, as Draco is to Hermione (whose parents are both Muggles). One might wonder if the Slytherins' bigotry goes beyond race to include gender since there are no girls on the Slytherins' Quidditch team (although this may change in later books). We also see a measure of hatred and contempt toward those of lower social class or economic level among the Slytherins.

When we learn more about the Heir of Slytherin, it is interesting to note that he is actually not pure-blooded himself. He proudly states that he has the blood of Salazar Slytherin flowing through his veins on his mother's side, but that his father was a Muggle. Future books reveal the lengths to which his hatred of his Muggle parentage will take him. What is clearly seen in this story is that those following the Dark Lord have hatred toward others on the basis of their ancestry and bloodline, a murderous hatred!

Sadly, history reveals that some who have claimed to be Christians have practiced a kind of bigotry similar to that of Salazar Slytherin and his heir, even to the extreme of participating in the Nazi genocide on the basis of bloodline. Such genocidal bigotry can be found in other religious traditions and political regimes as well, where bigotry and hatred motivate killing others on the basis of ethnicity. Such murderous bigotry, seen as the outworking of evil in the Harry Potter stories, is contrary to the gospel message.

The Old Testament says, "[God] shows no partiality to nobles, nor regards the rich more than the poor, for they are all the work of his hands" (Job 34:19). Jesus stunned his disciples and the religious leaders by disregarding the accepted bigotry of his day. He offered the gift of God to a Samaritan woman. Samaritans were hated by most Jews, and this particular woman had also raised a few eyebrows by being married five times and living with a man who was not her husband. He did miracles for Gentiles as well as Jews, although he did acknowledge that his ministry to Jews came first. He allowed women to be his disciples and to listen to his teaching, contrary to other rabbis of the time. He welcomed the poor along with the rich. He lived out the pronouncement made throughout the Old and New Testaments that "God shows no partiality" (Rom. 2:11). (See Acts 10–11 for a story that reveals what a revolutionary concept this was, even to Jesus' disciples and the early church.)

The good news Jesus came to bring was revolutionary, in large measure because it took the promise of blessings God had made to Abraham and his seed (commonly thought to mean only the Jews) and threw the doors wide open for everyone who would believe in Jesus. The Letter to the Galatians sums it up this way: "There is no longer Jew or Greek, there is no longer slave or free, there is no longer male and female; for all of you are one in Christ Jesus. And if you belong to Christ, then you are Abraham's offspring, heirs according to the promise" (Gal. 3:28–29).

The book of Revelation includes a remarkable vision of heaven: "There was a great multitude that no one could count, from every nation, from all tribes and peoples and languages, standing before the throne and before the Lamb, robed in white, with palm branches in their hands" (Rev. 7:9). The only "pure blood" recognized by God is the blood of Jesus. That is the only password necessary to open the doors and gain admittance to the kingdom of heaven.

Professor Dumbledore's Parting Words

"However," said Dumbledore, speaking very slowly and clearly so that none of them could miss a word, "you will find that I will only truly have left this school when none

*here are loyal to me. You will also find that help will
always be given at Hogwarts to those who ask for it."*
—Dumbledore to Harry and Ron,
Book Two, pp. 263–64

When Hermione and Penelope Clearwater were petrified by the monster, everyone at Hogwarts became distressed. The school would be closed if the attacks did not stop. Tom Riddle had led Harry to suspect Hagrid, so at that point Ron and Harry took the Invisibility Cloak and went to Hagrid's hut. Hagrid greeted them with a crossbow, terribly nervous and expecting company. When a knock came at the door, Harry and Ron hid under the Invisibility Cloak while Dumbledore and Cornelius Fudge, Minister of Magic, entered. Over the protests of Dumbledore, Fudge had come to take Hagrid away to Azkaban as a precaution against future attacks.

The next knock brought Mr. Malfoy, who had managed to "persuade" the school governors to suspend Dumbledore as headmaster because he was unable to stop the attacks. At this Fudge exclaimed, "See here, Malfoy, if *Dumbledore* can't stop them . . . who *can*?" But Dumbledore remained calm and agreed to go away. However, he had some parting words that seemed to be intended for the boys hiding under the cloak. Much later, when Harry faced off with Tom Riddle, Tom bragged that Dumbledore had been driven from the school by the mere memory of him. Harry countered, "He's not as gone as you might think!" And just then, the music of the phoenix could be heard.

While Jesus was on earth, his disciples could go to him with all the problems they could not handle—which were plentiful. When the time came for Jesus to depart and go (back to the Father in heaven), he prepared his disciples to function in a new way. They were assured that even though he was gone, he was not really gone. Jesus promised that he was available to them whenever "two or three are gathered in my name"; those who took his name and remained loyal to him could trust that he was with them (Matt. 18:20). After he had risen from the dead, he gave them final instructions before ascending back into heaven: "All authority in heaven and on earth has been given to me. Go therefore and make disciples of all nations, baptizing them in the name of the Father and of the Son and of the Holy Spirit, and teaching them to obey everything that I have commanded you. *And remember, I am with you always, to the end of the age*" (Matt. 28:18–20).

Dumbledore's promise that help would be given at Hogwarts to all who ask for it is also reminiscent of something Jesus promised his followers: "Very truly, I tell you, if you ask anything of the Father in my name, he will give it to you. Until now you have not asked for anything in my name. Ask and you will receive, so that your joy may be complete" (John 16:23–24). The time came when Harry especially needed to know Dumbledore was not really gone, and when he needed to call out for help, which he did while fighting the basilisk.

Likewise, the real good news of the gospel is not that Jesus lived two thousand years ago, did amazing things we should remember, and was a remarkable moral teacher. The good news is that Jesus will only truly have left this world when none here are loyal to him (that is, when he takes them out). Even though we cannot see him bodily now, Jesus is here, and help will always be given to those who ask for it in his name.

Gilderoy Lockhart Goes Down!

"It's not all book signings and publicity photos, you know. You want fame, you have to be prepared for a long hard slog."
—Gilderoy Lockhart to Harry, Book Two, p. 298

Gilderoy Lockhart created quite a lofty reputation for himself, albeit by questionable means—but that seemed beside the point to

Professor Lockhart. The entire collection of books he claimed to have authored was an assortment of the expertise, accomplishments, and conquests of others. Professor Lockhart appropriated these for himself, while looking down on those whose work he stole.

Lockhart viewed everything as an opportunity to exalt himself. At book signings, before the media, among the faculty at Hogwarts—Lockhart was puffed up with conceit. He created quite the image: winning *Witch Weekly*'s Most-Charming-Smile Award five times in a row, always dressed to color-coordinated perfection, with his hat set at a jaunty angle. Lockhart pursued the adulation of his fans, and was usually prepared to hand out autographed photos.

His elevated view of himself caused him to lose perspective, however. He claimed to know more than everyone else—Dumbledore included. He openly bragged that he knew where the Chamber of Secrets was hidden, and could have rid the school of the monster if he had been given free reign. He also assumed that Harry shared his quest for fame. This was not the case, as attested to by Harry's resistance to Colin Creevy's hero worship. In a flash of arrogance, Lockhart presumed Harry wanted to be just like him. Lockhart told Harry, "Yes, yes, I know what you're thinking! 'It's all right for him, he's an internationally famous wizard already!' But when I was twelve, I was just as much of a nobody as you are now. In fact, I'd say I was even more of a nobody! I mean, a few people have heard of you, haven't they? All that business with He-Who-Must-Not-Be-Named!" (Book Two, p. 91).

The other professors knew Lockhart for the fraud he was, so when the monster had taken a student down into the Chamber of Secrets, they were delighted at the chance to bring him down a few pegs. Professor McGonagall's invitation for him to have free reign at catching the monster and saving the girl gave Lockhart's peers a measure of pleasure even in that dark moment. However, they had no idea how far down Professor Lockhart would be forced to go.

The Bible makes this declaration: "All who exalt themselves will be humbled, and all who humble themselves will be exalted"

(Matt. 23:12). We can see this in a parable Jesus told to put people like Gilderoy Lockhart in their place:

> Two men went up to the temple to pray, one a Pharisee and the other a tax collector. The Pharisee, standing by himself, was praying thus, "God, I thank you that I am not like other people: thieves, rogues, adulterers, or even like this tax collector. I fast twice a week; I give a tenth of all my income." But the tax collector, standing far off, would not even look up to heaven, but was beating his breast and saying, "God, be merciful to me, a sinner!" I tell you, this man went down to his home justified rather than the other; for all who exalt themselves will be humbled, but all who humble themselves will be exalted. (Luke 18:10–14)

Another parallel in looking at what happened to Gilderoy Lockhart speaks more directly to the gospel message. Professor Lockhart, who exalted himself, was indeed humbled. He was brought down not only figuratively but literally when Ron and Harry forced him to go down far under the school, into the Chamber of Secrets. Once there, Lockhart got exactly what was coming to him. When he tried to cast his Memory Charm on Ron and Harry, it came back on him.

Gilderoy Lockhart exalted himself and was brought down, but this story also shows that those who humble themselves will be lifted. Harry and Ron (who had been humble all along and willingly lowered themselves into the depths under the school to save Ginny) were raised up by the phoenix. After being raised up, they were honored by Dumbledore. Both received Special Awards for Service to the School and two hundred points apiece for Gryffindor. This could serve to illustrate a theme taught in the book of Philippians:

> Do nothing from selfish ambition or conceit, but in humility regard others as better than yourselves. Let each of you look not to your own interests, but to the interests of others. Let the same mind be in you that was in Christ Jesus,
>
>> who, though he was in the form of God,
>>   did not regard equality with God
>>   as something to be exploited,
>> but emptied himself,

taking the form of a slave,
being born in human likeness.
And being found in human form,
he humbled himself
and became obedient to the point of death—
even death on a cross.
Therefore God also highly exalted him
and gave him the name
that is above every name,
so that at the name of Jesus
every knee should bend,
in heaven and on earth and under the earth,
and every tongue should confess
that Jesus Christ is Lord,
to the glory of God the Father.

(Phil. 2:3–11)

Harry and Ron's attitude and actions of going down into the Chamber of Secrets to save Ginny, then being raised up can serve to remind us of Christ, who humbled himself to come down to save us, then was raised up from death and exalted to the heights of heaven. And Gilderoy Lockhart can remind us that everyone who exalts himself will be brought down.

A Songbird and an Old Hat

"This is what Dumbledore sends his defender! A songbird and an old hat! Do you feel brave, Harry Potter? Do you feel safe now?"

—Tom Riddle to Harry, Book Two, p. 316

When Fawkes, Dumbledore's pet phoenix, showed up piping its weird music, Tom Riddle knew Dumbledore was behind it. He laughed at Harry as the bird dropped the Sorting Hat at Harry's feet. Even Harry did not quite see how these could help him in a duel with Tom Riddle—especially without his wand, which Tom still held. But as things progressed, it turned out that these unlikely things were precisely what Harry needed.

Previously, when Harry had been alone in Professor Dumbledore's office with Fawkes, the sickly looking bird suddenly burst into flames. He watched in amazement as it was reborn out of the ashes. Dumbledore explained that this was the nature of phoenixes, their other fascinating characteristics being that they "can carry immensely heavy loads, their tears have healing powers, and they make highly *faithful* pets" (Book Two, p. 207).

Consider the characteristics of Professor Dumbledore's pet phoenix. Each of these can be related to the gospel. Its ability to rise from the ashes can be seen as symbolic of the promise of resurrection. Fawkes was the one who pecked out the basilisk's eyes, thereby destroying its murderous gaze. The ability of the phoenix to carry heavy loads served to lift up all who would hold on and carried them out of the Chamber, where Tom Riddle and the basilisk did their best to kill Harry. The tears the phoenix shed as Harry lay dying showed compassion. The same tears also brought healing from the poisonous venom of the King of Snakes. If it had not been for the healing tears of the phoenix, Harry's wound would surely have been fatal.

As for the other item Dumbledore provided for Harry, the Sorting Hat declared which house each student at Hogwarts would be in. Although the Sorting Hat had considered putting Harry in Slytherin, and said he could have been great there, it had openly declared Harry to be a Gryffindor. In his showdown with Tom Riddle, Harry needed to have confidence that he *belonged* in Gryffindor while fighting against evil. The battle this time was partly in the form of Tom Riddle playing with Harry's mind by suggesting that they had a lot in common. Perhaps this was an attempt to keep Harry from fighting against him by undermining his confidence about belonging in Gryffindor. The Sorting Hat reminded Harry that he was a Gryffindor, and later supplied proof when he was able to pull the sword of Godric Gryffindor out of the hat.

How do a songbird and an old hat relate to the gospel? First, let's consider the symbolism of the phoenix. An Old Testament prophecy says, "But for you who revere my name the sun of righteousness shall rise, with healing in its wings. You shall go out leaping like calves from the stall. And you shall tread down the wicked, for they will be ashes under the soles of your feet, on the day when I act, says the LORD of hosts" (Mal. 4:2–3). Here we see the imagery of a bird with healing powers rising up to help the righteous triumph over the wicked. Most commentaries consider this a messianic prophecy. Although no use is made directly in the New Testament of the exact phrases "sun of righteousness" or "healing in his wings," there is an image of the glorified Son of Man (Jesus) in which his face is described like "the sun shining with full force" with a two-edged sword coming from his mouth (Rev. 1:16).

Consider these parallels: Jesus was sent by the Father, and was *faithful* to his mission. He was so faithful that when he struggled in prayer on the night he was to be betrayed, he was able to say, "Father, if you are willing, remove this cup from me"—referring to the cup of God's wrath and the suffering that awaited him on the cross—"yet, not my will but yours be done" (Luke 22:42).

Jesus offers to carry our heavy burdens: "Come to me, all you that are weary and are carrying heavy burdens, and I will give you rest" (Matt. 11:28). What are these heavy burdens that the Messiah would bear for us? Christians cherish the prophecy found in Isaiah:

> Surely he has borne our infirmities
>   and carried our diseases;
> yet we accounted him stricken,
>   struck down by God, and afflicted.
> But he was wounded for our transgressions,
>   crushed for our iniquities;
> upon him was the punishment that made us whole,
>   and by his bruises we are healed.
>   (Isa. 53:4–5)

Since Jesus carried these burdens, he has compassion for us. He was a man of sorrows and acquainted with grief. He wept at the grave of his friend, Lazarus, even though he knew that moments later he would raise him back to life. The phoenix wept at Harry's side when Tom Riddle enjoyed watching him die: "'You're dead, Harry Potter,' said Riddle's voice above him. 'Dead. Even Dumbledore's bird knows it. Do you see what he's doing, Potter? He's crying.'" Harry was dying from the basilisk's deadly venom, but his death was interrupted and reversed by the ministry of the phoenix. Similarly, the Bible says, "And you were dead in your trespasses and sins" (Eph. 2:1 NASB), but Christ came to interrupt and reverse death to give us new life. The bird's tears healed Harry of the fatal wound. Likewise, the one who has died and rose again himself has the power to heal us from the fatal venom of sin and raise us back to eternal life.

With regard to the Sorting Hat, does the Bible speak of a head covering that can assure us that we belong in a house other than the one ruled by the evil one? The apostle Paul declares, "For our struggle is not against enemies of blood and flesh, but against the rulers, against the authorities, against the cosmic powers of this present darkness, against the spiritual forces of evil in the heavenly places. Therefore take up the whole armor of God, so that you may be able to withstand on that evil day, and having done everything, to stand firm" (Eph. 6:12–13). This passage goes on to describe the full armor of God, which includes a head covering: the helmet of salvation. Like Harry we need to *know* we are saved in order to have courage for the battles with the evil one.

The Sorting Hat that was handed to Harry during his battle reminded him that he had been chosen to be in Gryffindor. God wants his children to remember that they were securely placed in Christ by the Holy Spirit. Therefore, we can confidently resist the accusations of the enemy when he tries to undermine our confident faith. It is from such assurance of mind that the Christian can draw the "sword of the Spirit," which is the word of God to defeat the evil one while engaged in spiritual battles. So the weapons Dumbledore sent Harry were formidable indeed, as are the ones provided to those in Christ.

The Rescue of Ginny Weasley

"Ginny, please wake up," Harry muttered desperately,
shaking her. Ginny's head lolled hopelessly from side to
side.
   "She won't wake," said a soft voice.

Book Two, p. 307

As improbable as it seemed, Ginny Weasley was the guilty one.
She had trusted herself to Tom Riddle, who reached her through
his enchanted diary. Progressively she poured herself into that
diary, and Tom Riddle poured himself back into her. She was soon
following the course he set out for her. He became her ruler, causing her to do terrible things. She was the one killing Hagrid's roost-
ers to protect the basilisk. She had loosed the monstrous snake on
the school. In the end, she was taken captive by Tom Riddle to lure
Harry down into the Chamber of Secrets. This left Ginny as good
as dead, under the control of one whose nature was murderous.

Then Harry arrived, killed the basilisk, defeated Tom Riddle,
and sent him back where he came from. When Tom Riddle's memory was destroyed by the venom of his own snake, Ginny's life
came streaming back into her. Then Fawkes raised them all up
through the pipes and guided them to Professor McGonagall's
office. There they were greeted with loving embraces. The whole
story came out, even the troublesome truth that Ginny had been
enchanted by Voldemort himself and that she was guilty.

Ginny was terribly afraid she would be expelled. After all, that
was what happened to Hagrid, the last person thought to have
opened the Chamber of Secrets. And he had been framed, while
Ginny actually did the deeds. However, Dumbledore waived the
punishment and sent her to Madam Pomfrey in the hospital wing
with a prescription for hot chocolate. Ginny had not done anything
to deserve such favor. She deserved to be expelled, maybe worse.
But Headmaster Dumbledore extended his gracious kindness to her.

This sequence of events can be likened to a retrospective of what happens to those who put their faith in Christ for salvation. The Letter to the Ephesians says, "You were dead through the trespasses and sins in which you once lived, following the course of this world, following the ruler of the power of the air, the spirit that is now at work among those who are disobedient" (Eph. 2:1–2).

Even though few of us have done something as destructive as to loose the king of snakes on our classmates, "All of us once lived among [those who are disobedient] in the passions of our flesh, following the desires of flesh and senses, and we were by nature children of wrath, like everyone else. But God, who is rich in mercy, out of the great love with which he loved us even when we were dead through our trespasses, made us alive together with Christ" (Eph. 2:3–5). We were not physically dead, but as long as we were without rescue, under the control of the evil one, we were as good as dead and sure to end up dead if Christ had not rescued us, apart from anything we could have done to save ourselves.

The Bible goes on to explain, "[God] raised us up with him and seated us with him in the heavenly places in Christ Jesus, so that in the ages to come he might show the immeasurable riches of his grace in kindness toward us in Christ Jesus" (Eph. 2:6–7). When the King of Snakes was defeated, Ginny came back to life. Similarly, Christ's death on the cross destroyed the "snake" that strikes with the venom of sin that brings death. Christ took the venom of sin and death for us. He died and conquered death for us. All who put their trust in Christ are raised up with him. Satan has not been utterly destroyed yet, just as Tom Riddle's memory only went away, to rise again another time. The good news of the gospel includes God's firm assurance that the snake (Satan) will ultimately be defeated and cast into hell forever, never to torment anyone ever again for all eternity. We are just not to that part of our story yet.

The Bible describes all of this as a work of grace: "For by grace you have been saved through faith, and this is not your own doing; it is the gift of God—not the result of works, so that no one may boast" (Eph. 2:8–9). What is this grace? Unmerited favor on top of mercy. It would have been mercy if Dumbledore simply did not punish Ginny as she deserved. God's goodness toward us includes mercy, not receiving the punishment we deserve, but also grace, receiving the favor we know we do not deserve. As Ginny was treated with such love and kindness by Dumbledore after she was rescued, so too God will treat all who are saved. As we think of how Ginny headed toward the hospital wing, looking forward to a steaming mug of hot chocolate instead of packing her bags, she can represent a small taste of what the grace of God is like.

Dumbledore's Remedy for Doubt

"Only a true Gryffindor could have pulled that out of the hat, Harry."
—Dumbledore to Harry, Book Two, p. 334

*A*fter Harry survived his battle with Tom Riddle and the basilisk, he was still deeply disturbed by some things Tom Riddle suggested to him about their apparent similarities. Dumbledore did not deny these, including a "certain disregard for rules," but reminded Harry that the Sorting Hat had put him in Gryffindor even though it could see the similarities that Tom Riddle pointed out. Dumbledore had a remedy for Harry's doubt. His proof that Harry belonged in Gryffindor was to point him to the blood-stained silver sword, with the name of Godric Gryffindor engraved above the hilt.

Harry had been declared to be *in Gryffindor* when the Sorting Hat sorted him. Those who trust Christ are declared to be *in Christ*. The Bible explains that we have been *chosen* to be *in Christ*. This is not something earned, but declared. Harry's place in Gryffindor was not based on him being perfectly good. Likewise, our security in Christ is not based on our being perfectly good, although we do want to please God who calls us to be holy (which could be compared to how Harry wants to please Dumbledore). Dumbledore put Harry's doubts to rest with assurance that he had the sword that proved he belonged in Gryffindor. It is being *in Christ* and relying on his righteousness that gives us confidence that we belong in God's family and will remain accepted there. Even the apostle Paul had to come to grips with the fact that he sometimes did the very things he hated, and did not do the very good he sought to do. In light of recognizing this inner struggle with evil inclinations, Paul exclaims, "Wretched man that I am! Who will rescue me from this body of death? Thanks be to God through Jesus Christ our Lord!" (Rom. 7:24–25). His assurance that he is *in Christ* is key.

The gospel shows that it is not being perfectly good, without any sinful inclinations, that makes one right with God. Rather, it is knowing that even on our best day, with the best intentions, when we still struggle against evil externally and internally, our hope is found by being *in Christ*. Later in the same letter, Paul gives strong assurance to help Christians put doubts to rest: "For I am convinced that neither death, nor life, nor angels, nor rulers, nor things present, nor things to come, nor powers, nor height, nor depth, nor anything else in all creation, will be able to separate us from the love of God in Christ Jesus our Lord" (Rom. 8:38–39; see also 8:31–37).

Since the "sword of the Spirit" is the word of God, perhaps the passage above from God's word will give us a confidence similar to that which put Harry's doubts to rest when Dumbledore pointed him to the name engraved on the hilt of the sword of Godric Gryffindor.

Dobby's Sock and Other Tales of Redemption

"Got a sock," said Dobby in disbelief. "Master threw it, and Dobby caught it, and Dobby—Dobby is free."
—Book Two, p. 338

*I*n introducing himself to Harry, Dobby explained that he is a house-elf and therefore bound to serve one house and one family forever. Unfortunately for Dobby, the house he served was the house of Malfoy. House-elves are slaves, without possessions. A house-elf wears rags of some sort because the terms of his enslavement declares that if anyone in his family gives him a piece of clothing, he will be free. That is why Dobby was wearing a pillowcase when he met Harry. Dobby explained that his master and family were careful not to even give him so much as an old sock, so as to keep him enslaved.

Harry's triumph over the Dark Lord had given hope to the house-elves:

> "Ah, if Harry Potter only knew!" Dobby groaned, more tears dripping onto his ragged pillowcase. "If he only knew what he means to us, to the lowly, the enslaved, we dregs of the magical world! . . . But mostly, sir, life has improved for my kind since you triumphed over He-Who-Must-Not-Be-Named. Harry Potter survived, and the Dark Lord's power was broken, and it was a new dawn, sir, and Harry Potter shone like a beacon of hope for those of us who thought the Dark days would never end, sir." (Book Two, pp. 177–78)

When Dobby met Harry it had been twelve years since Voldemort's power was broken, but Dobby himself had not benefited much personally. He was still enslaved to a cruel master, Lucius Malfoy. When the whole story came out, we learned that Mr. Malfoy played a key role in the dark deeds that happened at Hogwarts that year. He had slipped Tom Riddle's diary into Ginny's book. When Mr. Malfoy came storming into Hogwarts at the end of Book Two, Dobby was bobbing at his feet, still trying to polish his shoes. Dumbledore set Mr. Malfoy straight by letting him know that he was back in power and knew what Mr. Malfoy had done. As Mr. Malfoy stormed out, kicking Dobby down the hall, Harry had a great idea.

Harry tricked Mr. Malfoy into tossing Dobby his old sock. Once Dobby caught the sock, he realized that he was free. Mr. Malfoy was furious that his unwitting gift of a garment had cost him his slave, but there was nothing he could do. Dobby was free, and once free, he could use his considerable magical powers to protect himself and others from Mr. Malfoy. So when Dobby said that Mr. Malfoy had to leave, Mr. Malfoy *had* to leave.

The house-elves saw Harry as a light in their darkness. He gave them hope that there was some way to break the power of the Dark Lord who ruled so cruelly. Likewise, the prophecies of a coming Jewish Messiah were a light of hope even to non-Jewish people. Indeed, the promised Messiah gave hope to all those who were oppressed and who longed for freedom from cruel masters. Long before Jesus was born, the Bible prophesied that the Messiah would be a light to the Gentiles, like a light dawning for people who sat in darkness (see Matt. 4:16). Jesus fulfilled the specific prophecies when he went to live in "Galilee of the Gentiles." Jesus came to those who had no claim on salvation. He did not come to call the righteous—or self-righteous—but those enslaved to sin. When Jesus died and rose again, he broke the curse and offered a new dawn of hope, not just to the Jews, but to all who would believe in him.

This sense that Jesus was the promised light in the darkness was reinforced by the prophecy John the Baptist's father gave about his son:

> And you, child, will be called the prophet of the Most High;
>   for you will go before the Lord to prepare his ways,
> to give knowledge of salvation to his people
>   by the forgiveness of their sins.
> By the tender mercy of our God,
>   the dawn from on high will break upon us,
> to give light to those who sit in darkness and in the shadow
>   of death,
>   to guide our feet into the way of peace.
>
> (Luke 1:76–79)

When Jesus began his public ministry, he came to the synagogue in his home town of Nazareth. He publicly read a familiar passage from the prophet Isaiah. This passage was commonly understood as a prediction of what the awaited messiah would do. Jesus astounded the audience by announcing that this prophecy had been fulfilled that day, in their hearing. Here is what Jesus read:

> The Spirit of the Lord is upon me,
>> because he has anointed me to bring good news to the poor.
>
> He has sent me to proclaim release to the captives
>> and recovery of sight to the blind,
>>
>> to let the oppressed go free,
>
> to proclaim the year of the Lord's favor.
>
> (Luke 4:18–19, reading from Isa. 61:1–2)

This "year of the Lord's favor" refers to the Year of Jubilee, when once each fiftieth year all the slaves in Israel were to be set free. Jesus declared himself to be the one who would release the captives and let the oppressed go free. This is backed up later in the Letter to the Galatians: "For freedom Christ has set us free. Stand firm, therefore, and do not submit again to a yoke of slavery" (Gal. 5:1). This theme carries on throughout the New Testament.

The Bible describes people as slaves to sin, under a malevolent master. Unless we are freed, we are destined to be slaves forever. We too are clothed in spiritual rags, because the Bible says that even our best efforts are like "filthy rags" when what we really need are "garments of salvation" and "robes of righteousness": "I will greatly rejoice in the LORD, my whole being shall exult in my God; for he has clothed me with the garments of salvation, he has covered me with the robe of righteousness" (Isa. 61:10).

Dobby's sock can be a symbol of redemption. The idea is that something is given as a ransom to buy back or purchase the freedom of something or someone held captive. When the payment is made, the captive can go free. Our "garments of salvation" come in the form of the righteous blood of Jesus Christ that he gave as a ransom to pay our debt of sin. Therefore, "You know that you were ransomed from the futile ways inherited from your ancestors, not with perishable things like silver or gold, but with the precious blood of Christ" (1 Pet. 1:18–19).

We cannot be freed until someone gives us these robes of righteousness. We cannot get our own righteousness, and our master certainly is not going to help us out. He wants us to stay enslaved to him. The robes of righteousness have been purchased for us by Christ. In effect, they were tossed to us—unwittingly—by those acting under Satan's influence who put Jesus to death. They thought they were just killing him, when really they were acting to deliver the redemption God wanted us to receive.

Even though Christ came a long time ago, many individuals have not personally experienced the freedom he came to bring. Jesus has purchased the "garments of salvation" for us; he offers us his own righteousness in exchange for our old rags of our best efforts. But we have to take hold of it for ourselves, like Dobby catching that sock that set him free. Now that this garment has been offered, we each have to lay hold of it by faith. Then we can exclaim, as Dobby did, "I am free! I am free!"

Once we are freed by Christ, our obligation to live as slaves to sin and in Satan's control is over. Thereafter, we are commanded to be careful not to submit again to such slavery. We are given the power of the Holy Spirit so that we can resist our old master's attempts to enslave us again. We would do well to behave like Dobby and send our old master packing.

Glimmers of the Gospel in Book Three
Harry Potter and the Prisoner of Azkaban

Introduction to Book Three

*I*n Book Three we see the tenacious struggle required to bring about justice in a world fraught with injustice. Sirius Black had been wrongly accused, convicted, and imprisoned for more than a decade for a crime he did not commit, while the guilty one went free. Buckbeak the Hippogriff was unjustly condemned to death on the false accusations of one who gave and garnered false testimony. In Book Two, Hagrid was imprisoned unjustly because of the cloud of suspicion that remained over him based on a false accusation and conviction for something he had not done. He had been wrongfully expelled from Hogwarts because he had been framed for opening the Chamber of Secrets fifty years earlier, although he had not done so.

To counter these acts and effects of injustice, Dumbledore allows Harry, Ron, and Hermione to uncover the truth, which helps to correct some of the effects of injustice. Harry and Hermione are commissioned to do what they can to save innocent lives, and at least free them from the ultimate infliction of unjust punishments until the injustice can be overcome with true justice.

A secondary theme of Book Three is learning to find ways to overcome our fears and painful memories of the worst times of our lives rather than to give in to despair or fear. This is addressed by learning to counteract the power of the boggarts and the dementors. We also see a corollary in the life of Professor Lupin, who does not let the personal challenges associated with being a werewolf keep him from trying his best to be a productive member of society. We see that he is poor, probably because it is hard for a werewolf to find work in the wizarding world, but he still risks misunderstanding and criticism in order to contribute by teaching Defense Against the Dark Arts.

In the Company of Albus Dumbledore

Harry happened to agree wholeheartedly with Mrs.
Weasley that the safest place on earth was wherever Albus
Dumbledore happened to be.
—Book Three, p. 67

*A*lbus Dumbledore, Headmaster of Hogwarts, is a somewhat mysterious character. The reader gets the impression that there is far more to him than anyone yet knows. However, we do know that Dumbledore engenders trust among those on the side of good, making them feel safer for being in his presence. In his first year, when Harry knows someone is trying to hurt or kill him, he is tremendously relieved to see Professor Dumbledore in the stands for the Quidditch match. And Dumbledore makes evildoers think twice before doing anything amiss while he is around.

Here is some of what we know so far: Dumbledore was the Transfiguration teacher fifty years earlier, when Tom Riddle was a student. When Tom framed Hagrid for opening the Chamber of Secrets, Dumbledore was the only one who was not fooled. He kept a close watch on Tom thereafter, so it was not safe for him to open the Chamber again. He is one of the few people unafraid to call Voldemort by name. When Harry's parents were murdered, Dumbledore decided Harry would be better off living with his Muggle aunt and uncle and delivered him to their doorstep personally. Dumbledore gave Harry the Invisibility Cloak his father left him, and permission to be on the Gryffindor Quidditch team his first year. Dumbledore is famous for his defeat of the dark wizard Grindelwald in 1945. He doesn't need an Invisibility Cloak to become invisible. He made sure Harry found the Mirror of Erised, understood how it worked, and was prepared if he should ever run across it again. We later learn that Dumbledore had hidden the Sorcerer's Stone in the mirror. The knowledge Dumbledore arranged for Harry to learn is what helped him defeat Quirrell and Voldemort. In Harry's second year, again it was Dumbledore who gave Harry the knowledge he needed to prepare for his battle with Tom

Riddle (aka: You-Know-Who), by explaining that his presence would be available to anyone who remained loyal to him and that help would come to anyone at Hogwarts who asked for it. In the battle, Harry's survival and victory hinged on his loyalty to Dumbledore. And it was the weapons Dumbledore sent that Harry used to defeat the basilisk and Tom Riddle.

When injustice is in the works, Dumbledore manages to help set things right—as right as things can be while people are either too afraid to stand up to evil or unable to see the truth. He made sure Sirius and Buckbeak escaped, and that Hagrid was released from Azkaban. He gave Hagrid a teaching post once his name was cleared of the crime Tom Riddle framed him for. (This took fifty years, but it seems that Dumbledore is extremely patient or has a different view of time than most.)

While Dumbledore is staunchly on the side of good, and tremendously powerful, he often stands back to let those on the good side take up the battle (providing overarching security, guidance, weapons, and instruction). When Hermione and Harry told him the truth about Peter Pettigrew and asked if he believed them, he answered, "Yes, I do. . . . But I have no power to make other men see the truth, or to overrule the Minister of Magic." Instead of providing the solution for them, Dumbledore pointed the way for them to bring about justice and help save innocent lives. While it seems that he could set everything right in an instant, he allows the battle to play out and helps those looking up to him to engage in the battle themselves.

Dumbledore seems unusually open to giving people second chances, and redeeming those who have been rejected in wizarding society: He hired Professor Lupin even though he knew he was a werewolf. When Hagrid was expelled, he arranged for Headmaster Dippet to keep him at Hogwarts and train him as Keeper of Keys. Dumbledore lets students attend Hogwarts without discriminating on the basis of their bloodline and magical heritage. Dumbledore never endorses breaking the rules, but exercises authority at Hogwarts in the form of humane punishments. He also exercises his prerogative to show mercy, forbearance, and grace to those caught breaking the rules.

While Dumbledore's power is greater than Voldemort's, he refuses to resort to the Dark Arts. Dumbledore is Ron's hero. Hagrid repeatedly calls him a great man, and will not tolerate anyone speaking against him. His staff respects him. The dementors fear him. When Harry and friends are really in trouble, they run to Dumbledore. As Harry realized his first year, Dumbledore seems to know everything that is going on, but holds back to let his students fight the battles. Then he shows up afterward, to give some insight and provide lessons. His provision of safety does not preclude casualties—which do occur when evil is on the loose—but Dumbledore is actively engaged in the fight against evil.

We also see that Dumbledore presents a danger for those on the side of evil. When Professor Quirrell admitted that he had tried to knock Harry off his broom, he also said that Snape's countercurse was unnecessary since he could not have done anything to harm Harry with Dumbledore watching. Before Harry and friends went down the trapdoor, someone lured Dumbledore away (presumably because that would remove a measure of protection for those on the good side). Lucius Malfoy did all in his power to have Dumbledore removed as Headmaster, but when Dumbledore bested him, Malfoy dared not challenge him directly. Tom Riddle admitted that he could not let the monster out of the Chamber of Secrets again while he was a student at Hogwarts because of Dumbledore. He had to preserve his memory in the diary, hoping for a time when Dumbledore would be less of a threat to his evil plans. As it turned out, that was not the case.

Dumbledore's attitude is typically cheerful, kind, long-suffering, calm, and there is usually a twinkle in his eye. However, when faced with an assault of evil, he is strong and unyielding. He is compassionate toward those who are weak or who have fallen under the influence of the evil one, but he does not interfere with the consequences they bring upon themselves if they have willingly conspired to do evil. When someone such as Ginny Weasley is overtaken by evil unwittingly or against her will, he does not punish severely, but corrects. Overall, Dumbledore seems to genuinely love people. He stands staunchly on the side of good, but hates evil, even while showing compassion for those destroyed by the evil they embrace.

Hmmm . . . Perhaps you can draw your own parallels here.

Let the Feast Begin!

"Let the feast begin!" [said Dumbledore.]
    The golden plates and goblets before them filled sud-denly with food and drink.
                                                —Book Three, pp. 93–94

*O*ne of the most marvelous and enjoyable aspects of life at Hogwarts is the magical meals. It is great fun for the students to sit down at a table and to watch all their favorite foods appear—especially for Harry, who had never been allowed to eat enough to really satisfy his hunger: "The Dursleys had never exactly starved Harry, but he'd never been allowed to eat as much as he liked" (Book One, p. 123). The feasts were especially lavish, but every day, at every meal, the food magically appeared on their plates in the Great Hall. Then, when the meal was over the plates were magically clean again. (Of course, we later learn that even such magic requires the service of willing house-elves working in the kitchens.)

When Jesus went about teaching people about the kingdom of God, he attracted massive crowds because of the miracles he was performing, mostly healing the sick and casting demons out of people tormented by them. Kurt Bruner, author of *Finding God in the Lord of the Rings,* pointed out in a radio interview that the use of good magic in fantasy stories could be compared to that which is miraculous in the real world. Some people who saw the miracles of Jesus may have thought of him as a magician.

Jesus was far more than a magician, however. He would soon make this clear to the gathering crowd by the message that accompanied his miraculous signs. This complimentary meal would be followed by an after-dinner talk they would never forget. The miracle Jesus was about to perform would speak a language everyone understands: hunger satisfaction.

John 6:1–13 tells the familiar story about Jesus feeding the crowd by the Sea of Galilee: "One of his disciples, Andrew, Simon Peter's brother, said to him, 'There is a boy here who has five barley loaves and two fish. But what are they among so many people?' " (John 6:8–9). Notice here that Jesus let a small but willing servant help deliver up the miracle meal, not unlike what Dumbledore did by employing the house-elves in his kitchens. "Then Jesus took the loaves, and when he had given thanks, he distributed them to those who were seated; so also the fish, *as much as they wanted*. When they were satisfied, he told his disciples, 'Gather up the fragments left over, so that nothing may be lost.' So they gathered them up, and from the fragments of the five barley loaves, left by those who had eaten, they filled twelve baskets" (John 6:11–13).

As at Hogwarts, this was an all-you-can-eat meal and cleanup was provided! But Jesus was not just doing tricks with fish and bread, nor was he only concerned with his audience's physical hunger. He was aiming to teach the people a vital spiritual truth. This crowd was expecting a prophet to arise to free them from the oppressive Roman government under which they lived. Moses had promised the people of Israel, "The LORD your God will raise up for you a prophet like me from among your own brothers. You must listen to him" (Deut. 18:15 NIV). They remembered how Moses was good at serving up regular meals and were now wondering if Jesus could be the one Moses told them to expect.

"When the people saw the sign that he had done, they began to say, 'This is indeed the prophet who is to come into the world'" (John 6:14). A political action committee formed right then and there. Someone came to the conclusion that they should make Jesus their king and have him fulfill all the other prophecies the Messiah would fulfill. They especially liked the part about their enemies being overthrown. John continues, "When Jesus realized that they were about to come and take him by force to make him king, he withdrew again to the mountain by himself" (John 6:15).

What's the point? These people were focused on earthly food and political power. Jesus went on to explain, "Do not work for the food that perishes, but for the food that endures for eternal life, which the Son of Man will give you. For it is on him that God the Father has set his seal" (John 6:27).

But the people still did not understand; they were seeking bread to satisfy a mere physical hunger. Jesus put it to them this way: "I am the bread of life. *Whoever comes to me will never be hungry, and whoever believes in me will never be thirsty*" (John 6:35).

Jesus used a "magical meal" to get their attention and then to aim it at the deeper hunger of the soul. The Bible is replete with imagery and events that relate to satisfying our hunger. The promises of heaven include a banquet where Jesus will once again sit with his disciples, to eat and drink. Psalm 23 looks forward to a time when God will prepare a banquet for us in the presence of our enemies. All of this correlates our experience of never quite getting enough, knowing recurrent hunger, and ultimately receiving the satisfaction available through that which God has provided. On a spiritual level, Jesus declared that he is the "true bread" that alone can satisfy the hunger of our souls.

But Jesus was not avoiding the practical need of people—he was getting first things first. He would teach those who became his disciples to pray to the Father for all they would need in body and soul. That prayer includes this provision: "Give us this day our daily bread" (Matt. 6:11). So when we enjoy reading about the magical meals at Hogwarts and seeing Harry finally be satisfied, let us remember that God wants nothing less for us.

Grim Omens of Death
Prove Misleading

"The Grim, my dear, the Grim!" cried Professor Trelawney. . . . "My dear boy, it is an omen—the worst omen—of death!"
—Professor Trelawney to Harry, Book Three, p. 107

*I*t was a bit unsettling for Harry to start his third year at Hogwarts the way he did. After losing his temper, blowing up Aunt Marge, and running away, he was rescued by the Knight Bus and taken to the Leaky Cauldron. There he overheard that an escaped prisoner was probably on his way to try to murder him. Harry was troubled by his own conscience, but also by the sighting of a giant black dog, which he learned could be called "the Grim." According to his rather odd divination teacher, Professor Sibyll Trelawney, the Grim is the giant, spectral dog that haunts churchyards and is an omen of death.

No wonder Harry did not want to tell anyone about the black dog he had seen the night he ran away. Harry had looked it up in a book called *Death Omens: What to Do When You Know the Worst Is Coming,* but that had not helped. The bookshop manager had tried to turn him to other interests, saying, "Oh, I wouldn't read that if I were you. . . . You'll start seeing death omens everywhere. It's enough to frighten anyone to death" (Book Three, p. 54). When Professor Trelawney claimed to have seen the Grim in Harry's teacup on the first day of class, the implications were truly upsetting.

Professor McGonagall tried to set her students straight: "You should know, Potter, that Sibyll Trelawney has predicted the death of one student a year since she arrived at this school. None of them has died yet. Seeing death omens is her favorite way of greeting a new class. If it were not for the fact that I never speak ill of my colleagues—" (Book Three, p. 109).

Even though Professor Trelawney's belief in death omens is belittled by a more sensible professor, Harry still endures much worry under the shadow of his own superstitions. Then it turned out that the black dog he saw was not the Grim at all; it was really someone who cared for him very much, in the form of an Animagus. Harry's belief in omens misled him, and caused him much unnecessary worry.

The Bible has this to say about those who believe in omens:

> Thus says the LORD, your Redeemer,
>   who formed you in the womb:
> I am the LORD, who made all things,
>   who alone stretched out the heavens,
>   who by myself spread out the earth;
> who frustrates the omens of liars,
>   and makes fools of diviners;
> who turns back the wise
>   and makes their knowledge foolish;
> who confirms the word of his servant
>   and fulfills the prediction of his messengers.
>   (Isa. 44:24–26a)

This certainly seems to have something to say in reference to Professor Trelawney.

The Bible tells us not to look to omens; rather, we are to look to and trust the predictions of God's messengers recorded in the Bible. Jesus also directly warned against false prophets who would come producing signs and omens, with the result of leading people astray. Jesus said this in regard to the time of his own return:

> For false messiahs and false prophets will appear and produce great signs and omens, to lead astray, if possible, even the elect. Take note, I have told you beforehand. So, if they say to you, "Look! He is in the wilderness," do not go out. If they say, "Look! He is in the inner rooms," do not believe it. For as the lightning comes from the east and flashes as far as the west, so will be the coming of the Son of Man. (Matt. 24:24–27)

The omen of death Harry thought he saw was really in his mind, which had been filled with superstitious fears. These proved to be unfounded and counterproductive. Instead of looking for omens, Jesus said we should be looking for the signs of his coming, which will not be nearly as obscure or open for speculation as an omen.

One might wonder why Dumbledore would leave Professor Trelawney in her position when he makes clear to Harry that he knew she did not give accurate predictions, and that she may have even been the mouthpiece for a prophecy that Voldemort's servant would return to him and aid in his return to power. Does this have any biblical parallel? Indeed it does. It is an explanation for why questionable characters are allowed to remain in the ranks of those who claim to be representatives of God's kingdom.

Jesus told this parable:

> The kingdom of heaven may be compared to someone who sowed good seed in his field; but while everybody was asleep, an enemy came and sowed weeds among the wheat, and then went away. So when the plants came up and bore grain, then the weeds appeared as well. And the slaves of the householder came and said to him, "Master, did you not sow good seed in your field? Where, then, did these weeds come from?" He answered, "An enemy has done this." The slaves said to him, "Then do you want us to go and gather them?" But he replied, "No; for in gathering the weeds you would uproot the wheat along with them. Let both of them grow together until the harvest; and at harvest time I will tell the reapers, Collect the weeds first and bind them in bundles to be burned, but gather the wheat into my barn." (Matt. 13:24–30)

This seems to parallel Dumbledore's policy with regard to his staff. As is true throughout the Harry Potter books, it is not always easy to tell who is truly on the side of good or evil. If those who presumed some were evil and had eliminated them when they had the chance (Sirius Black comes to mind), tragedy would have occurred. Likewise, one cannot trust that those who claim to be on the side of good truly are (think of Professor Quirrell and Gilderoy Lockhart). In these stories, and in life, we must always remain on the alert and recognize that just because someone claims to be on the "good" side, it does not mean he or she truly is. By their deeds we will know them: A true prophet is known by an accuracy rate of 100 percent. Apparently we can expect some weeds to grow up with the good seed.

Judging from Professor Trelawney's dismal track record with her predictions and recurrent sightings of the death omen, one might suspect that she will turn out to be a weed. However, there is much we cannot know until the story is fully told, both in the Harry Potter books and in human history.

The good news here is that Professor Trelawney's death omen for Harry proved misleading. Instead of an omen of death, the giant black dog turned out to be a watch dog looking to protect Harry. He did not have to fear death because someone—his godfather—was watching over him to protect him all along. So too for those who put their trust in their God-Father in heaven rather than superstitions.

Fred and George and Original Sin

"Well . . . when we were in our first year, Harry—young, carefree, and innocent—"
   Harry snorted. He doubted whether Fred and George had ever been innocent.
                                             —Book Three, p. 191

*F*red and George Weasley are confirmed mischief makers, albeit good-hearted and fun-loving ones. Innocent? No! No one would ever buy that line. Fred and George continually get in trouble for sneaking out, swiping food from the kitchens, and pulling off practical jokes like when they left Ton-Tongue Toffees where Dudley was sure to find them. When they bequeathed their prized possession—the Marauder's Map—to Harry, it was intended as a supreme act of goodwill. However, Fred and George explained that in order to use the map the user had to say, "I solemnly swear that I am up to no good."

It is easy to see through Fred and George's claims of innocence, but not so easy with other characters who put more stock in being good and keeping the laws of the wizarding world. Hermione Granger could rightly be characterized as the conscience of her group, often dissuading them from wrongdoing. Mr. Weasley works in law enforcement for the Ministry of Magic. And yet, even these characters who aim to keep the law end up sometimes breaking the rules and laws they seemed so committed to uphold.

Hermione never stops being keenly aware of what is right, and feels deep pangs of conscience when she breaks the rules; however, she does break them at times. Mr. Weasley, who patrols others to make sure they are not misusing Muggle artifacts, cannot resist doing so himself. The flying car he rigged up secretly in his garage got Harry and Ron to school their second year, but also got them—and Mr. Weasley—into a lot of trouble. So, Fred, George, Hermione, Mr. Weasley, and all the "good" characters share a troubling flaw in common even with the Slytherins (except that Slytherins seem to be lacking pangs of conscience).

Many Christians would explain such universal inclinations toward wrongdoing—whether occasional or chronic—with the doctrine of original sin. The Bible makes it clear that every person is born a sinner, and comes from a long line of sinners dating all the way back to the first man and woman God created. They were created with free will, but when they chose to disobey God, a compulsion toward disobedience became inherent in human nature. The only exception to this in those born of a woman was Jesus Christ, the only begotten Son of God, conceived of the Holy Spirit.

This realization that even the best of the "good" characters are not constantly good may be disturbing to some. It reminds me of a line from the animated sitcom *The Simpsons,* when Homer buys a Bible at a yard sale. After flipping through it, he remarks, "Talk about a preachy book! Everybody in here is a sinner, except this guy"—presumably referring to Jesus.

This realization that "everybody in here is a sinner"—even those who try their very best to be good, and some like Fred and George who don't try as hard as others—is a necessary realization before one can go on to find the remedy for sin. In short, the gospel cannot be good news until you realize the bad news that you too are a sinner in need of a Savior. While such a realization may be troubling to folks like Hermione, this is a fundamental teaching of the Bible: "There is no one who is righteousness, not even one" (Rom. 3:10).

The Bible upholds a supremely high absolute moral standard, but being able to live according to that moral standard requires the help of God's Holy Spirit. As in the Harry Potter stories, Bible characters run the gamut between those who stay well within God's moral law most of the time with only occasional lapses, those who seem to make a career of breaking the rules (Jacob comes to mind) then have a dramatic turnaround, or those like Saul of Tarsus (who became Paul the apostle) who strictly followed God's law and were stunned to learn they were sinners like the rest.

The characters God singles out as heroes of the faith are listed in Hebrews 11, which is sometimes called the faith hall of fame. If we read this list in order to see if these are people who always did the right thing, we discover a wide range of sins in their lives. Everybody on that list was a sinner.

Fred and George could be seen as poster boys for the doctrine of original sin, but so too could all the other characters. Considering this can be instructive as we reflect on the sinful human condition. So when the Bible says, "All have sinned and fall short of the glory of God" (Rom. 3:23), we won't count ourselves out. This is good, because that leaves us open to be justified—not by our own presumed goodness but by God's grace received as a gift that comes through Jesus Christ (see Rom. 3:24). In understanding this, we can each come to agree with the apostle Paul: "The saying is sure and worthy of full acceptance, that Christ Jesus came into the world to save sinners—of whom I am the foremost" (1 Tim. 1:15).

Understanding that even the Hermiones and Mr. Weasleys of our world cannot be completely righteous can make those who identify more with Fred and George breathe a bit easier. It also paves the way to receive the good news that God loves all of us sinners and has a remedy for our sinful nature that cannot be achieved by keeping external laws alone.

The Department of Mysteries

"You've got to listen to me," Black said, and there was a note of urgency in his voice now. "You'll regret it if you don't. . . . You don't understand. . . ."
—Sirius Black to Harry, Book Three, p. 342

*T*hroughout the Harry Potter books it becomes apparent that the characters often think they have everything figured out, and they do—they have figured it out wrong. They see clues, they see suspicious behavior, they may see what they think is an omen or something incriminating about a particular character, but when the story unfolds they discover they had it all wrong. They did in fact see what they thought they saw, but they did not see it clearly: like when Hermione saw Snape muttering while looking up at Harry and his bucking broomstick in Book One and assumed Snape was jinxing it. It turned out that Professor Quirrell was the one trying to knock Harry off his broom, while Professor Snape was trying to protect him. Throughout the story, these characters' assumptions led to wrong conclusions, and sometimes wrong treatment of those whom they misunderstood.

Book Three is filled with suspense because what people believe, and sincerely think to be true, turns out to be very different from the truth. Indeed, if Harry had acted rashly on the basis of what he saw with his own eyes, what he believed on the basis of newspaper reports and the stories he heard from trusted friends, even adults he respected, he could have made terrible life-changing mistakes.

At one point, Mr. Weasley mentions that the Ministry of Magic has a Department of Mysteries, which handles things that are top secret. The Department of Mysteries could be a good description of how these stories unfold. Each one contains a mystery. Along with the characters, the reader begins to understand the importance of not being hasty in judgment because there is much that we may not see clearly. So we learn to reserve final judgment until we gain greater insight as the whole story unfolds.

According to the Bible, we should exercise that same caution in our own world and in the lives of the people with whom we have relationships. Paul wrote a letter to a church in the city of Corinth. These people had become Christians, but were having all kinds of problems with each other and in their worship practices. Paul goes over the problems they are having, addressing the specifics, but then he gets to the heart of his message, which is love: "Love is patient; love is kind; love is not envious or boastful or arrogant or rude. It does not insist on its own way; it is not irritable or resentful; it does not rejoice in wrongdoing, but rejoices in the truth. It bears all things, believes all things, hopes all things, endures all things. . . . Love never ends" (1 Cor. 13:4–8a).

Later on in the chapter he writes, "For now we see in a mirror, dimly, but then we will see face to face. Now I know only in part; then I will know fully, even as I have been fully known. And now faith, hope, and love abide, these three; and the greatest of these is love" (1 Cor. 13:12–13). Therefore, when we are not sure about someone, or even when we believe we have that person figured out, let's remember that we could be wrong, and pause before condemning someone. That is where the patience of love pays off.

God's good news really does come down to love. God loving us. Us loving God. Us loving each other with God's help. "In this is love, not that we loved God but that he loved us and sent his Son to be the atoning sacrifice for our sins. Beloved, since God loved us so much, we also ought to love one another. No one has ever seen God; if we love one another, God lives in us, and his love is perfected in us" (1 John 4:10–12).

Some people reject the Bible or the gospel because they don't have it all figured out. We are not going to have it all figured out or see everything clearly in this life. But we can see enough to respond to God's love.

The Rat Who Betrayed Harry's Parents

"You sold Lily and James to Voldemort," said Black, who was shaking too. "Do you deny it?"
Peter Pettigrew burst into tears.
—Book Three, p. 374

*R*on never suspected that his rat, Scabbers, was a rat in a far more significant way. It turns out that Scabbers was really Peter Pettigrew, who had gone to Hogwarts with Harry's father. Peter had been one of a band of friends that included James Potter, Remus Lupin, and Sirius Black. When Voldemort terrorized the wizarding world, James and Lily Potter stood against him. Their friends were all thought to be staunchly on the side of good, but it turned out there was a traitor in their midst.

James and Lily went into hiding in Godric Hollow with their baby, Harry. They depended on their friends to keep their whereabouts secret. By means of a Fidelius Charm, Voldemort would have been unable to find them as long as the friend they trusted as their Secret-Keeper kept their secret. They made Peter Pettigrew their Secret-Keeper, but he gave in to Lord Voldemort and betrayed them. His betrayal led directly to their deaths and to Voldemort's attack on Harry.

When Jesus lived on earth, he chose twelve disciples, whom he called his friends. One of them turned against him and betrayed him to the forces that had aligned themselves against him. Those who wanted to arrest and kill Jesus did not dare do it in daylight, for they feared the crowds who regarded Jesus as a prophet or as the Messiah. So they had to find out where he was staying at night. Judas, one of the twelve, went to those seeking to kill Jesus and offered to betray him. They paid him thirty pieces of silver. Then Judas went back to Jesus. He sat down to dinner with him for the Passover meal, where Jesus let him know that he was on to him. The Bible says that Satan entered into Judas and he went out. Later that night Judas went to the chief priests, who had assembled a military force to arrest Jesus. Judas led them to the Garden of Gethsemane, where Jesus had been praying. Judas gave the sign he had promised—the one whom he kissed was the one they should arrest: "While [Jesus] was still speaking, suddenly a crowd came, and the one called Judas, one of the twelve, was leading them. He approached Jesus to kiss him; but Jesus said to him, 'Judas, is it with a kiss that you are betraying the Son of Man?'" (Luke 22:47–48).

Sirius understood the demands of friendship and confronted Peter Pettigrew after forcing him to reveal himself (after he had been hiding as a rat for over a decade). Peter pleaded that he had given in to Voldemort because he was afraid the Dark Lord would have killed him. "'THEN YOU SHOULD HAVE DIED!' roared Black. 'DIED RATHER THAN BETRAY YOUR FRIENDS, AS WE WOULD HAVE DONE FOR YOU!'" (Book Three, p. 375).

We do not know whether James, Remus, and Sirius really would have died for their friend, but that is the ideal. Even Jesus upheld it: "No one has greater love than this, to lay down one's life for one's friends" (John 15:13). We do know that even though Jesus was betrayed by one of his friends, like James and Lily Potter he showed us the greatest act of love and friendship one can possibly demonstrate when he laid down his life for us.

Glimmers of the Gospel in Book Four

Harry Potter and the Goblet of Fire

Introduction to Book Four

*B*ook Four's major theme is that the aggressive nature of evil must be aggressively resisted. One dare not ignore or try to pacify or appease the forces of evil; those who do so, do so to their own peril. The only way to deal with the forces of evil is to identify them, resist them, reveal their evil deeds, and aggressively seek to counteract their evil schemes. This is carried out by showing what Voldemort is setting out to do, the elaborate nature of his schemes, and that he thinks nothing of murdering the innocent once they are no longer useful to his aims. This is countered by Dumbledore's call for a parting of the ways and for all to declare which side they are on—good or evil—as the forces of good prepare to actively fight against evil with all their might.

Secondary themes include the following:

1. Those on the side of good must employ constant vigilance against an evil enemy who uses deception as a key tactic to accomplish evil aims. We see this primarily in the deception carried out by Barty Crouch Jr. in the guise of Mad-Eye Moody. The success of his ability to deceive the characters in the story as well as the readers is a powerful theme to reflect on when considering the message of the book.

2. The destructive influence of those who bear false witness is depicted in the character of Rita Skeeter. She continually twists the truth, generates gossip, and writes reports that include untrue statements along with half-truths and just enough facts to give her stories credibility. The destructive effects of false and misleading reports can be clearly seen throughout the story. We also see how hard it is to counteract such destructive practices, but that it is good when this is done by those who are able to discover the truth, as Hermione did with Rita Skeeter.

3. The concern for social justice is also raised by Hermione's campaign to lift the house-elves up from their oppressive conditions. Her Society for the Promotion of Elf Welfare (S.P.E.W.)

desires to help those less fortunate. This also acknowledges the challenges of helping those long enslaved to learn to function in a new way of life while treating them respectfully (as Albus Dumbledore did with Dobby and Winky).

4. Book Four ends with one of the most important themes summed up in this quote from Dumbledore: "Remember, if the time should come when you have to make a choice between what is right and what is easy, remember what happened to a boy who was good, and kind, and brave, because he strayed across the path of Lord Voldemort" (Book Four, p. 724). We are challenged to choose that which is right over that which is easy. When faced with such choices, we are called upon to remember the lost lives of innocent victims murdered by forces of evil, reminding ourselves that the forces of evil will justify any means to achieve their aims.

A Murderer from the Beginning

All the villagers cared about was the identity of their murderer—for plainly, three apparently healthy people did not all drop dead of natural causes on the same night.
—Book Four, p. 2

*B*ook Four reveals Voldemort as a murderer from the beginning of the story. He killed his own father and grandparents, partially because his Muggle father abandoned his mother before he was born. We already knew he had killed Harry's parents and many others during his reign of terror when he was at his full power. Book Four opens with the revelation that he also killed Brenda Jorkins, and then recounts his murder of Frank Brice, who happened upon him hiding in the old Riddle House. Voldemort is still plotting his return to power; his aims have not changed. The way he terrorizes his own follower, Peter Pettigrew, shows his nature has not changed either; only his form is diminished. The Dark Lord cannot be dismissed. Thus, we see that the nature of evil is aggressive and must be stopped by force.

While some people may think of "sweet Jesus, meek and mild," the revelation of Jesus in the Bible shows that he was never soft on evil. He recognized the nature of evil as murderous, and that those who serve evil do their master's bidding—which is to hate, murder, and destroy all that is good. Jesus certainly did not bow to political correctness when he addressed his opponents. He publicly told them, "You are from your father the devil, and you choose to do your father's desires. He was a murderer from the beginning and does not stand in the truth, because there is no truth in him" (John 8:44). Another time he said to them, "You snakes! You brood of vipers! How can you escape being sentenced to hell?" (Matt. 23:33).

Given that Voldemort has been shown to be devoted to the side of evil in these stories, we should not be surprised to find that he was a murderer from the beginning and that his followers will seek to carry out his murderous plans. In our world, when we see those who aggressively pursue and grasp for power by murderous means, we can rightly conclude that they are working on the side of evil and must be opposed outright.

Harry's Dreams Warn of Danger

"It was only a dream," said Ron bracingly. "Just a night-mare."
"Yeah, but was it, though?" said Harry.
—Book Four, p. 149

Often in these stories Harry's sleep is disturbed by troubling dreams and pain in his scar. Sometimes these disturbances have come in the form of a warning that Voldemort was nearby. Sometimes, such as when the Death Eaters dared to attack Muggles at the Quidditch World Cup, Harry was awakened by danger happening nearby. In Book Four, Harry's dream—which Ron tried to convince him was just a nightmare—was a revelation of what the evil one was up to. It was a warning.

Throughout the Bible, God sometimes speaks to people by way of dreams. This does not mean that people should look to dreams as a means of knowing the future apart from God. Rather, we should take all our dreams, waking and sleeping, to God in prayer, understanding that dreams have been one way God has spoken in the past and that all impressions must be tested by God's word. In the Old Testament, Joseph had dreams that foretold his future rise to power in Egypt and his family bowing before him. The ability to interpret dreams was a gift God gave some, which was instrumental to God elevating them to positions of power, as was the case with Joseph (when he rightly interpreted the dreams of two of his fellow prisoners and of Pharaoh) and Daniel (who was able to interpret the dream of the king of Babylon when none of the sorcerers, seers, astrologers, or magicians could).

God gave the following guidelines to Moses' brother, Aaron, and sister, Miriam: "When there are prophets among you, I the LORD make myself known to them in visions; I speak to them in dreams" (Num. 12:6). However, Deuteronomy 13:1–3 records a test that must be applied to check those who say their dreams have spiritual significance:

> If a prophet, or one who foretells by dreams, appears among you and announces to you a miraculous sign or wonder, and if the sign or wonder of which he has spoken takes place, and he says, "Let us follow other gods" (gods you have not known) "and let us worship them," you must not listen to the words of that prophet or dreamer. The LORD your God is testing you to find out whether you love him with all your heart and with all your soul. (NIV)

In our world, God makes it clear that there may be people who show real supernatural signs and dreams that really do come true, even if they do not speak for God. Therefore, the test God gives us centers on whether or not a person's aim is to direct people to God (who revealed himself in the Bible), and not to any other god.

The four Gospels record dramatic communication that took place through dreams and other supernatural means. The Messiah's coming was foretold in Old Testament prophecies that mention the virgin birth ("Therefore the Lord himself will give you a sign: The virgin will be with child and will give birth to a son, and will call him Immanuel"[Isa. 7:14 NIV]) and Mary having to go to Bethlehem where the Messiah had to be born ("But you, O Bethlehem of Ephrathah, who are one of the little clans of Judah, from you shall come forth for me one who is to rule in Israel, whose origin is from of old, from ancient days" [Mic. 5:2]). When these prophecies began to be fulfilled, the evil one did not just sit idle. The battle lines were drawn up and the forces of evil took action to try to stop God's prophecies from being fulfilled. Spiritual forces of evil, and people under their control, sought to kill the baby Jesus to try to keep him from growing up to fulfill the messianic prophecies.

In the birth narrative in Matthew 1:13–2:23, much of the communication from God comes through supernatural means: prophecies recorded in the Old Testament, signs in the heavens, and through dreams. Note the similarities between the battle of those on the side of evil versus those on the side of Jesus and the kind of battle we see unfold between good and evil in the Harry Potter stories.

When we see how the Harry Potter stories use dreams, prophecies, and signs in the heavens, we can remember that these kinds of supernatural modes of communication are not only part of fantasy stories. That which we see in the wizarding world of Harry Potter as merely magical is quite similar to the miraculous ways God has communicated with people so they could do their part to protect the Christ child and help carry out his mission.

The Muggle Protection Act

*"Harry, that's their idea of fun. Half the Muggle killings
back when You-Know-Who was in power were done for
fun."*

—Mr. Weasley, Book Four, p. 143

*I*n Book Three, Arthur Weasley introduced a Muggle Protection Act
at the Ministry of Magic. Few details were provided, but those on
Voldemort's side opposed this. Mr. Malfoy called Mr. Weasley a disgrace because of his desire to protect Muggles. Those on the side of
good—Dumbledore, the Weasleys, Harry—share this love of Muggles. Mr. Weasley even tried to be kind to the Dursleys despite their
rudeness to his family, mistrust, and outright meanness to Harry.

At the Quidditch World Cup, hooded Death Eaters attacked
Muggles and threatened Muggle-born wizards. Mr. Weasley took
immediate action to try to stop the attacks and catch the perpetra-
tors. This concern for the welfare of Muggles shows a desire to
protect them even though they are not in the wizarding world.
Readers also see that those on the side of good do not discriminate
against those who are of mixed blood or Muggle heritage, while
many of the Slytherins and followers of Voldemort do.

The Muggle Protection Act can be seen as a parallel of how God
loves the whole world, not just those who are already in the kingdom of God or even aware of the goings-on of the supernatural
world. It reminds me of how Jesus treated the crowds of all sorts
of people who came to him:

> Jesus went throughout Galilee, teaching in their synagogues
> and proclaiming the good news of the kingdom and curing
> every disease and every sickness among the people. So his
> fame spread throughout all Syria, and they brought to him all
> the sick, those who were afflicted with various diseases and
> pains, demoniacs, epileptics, and paralytics, and he cured

them. And great crowds followed him from Galilee, the Decapolis, Jerusalem, Judea, and from beyond the Jordan. (Matt. 4:23–25)

These crowds were not just made up of those in the Jewish religious establishment. Indeed, these masses of humanity were made up of Gentiles (non-Jews), Samaritans (persons of Jewish heritage who worshiped on Mount Gerizim rather than Jerusalem), and people of various ethnic and religious backgrounds. This showed God's compassion for all people, even those who were not yet faithful to him or even fully aware of the spiritual battle Jesus was embroiled in while walking in their midst. "When he saw the crowds, he had compassion for them, because they were harassed and helpless, like sheep without a shepherd" (Matt. 9:36).

When we see how those on the side of good show compassion for the Muggles, let us call to mind the compassion of God for *all people* that is expressed in the life and ministry of Jesus Christ.

Mad-Eye Moody's Ironic Warnings

"A wizard who's about to put an illegal curse on you isn't going to tell you what he's about to do. He's not going to do it nice and polite to your face. You need to be prepared. You need to be alert and watchful."
—Mad-Eye Moody to Defense Against the Dark Arts class, Book Four, p. 212

*M*ad-Eye Moody was introduced as a renowned fighter of evil, having put many of Voldemort's followers in prison. He is an auror, someone who sees what others miss, aided by his "mad eye" that can see all around and by other means, such as his foe glass, which warns him of approaching foes. His name also reveals that he was considered somewhat mad—good, but a bit mad. Throughout the greater part of Book Four, no one suspected that an evil impostor was merely replicating the real Mad-Eye Moody with the help of Polyjuice Potion.

"Professor Moody" taught his students about the three Unforgivable Curses: Cruciatus (pain), Imperius (total control), *Avada Kedavra* (instant death). These curses were presented as evil, extremely dangerous, and against the laws of the wizarding world. "Professor Moody" feigned not to promote these but to show the students how to protect themselves. He stressed that these must be resisted, saying, "That's what you're up against. That's what I have got to teach you to fight. You need preparing. You need arming. But most of all, you need to practice *constant, never-ceasing vigilance*" (Book Four, p. 217). In retrospect, the reader can see how ironic the lessons against the forbidden curses were. In reality, the one giving the lesson was fully devoted to Voldemort and to using these curses.

In the New Testament, Paul likewise warned his students when he was preparing to leave them, "I know that after I have gone, savage wolves will come in among you, not sparing the flock. Some even from your own group will come distorting the truth in order to entice the disciples to follow them. Therefore be alert, remembering that for three years I did not cease night or day to warn everyone with tears" (Acts 20:29–31).

The students in the third-year Defense Against the Dark Arts class taught by "Professor Moody" would have done well to note the nuances of such teaching, and so would we. The irony of Mad-Eye Moody's lesson on the need for constant vigilance is that he himself was an impostor they needed to be alert to detect. One wonders if Barty Crouch Jr., behind the facade of Mad-Eye Moody, got perverse pleasure out of such irony. He can serve to remind us that it is not enough to trust someone just because that person is part of some approved group or even in a position of authority.

What must be paramount in discerning good from evil is knowing the truth, not just deciding whether the one delivering the message seems trustworthy or not. The distortion of the truth is what we must guard against. Therefore, even in our world, when we know the truth about God revealed in the Bible, we can use that to discern whether any teaching is true, regardless of who delivers the message. It is far better, however, to receive a true message from someone who lives in keeping with the message proclaimed.

Luke was not a follower of Jesus when he lived on earth. Luke was more like an investigative reporter who became a disciple of Jesus after the resurrection. Then he made careful inquiry to record the truth about the life and teachings of Jesus. He begins his Gospel with this introduction:

> Since many have undertaken to set down an orderly account of the events that have been fulfilled among us, just as they were handed on to us by those who from the beginning were eyewitnesses and servants of the word, I too decided, after investigating everything carefully from the very first, to write an orderly account for you, most excellent Theophilus, so that you may know the truth concerning the things about which you have been instructed. (Luke 1:1–4)

The record was set down after being carefully examined to see if it could be trusted as true. Even Jesus' opponents said to him, "Teacher, we know that you are right in what you say and teach, and you show deference to no one, but teach the way of God in accordance with truth" (Luke 20:21). However, one might detect a note of sarcasm in this comment since it was followed by a question meant to trap Jesus.

At the trial of Jesus, John relates the following exchange: "Pilate asked him, 'So you are a king?' Jesus answered, 'You say that I am a king. For this I was born, and for this I came into the world, to testify to the truth. Everyone who belongs to the truth listens to my voice.' Pilate asked him, 'What is truth?'" (John 18:37–38). Elsewhere, Jesus said of himself, "I am the way, and the truth, and the life. No one comes to the Father except through me" (John 14:6).

The whole weight of Jesus' ministry stands or falls on whether or not this statement he made about himself is true. If true, he is the *only* way to the Father, thus the only way to heaven. If this statement is not true, we dare not trust any of his claims or promises of eternal life. If this claim he made about himself is not true, he is shown to be a liar and a cruel impostor. Just as Barty Crouch Jr. impersonated a good teacher but was unmasked as an impostor, so too, if these statements by Jesus (and many of his other claims about himself) are not true, he cannot be called a good moral teacher.

Here is what C. S. Lewis had to say on this matter in his classic work, *Mere Christianity*:

> I am trying here to prevent anyone saying the really foolish thing that people often say about Him: "I'm ready to accept Jesus as a great moral teacher, but I don't accept His claim to be God." That is the one thing we must not say. A man who was merely a man and said the sort of things Jesus said would not be a great moral teacher. He would either be a lunatic—on a level with the man who says he is a poached egg—or else he would be the Devil of Hell. You must make your choice. Either this man was, and is, the Son of God: or else a madman or something worse. You can shut Him up for a fool, you can spit at Him and kill Him as a demon; or you can fall at His feet and call Him Lord and God. But let us not come with any patronising nonsense about His being a great human teacher. He has not left that open to us. He did not intend to.[6]

As with Defense Against the Dark Arts at Hogwarts, knowing whether or not someone is an impostor is important. It is even more important that we know what truth is. Jesus made dramatic claims about who he is and why he came. If these are true, he deserves to be accepted as Messiah and worshiped as Lord and God; if they are not true, there is no place to call him a "good moral teacher" any more than one could rightly say that of Barty Crouch Jr.

The Only Known Survivor
of the Killing Curse

"There's no countercurse. There's no blocking it. Only one known person has ever survived it, and he's sitting right in front of me."
—Professor Moody to his Defense Against the Dark Arts class, Book Four, p. 216

*H*arry is famous because he is the only known survivor of the Killing Curse. This has not been spelled out completely yet, but we do know that the key to Harry's survival was that his mother took the curse on herself and died in his place. Dumbledore said Voldemort could not understand such love. Tom Riddle seemed baffled by it when he quizzed Harry on how he had survived, wanting to know how a skinny boy like Harry "with no extraordinary magical talent" managed to defeat Voldemort and break his power. Harry replied that no one knew why Voldemort had lost his powers, but that he did know that the Dark Lord could not kill him because his mother had died to save him.

While Harry is the single survivor of the Killing Curse in these books—so far—the Bible actually has several stories that show how God sent a way of escape for impending death. When the people of Israel were warned that God was about to send a plague of death on the firstborn of the Egyptians, they were given a way to survive: "Thus says the LORD: 'About midnight I will go out through Egypt. Every firstborn in the land of Egypt shall die, from the firstborn of Pharaoh who sits on his throne to the firstborn of the female slave who is behind the handmill, and all the firstborn of the livestock'" (Exod. 11:4–5). (Since this decree was made by God, it is not directly analogous to the Killing Curse used by Voldemort.) The only way to block this action was to put the blood of an unblemished male lamb on the doorposts and lintel of one's doorway. God said, "The blood shall be a sign for you on the houses where you live: when I see the blood, I will pass over you, and no plague shall destroy you when I strike the land of Egypt" (Exod. 12:13). God was true to his promise. Death passed over those homes covered by the blood of the Passover lamb. The celebration of Passover, which commemorates this, is a sacred celebration of this day for Jews, and many Christians incorporate elements of the Passover Seder in their traditions of worship.

The New Testament associates Passover with the death of Christ. When Jesus first began his ministry, John the Baptist announced him by saying, "Here is the Lamb of God who takes away the sin of the world!" (John 1:29). This signified that Jesus would die as the sacrificial lamb to pay for the sins of the people and make atonement for them. But it also relates Jesus to the Passover lamb. Indeed, Jesus died at Passover: "Now it was the day of Preparation for the Passover; and it was about noon. He said to the Jews, "Here is your King!" They cried out, "Away with him! Away with him! Crucify him!" (John 19:14–15). So, as it was prophesied, Jesus became our Passover lamb. All who apply the blood Jesus shed on the cross to the "door of their hearts" by faith will escape the "Killing Curse."

When Tom Riddle heard Harry say it was his mother's self-sacrificial death that saved him, he said, "Yes, that's a powerful counter-charm" (Book Two, p. 317). Likewise, the sacrifice of Jesus laying down his life to be our Passover lamb is a powerful way to counteract the curse of sin and death. In Harry's story, he is the only one so far who has been able to survive the fatal curse from the Dark Lord. We do not yet know if there will be some way for the whole wizarding world to take cover under some kind of "counter-charm" like the one that saved Harry, but the blood of Jesus offers a way for everyone in our world to be protected from the curse of death.

The final outcome for all who escape the curse of death will be to stand triumphant before God, as death is destroyed once and forever:

And I heard a loud voice from the throne saying,

"See, the home of God is among mortals.
He will dwell with them as their God;
they will be his peoples,
and God himself will be with them;
he will wipe every tear from their eyes.
Death will be no more;
mourning and crying and pain will be no more,
for the first things have passed away."

(Rev. 21:3–4)

In our world, as in Harry's world, though some are safe, the Killing Curse still threatens many people. The Bible points us to a day when the curse of death will be destroyed entirely. We will have to wait and see what becomes of it in Harry's story.

Harry's Heroism in the Triwizard Tournament

"The Merchieftainess informs us that Mr. Potter was first to reach the hostages, and that the delay in his return was due to his determination to return all hostages to safety, not merely his own."

—Ludo Bagman, Book Four, p. 507

The Triwizard Tournament consisted of three tasks. One was to get past a dragon, another to get through a maze, and another to rescue a hostage from under the lake. Harry was to rescue his friend, Ron; Fleur was to rescue her sister, Gabrielle; and Krum was to rescue Hermione. Harry got to the hostages first, and could have had a distinct advantage by saving Ron and moving on. But Harry was concerned about the safety of Hermione, because she was also his friend, and also Gabrielle, whom he barely knew. So Harry waited to make sure Krum got there to save Hermione, and then waited to see if Fleur was coming. When she did not show up, Harry rescued Gabrielle along with Ron. In doing so, he slowed himself down so much he missed the time limit.

In this act of heroism on Harry's part, we see his concern for all the hostages. He did not know what would happen to the hostages if they were not rescued, but he feared that they might die. He did know they could not save themselves. Fleur seemed to share Harry's concern that there was real danger for the hostages. When Harry saved her sister, she saw it as a gift of life for which she was ever grateful.

The Bible tells us that there will come a time when it is too late to be saved. God the Lord will return, the heavens and the earth will melt with intense heat (see 2 Pet. 3:3–7) and God will create a new heaven and a new earth in which righteousness will dwell (see Rev. 21:1). This has been predicted throughout human history. We do not know precisely when that time will come, but it will. The way Harry behaved under the lake reminds me of something the Bible tells us about why God has taken so long (in the opinion of some) to fulfill the promise of his return to set up the kingdom of heaven: Peter writes, "But do not ignore this one fact, beloved, that with the Lord one day is like a thousand years, and a thousand years are like one day. The Lord is not slow about his promise, as some think of slowness, but is patient with you, not wanting any to perish, but all to come to repentance" (2 Pet. 3:8–9).

So when we think about how Harry was slow in getting back out of the lake because of his concern to try to save all the hostages, we can bear in mind the patience of God and his love for all who are in danger of perishing eternally. We may not understand fully what that means, just as Harry could not be sure of the full consequences for the hostages under the lake, but we show true heroism when we do all we can to make sure those within our reach are saved.

The *Daily Prophet*:
News from the World Beyond

*"Dumbledore!" cried Rita Skeeter, with every appearance
of delight—but Harry noticed that her quill and the parch-
ment had suddenly vanished.*

—Book Four, p. 306–7

*I*n the wizarding world, people get their news from the *Daily
Prophet,* a newspaper that employs reporters such as Rita Skeeter,
with her Quick-Quotes Quill. Rita Skeeter reports the juicy gossip
people love to read, she touches on real news stories, but pushes
the truth aside for the sake of sensationalism. Readers of the *Daily
Prophet* must be discerning to sift out the truth from that which is
false or manipulated.

The Bible declares, "First of all you must understand this, that no
prophecy of scripture is a matter of one's own interpretation,
because no prophecy ever came by human will, but men and
women moved by the Holy Spirit spoke from God" (2 Pet.
1:20–21). God has sent his message to our world from beyond by
means of prophets and others who were moved by the Holy Spirit
as they wrote down the Scripture. However, in an attempt to confuse God's message, the enemy has sent out many false prophets
who proclaim and write what people want to hear and messages
meant to confuse or contradict God's message. We are cautioned
to be discerning whenever we hear a message that claims to be
from God. The Bible declares itself to be the only true revelation
of the will of God, by which we will be judged.

In our world, we read all kinds of reports and religious documents that claim to be messages from God, some about as reliable
as Rita Skeeter's reporting. People argue over the Bible: Some
declare it to be the true and infallible word of God, others are not

so sure, still others scoff and try to discredit it. The Bible claims to be holy, which means set apart from all the rest, unique, the only true revelation of God. God says throughout his word that while he may add to his revelation during the formation of the canon of Scripture, we are not to add to his word, or take away from it. We see such warnings with the giving of God's law in Deuteronomy 4:2 and 12:32, in the wisdom of Proverbs 30:5–6, and in the last book of the New Testament, where it says: "I warn everyone who hears the words of the prophecy of this book: if anyone adds to them, God will add to that person the plagues described in this book; if anyone takes away from the words of the book of this prophecy, God will take away that person's share in the tree of life and in the holy city, which are described in this book" (Rev. 22:18–19). Obviously, if the Bible is God's holy word, this warning is not to be taken lightly.

What if the Bible is what it claims to be? Wouldn't it deserve at least as much attention and consideration as all the other sources of news and information that bombard us daily—things we read and watch that are less worthy of our consideration? If so, wouldn't it be a tragic success for the forces of evil if we became so confused or untrusting because of all the conflicting claims of the false prophets and Rita Skeeters of the world that we threw out the truth with the trivial?

Unlike the *Daily Prophet* in the wizarding world, the Bible is replete with fascinating elements that show the sincere seeker that it must be a true document sent by God from beyond. The unique qualities of the Bible are beyond mere human ingenuity and contradict mere human inclinations. Just the fulfilled prophecies alone are enough to substantiate its claims to be the authorized collection of God's message to humanity.

God appeals to this to cause us to see that he is the only one who could have written the Bible because it reveals much of human history before it has come to pass:

> I am the LORD, that is my name;
> my glory I give to no other,
> nor my praise to idols.

See, the former things have come to pass,
  and new things I now declare;
before they spring forth,
  I tell you of them.

(Isa. 42:8–9)

Even though the *Daily Prophet* was less than reliable, people in Harry's world still read it and were influenced by it—often with negative results. Dare we disregard or neglect the one book that claims to contain the true and authorized messages from the world beyond through God's holy prophets?

The Death Eaters and the Dark Mark

"Every Death Eater had the sign burned into him by the Dark Lord. It was a means of distinguishing one another, and his means of summoning us to him."
—Professor Snape, Book Four, p. 710

Voldemort's followers, called Death Eaters, bore the Dark Mark on their bodies as a sign of allegiance to the Dark Lord. They openly followed him when he was in power, but after his downfall many claimed they had been acting against their will. Some were convicted and put in Azkaban. Many blended back into the wizarding population. Some worked at Hogwarts (noted for its firm stance against the Dark Arts), others worked at schools such as Durmstrang (that reportedly still taught the Dark Arts), and some even went to work at the Ministry of Magic.

At the Quidditch World Cup, someone projected the Dark Mark in the sky and called the Death Eaters to unify. Seeing this sign struck terror in the hearts of those who remembered the terrible times of the past. Then the Dark Mark would be projected over any place where someone had been murdered by the forces of the Dark Lord.

The Dark Mark was also used to call the Death Eaters to Voldemort whenever it became visible on their bodies. Both Karkaroff and Professor Snape had been troubled because the mark they bore had become more and more pronounced throughout the Triwizard Tournament. Neither intended to return; Karkaroff feared retribution because he had turned in many of his fellow Death Eaters, sending them to Azkaban so he could go free. Snape's full story has yet to come out, but we know he had been a Death Eater who renounced his involvement with Voldemort, made a turnaround and—somehow—gained Dumbledore's trust. Dumbledore even accepted him as a teacher at Hogwarts. However, his experience with the Dark Arts left its mark—which he can hide, but apparently not erase entirely.

When one thinks of a "Dark Mark" in biblical terms, one might recall "the mark of the beast," which Revelation says is a mark that will be put on those aligned with the antichrist before the last battle. However, there are significant differences that make a correlation between the Dark Mark and the mark of the beast only serve as a secondary parallel at best. There is another parallel that is more in keeping with the story line of the Harry Potter books, and goes more directly to the heart of the gospel. It calls us to focus our attention on Professor Snape. The Bible says,

> Do you not know that wrongdoers will not inherit the kingdom of God? Do not be deceived! Fornicators, idolaters, adulterers, male prostitutes, sodomites, thieves, the greedy, drunkards, robbers—none of these will inherit the kingdom of God. *And that is what some of you used to be. But you were washed, you were sanctified, you were justified* in the name of the Lord Jesus Christ and in the Spirit of our God. (1 Cor. 6:9–11)

This passage is a declaration that even those who have become known as one of the "wicked" in all their various classifications can become something different. This passage names all kinds of people and behaviors God says will disqualify one from the kingdom of

God, then says "this is what some of you used to be. But . . ." It shows there is an opportunity for those who previously served the "Dark Lord" of our world to put their past behind them.

This passage declares: But you *were* washed. You *were* sanctified. You *were* justified. This declaration of acceptance regardless of one's past sinful classification leads into an understanding of the doctrines of absolution (washing), sanctification (being set apart as holy while God is at work transforming a person into one whose life is holy), and justification (being vindicated by God, declared not guilty).

The New Testament speaks of salvation as something that is simultaneously a done deal and an ongoing process. When people accept Christ as their new Lord, they are transferred instantly out of the kingdom of darkness and into the kingdom of God's Son. They are saved and sealed by the Holy Spirit, but they also begin a process of fully experiencing that salvation. God sees those who put their faith in Christ as already holy and blameless before him, while also calling them to progressively live lives marked outwardly by increasing holiness of character and conduct. This process of transformation involves being (1) washed: cleansed, having our past sins washed away, being absolved by God for what we have done; (2) sanctified: set apart by God as one of his own, but also the ongoing process of the working of the Word and the Spirit to equip us to serve God in the world and to live holy lives; and (3) justified: acquitted and vindicated by God, pronounced righteous (but not on the basis of what we have done; rather, on the basis of what Jesus did by dying on the cross to pay for our sins).

I am going to take a bit of a risk here by using Severus Snape and his relationship to Dumbledore as a parallel to how God works with those who have turned from allegiance to the Dark Lord of our world to join the ranks of those on God's side. This is a risk because we do not know what will become of Severus Snape in the Harry Potter stories. (I wonder if his name, Severus, might represent the fact that he severed his ties to the Dark Lord?) I believe the risk is worth taking because Dumbledore's treatment of Snape at this point in the book can be a good picture of a wonderful aspect of the gospel people often miss.

We know little about what Snape did while siding with Voldemort, except that he had been a Death Eater. But Dumbledore accepted Snape back, called him one of his own, and called on others to treat him as one who used to be but is no longer numbered among the Death Eaters. Somehow—and this is still unrevealed—Snape was absolved of former evildoing rather than being imprisoned. Dumbledore no longer sees him as a Death Eater or even just a former Death Eater, but as a trusted teacher at Hogwarts and a worthy ally of those on the good side.

Snape is one of the most curious of characters because it is not clear how or why Dumbledore would let one so dark in his demeanor be numbered on the side of good. Snape's sanctification can be seen in the way Dumbledore works with him, sometimes correcting him, sometimes calling him to serve him, sometimes calling him to make peace with old enemies. He has accepted him, but does not always accept the way he behaves. While he is treated as one who belongs fully to the good side, there are times Dumbledore must rein him in and even reprimand him. He works under Dumbledore's authority and ongoing supervision.

Perhaps the way Dumbledore deals with Snape could turn out to be a wonderful example of how God works with repentant sinners while transforming them into useful servants for his kingdom. In both cases, there are people in the process who do not seem to fit the image of someone on the side of good. In Christianity, all who trust Christ are called to holiness of life, but the actual transformation takes place from the inside out. So there are some people bearing the name of Christ who do not look the part, but we look on their outward appearance while God looks on the heart. We look at how they act now, while God looks at how far they have come from the wickedness they have left behind.

At some point, Dumbledore declared Snape justified, even though he used to be a Death Eater. The idea of being justified is a judicial concept. God is the ultimate judge. If he judged us just on the basis of what we have done—only by our "dark deeds"—no one could be justified. So in the Old Testament we see that David pleaded with God for mercy, knowing he was guilty of adultery and murder. He knew that God alone could free him from guilt, forgive his sins, and release him from the judgment he deserved (in that case, it was the death penalty). So when God punished David, but did not require the full death penalty, he was justified by God, even though acknowledged as a lawbreaker. In the New Testament, we are justified when God declares us "not guilty," because he has accepted Christ's crucifixion as payment and punishment for our sins. We do not know what the terms were between Dumbledore and Snape, but we do see that he has been justified somehow.

A character who is drawn in dark shades, like Snape, is the most likely kind of candidate to be thought of as what one might imagine a "sinner" or "wicked" person to be. So it is puzzling to see someone like Snape working at Hogwarts, even accepted and protected by Headmaster Dumbledore. Religious people have taken issue with the way God invites sinners to come to him. Indeed, Jesus said he came to call sinners to himself, not the righteous (or those who think of themselves as righteous). No matter how dark our past, how dark the stain our sins have left on our lives, or even how our sins have hurt others, there is a way back into God's good graces and a process of transformation that follows.

While sin will always have its consequences and leave a mark on us and our future, those who come back to God and repent can find assurance of God's acceptance, cleansing, sanctification, and justification. God can handle any "Dark Mark" for those who repent. This was prophesied by the prophet Isaiah:

> Come now, let us argue it out,
>   says the LORD:
> though your sins are like scarlet,
>   they shall be like snow;
> though they are red like crimson,
>   they shall become like wool.
> If you are willing and obedient,
>   you shall eat the good of the land;
> but if you refuse and rebel,
>   you shall be devoured by the sword;
>   for the mouth of the LORD has spoken.
>   (Isa. 1:18–20)

This was also promised in the New Testament: "If we confess our sins, he who is faithful and just will forgive us our sins and cleanse us from all unrighteousness. If we say that we have not sinned, we make him a liar, and his word is not in us" (1 John 1:9–10).

While still reserving final assessment of Severus Snape, I see the way Dumbledore treats him as a picture of hope for all who want to sever their ties with a past life of service to the Dark Lord of our world. There is hope for those who will come back to God and put the past away. They can receive absolution, a new position, and vindication. The one who is in authority over all our lives says we are not to indulge in the kinds of lifestyles that characterize those who will not enter the kingdom, but neither should we forget that such were some of us. The dark mark of our past does not have to brand our future.

The Wrath of Albus Dumbledore

There was no benign smile upon Dumbledore's face, no twinkle in the eyes behind the spectacles. There was cold fury in every line of the ancient face.

—Book Four, p. 679

*D*umbledore realized that Mad-Eye Moody was an impostor when he removed Harry from the field against his orders. At that point, Dumbledore understood that there had been one in their midst with evil intentions, a consummate deceiver. He also knew Harry was in immediate danger. That is why he followed as soon as he was free of obligations. Just as Mad-Eye Moody's wand was poised to murder Harry, a blast of red blew away the door and downed the evil impostor. Dumbledore, Snape, and McGonagall had arrived just in time to save Harry. The fact that they appeared in the foe glass also revealed that whoever was in Moody's form was not on the side of good. The occasion allows Harry a chance to see another dimension to Dumbledore: "At that moment, Harry fully understood for the first time why people said Dumbledore was the only wizard Voldemort had ever feared. The look upon Dumbledore's face as he stared down at the unconscious form of Mad-Eye Moody was more terrible than Harry could have ever imagined" (Book Four, p. 679).

Dumbledore's wrath displayed in this situation was not contrary to his loving kindness and goodness; it was an appropriate display of it. In similar fashion, the images of God as both loving and at times full of wrath are not contradictory. The Bible presents a God who is loving, kind, long-suffering, patient, willing to forgive, and to reach out to every living soul. And yet, God's loving nature is also displayed in his hatred of evil. As we saw here, evil is that which comes to kill and destroy that which is good and those who are loved. Therefore, evil is hated, and those who cling to evil even after seeing the goodness of God will be subjected to his wrath.

We see this several places in the Old Testament, of which these passages are only a few:

> If you are willing and obedient,
>   you shall eat the good of the land;
> but if you refuse and rebel,
>   you shall be devoured by the sword;
>   for the mouth of the LORD has spoken.
>   (Isa. 1:19–20)

> Hate evil and love good,
>   and establish justice in the gate.
>   (Amos 5:15)

> Your arrows are sharp
>   in the heart of the king's enemies;
>   the peoples fall under you.
> Your throne, O God, endures forever and ever.

> Your royal scepter is a scepter of equity;
>   you love righteousness and hate wickedness.
> Therefore God, your God, has anointed you
>   with the oil of gladness beyond your companions.
>
> (Ps. 45:5–7)

Isaiah's prophecy in chapter 61 is the messianic prophecy Jesus proclaimed himself to have fulfilled the day he spoke in the synagogue in Nazareth. Therein, Scripture puts God's love right alongside his vengeance, but notice that Jesus stopped short in his reading. Jesus read Isaiah's prophecy this far:

> The Spirit of the Lord is upon me,
>   because he has anointed me to bring good news to the poor.
> He has sent me to proclaim release to the captives
>   and recovery of sight to the blind,
>   to let the oppressed go free,
> to proclaim the year of the Lord's favor.
>
> (Luke 4:18–19)

Jesus stopped there—in mid-sentence—because his first coming was meant to offer the good news of God's love, comfort, and deliverance to the poor, the captives, and all who mourn. The sentence Jesus did not complete continues, "and the day of *vengeance* of our God . . ." (Isa. 61:2).

God's wrath is surrounded with his love and mercy, but to those who refuse and rebel, the wrath will be sure and severe. Therefore, the Bible says, "Let love be genuine; hate what is evil, hold fast to what is good" (Rom. 12:9). The wrath of Albus Dumbledore came out of his love for people and his commitment to hold fast to and protect that which was good.

The Bible clearly states, "For the wrath of God is revealed from heaven against all ungodliness and wickedness of those who by their wickedness suppress the truth" (Rom. 1:18). Barty Crouch Jr. acted as an impostor of one who was truly good, suppressing the truth with his Polyjuice Potion. He did so to carry out his wicked scheme to hand Harry over to Voldemort to be murdered, or to commit the murder himself. He deserved the wrath of Albus Dumbledore. Those on the good side did not have to fear such wrath; not so for those on the evil side.

Dumbledore waited for the Polyjuice Potion to wear off, knowing that when it did the identity of the deceiver would come to light. That brings to mind this bit of advice: "Let no one deceive you with empty words, for because of these things the wrath of God comes on those who are disobedient. Therefore do not be associated with them. For once you were darkness, but now in the Lord you are light" (Eph. 5:6–8).

Just as the wrath of Albus Dumbledore does not contradict his kindness or love, neither does the wrath of God contradict his. We must be careful not to be deceived by those who will rightly receive the wrath of God, and to make sure we live under the protection God provides so that we are not subject to his wrath.

Veritaserum: The Truth Will Be Told

"Severus, please fetch me the strongest Truth Potion you possess."
—Dumbledore to Professor Snape, Book Four, p. 680

*D*umbledore gave the impostor Veritaserum. It only took three drops to bring out the truth. He had no choice in the matter. Everything he had been hiding so deviously and for so long was revealed. This led to his condemnation.

The Bible tells us that God already knows everything. Everything we do, every idle word we speak, every thought—even the intent of our hearts is not hidden from God. However, we go through life trying to keep much hidden. The Bible makes it clear that the word of God is able to cut away all falsehood and get to the heart, to our most basic motives: "Indeed, the word of God is living and active, sharper than any two-edged sword, piercing until it divides soul from spirit, joints from marrow; it is able to judge the thoughts and intentions of the heart. And before him no creature is hidden, but all are naked and laid bare to the eyes of the one to whom we must render an account" (Heb. 4:12–13).

Barty Crouch Jr. had to give account to Dumbledore. Each human being will have to give account to God. As there was a "moment of truth" for Mr. Crouch, there will also be a specific moment when each of us will get the equivalent of Veritaserum and our secrets will become common knowledge. Hypocrites and impostors who have the most to hide also have the most to fear.

Consider what Jesus taught his disciples:

> Meanwhile, when the crowd gathered by the thousands, so that they trampled on one another, he began to speak first to his disciples, "Beware of the yeast of the Pharisees, that is, their hypocrisy. Nothing is covered up that will not be uncovered, and nothing secret that will not become known. Therefore whatever you have said in the dark will be heard in the light, and what you have whispered behind closed doors will be proclaimed from the housetops." (Luke 12:1–3)

While there will be a moment in the future when all the truth comes out, discretion must also be exercised wisely. In Book One, when Harry wanted to know the truth about some things, this was Dumbledore's reply: "'The truth.' Dumbledore sighed. 'It is a beautiful and terrible thing, and should therefore be treated with great caution'" (Book One, p. 298). Like Dumbledore, we should determine never to lie, but also be careful to handle the truth we know with consideration for the people to whom we would tell it. Like Harry, we do not know the whole truth yet, but we can be assured that one day it will all be revealed. On that day, those who have trusted the one who called himself "the truth" will be safe; those who have suppressed the truth in unrighteousness or tried to hide their evil deeds will be exposed and pay a terrible price similar to the price paid by Barty Crouch Jr.

The Kiss That Cost His Soul

He knew what the dementor must have done. It had administered its fatal kiss to Barty Crouch. It had sucked his soul out through his mouth. He was worse than dead.
—Book Four, p. 703

*D*umbledore never wanted the dementors at Hogwarts. He certainly did not want them threatening his students. When Cornelius Fudge came into the room with a dementor, Professor McGonagall told him Dumbledore would never allow dementors to set foot inside the castle, but that did not stop him. The moment the dementor was in the room it swept down on Barty Crouch Jr. and administered the kiss. His expectations of honor from the Dark Lord were lost along with his soul.

The dementors had been described as soulless and evil creatures that sucked every good feeling and happy memory out of those they came near, leaving those under their influence too long with nothing but memories of the worst experiences of their lives. But the worst fate anyone could have was to receive the dementor's kiss, which left the person technically alive but without his or her soul. Harry was right in thinking this was a fate worse than death. Even though Dumbledore dealt severely with Barty Crouch Jr., he did not want him to lose his soul.

The Bible and the Harry Potter stories agree that there is something worse than death. When God created human beings he gave them a soul, that part of them destined for eternity and capable of loving or rejecting him. The eternal soul of every person will either enjoy the blessings and comforts of God's presence forever or be lost in a tortured eternity apart from God. Everyone will die, seeing that mortality is part of the curse that came on humanity because of sin. But, compared to physical death, the loss of one's soul is far more important than when or how one dies. No earthly power or material wealth can compare to the worth of a human soul. As Jesus asked, "What good is it for a man to gain the whole world, yet forfeit his soul? Or what can a man give in exchange for his soul?" (Mark 8:36–37 NIV). This is repeated in three of the four Gospels.

Jesus never gave his disciples a guarantee of protection from pain, hardship, or death; indeed, he predicted that they would suffer and that some would be put to death because of their testimony about him. He did emphasize that the final and eternal destiny of each human soul is of far greater importance than temporary troubles in this life. The Bible says, "For this slight momentary affliction is preparing for us an eternal weight of glory far beyond all measure" (2 Cor. 4:17).

The fear and revulsion over the dementor's kiss can remind us of the gravity of one lost soul—even one as despicable as Barty Crouch Jr. Whenever the dementor's kiss is dealt with in Harry's world, it is always treated as worse than death. This is how the Bible treats the loss of one soul.

Jesus clearly rated death a distant second to the risk of losing one's soul. He told his disciples, "Do not fear those who kill the body but cannot kill the soul; rather fear him who can destroy both soul and body in hell" (Matt. 10:28). The Bible teaches that there is a real hell, which was created for the devil and his angels—never for human beings. Therefore, Jesus personally does everything he can to dissuade people from going to hell. Consider the story Jesus tells in Luke 16:19–31 of the rich man who learned too late of the power and permanence of hell. Jesus ended this story with a sad prophecy of what he could foresee. Even after he rose from the dead, there would still be those who would not listen to his warnings. But he made sure we had these warnings while there is still time for our souls to be rescued.

Just as Dumbledore took no delight in seeing even an evil man receive the dementor's kiss, God takes no delight in seeing any soul be lost and cast into hell. Jesus never made light of hell; instead he showed his urgent concern for and desire to save those whose souls were in danger.

What man among you, if he has a hundred sheep and has lost one of them, does not leave the ninety-nine in the open pasture, and go after the one which is lost, until he finds it? And when he has found it, he lays it on his shoulders, rejoicing. And when he comes home, he calls together his friends and his neighbors, saying to them, "Rejoice with me, for I have found my sheep which was lost!" I tell you that in the same way, there will be more joy in heaven over one sinner who repents, than over ninety-nine righteous persons who need no repentance. (Luke 15:3–7 NASB)

In reflecting on the kiss that cost a man his soul, consider the contrast of emotions at the end of Book Four as compared to the end of Book Three when Harry and Sirius Black both escaped the dementor's kiss. The dementor's kiss brought tragedy and solemn trepidation with no hope for the future. Rescue from the dementor's kiss brought exhilarating relief, comfort, and joy shared by Harry, Sirius, and all who loved them (along with expectations for a good future). That is like the contrast of emotions we feel toward the rich man in Jesus' parable who faced eternity in torment, as compared to the relief and joy we feel for the poor man in the story Jesus told who ended up in the afterlife comforted and celebrating with Abraham for all eternity.

The Parting of the Ways

"If your determination to shut your eyes will carry you as far as this, Cornelius," said Dumbledore, *"we have reached a parting of the ways. You must act as you see fit. And I—I shall act as I see fit."*

—Book Four, p. 709

Cornelius Fudge, Minister of Magic, reacted to the confessions of Barty Crouch Jr. and news of Voldemort's return in a very strange way. He sought to deny it and discredit the evidence. By allowing the dementor to administer its kiss, he effectively got rid of the star witness. His reaction toward Dumbledore revealed that he was unwilling to stand with him against evil. This is what brought them to a parting of the ways.

Fudge refused to believe the story Barty Crouch Jr. had told under the compulsion of Veritaserum (or perhaps just refused to admit it openly). Instead, he characterized Crouch as a lunatic murderer. He rejected the assembled testimony of trustworthy witnesses (Harry, Dumbledore, Snape, and McGonagall) who had no reason to lie or make up such a story. Even if they did want to concoct such a story, they could not have been so clever as to come up with a story that made sense of all the details and be able to agree on a cohesive story line with so little time to form a conspiracy. Fudge also swept aside or disregarded the mute evidence of Snape's Dark Mark that had appeared on his arm. Most significantly, he made no attempt to deal with the reality of Cedric's murder: that the boy's dead body had no mark was clear evidence that he had been the victim of the Killing Curse. If he wanted to go further, he could have sought to verify Barty Crouch Jr.'s testimony by exhuming the bone (that had once been the body of Mr. Crouch Sr.). But he did none of this.

Cornelius Fudge openly admitted that he did not *want* to believe their testimony because it would upset the status quo and threaten his political position. If the story as told by Harry and the others was true, it reflected poorly on some people with whom Fudge had aligned himself (and could possibly uncover other things Fudge may be hiding, which remain hidden at this point in the story). We do know that Harry could name the Death Eaters who returned to Voldemort at his call, those he saw in the graveyard. These included MacNair, whom Fudge had hired to work at the Ministry, and Lucius Malfoy, who held considerable power; Fudge had vouched for both of them. Rather than upset all of that, Fudge exhibited a determination to shut his eyes. Therefore, Dumbledore declared they had reached a parting of the ways.

Cornelius Fudge tried to turn this around to make it look like Dumbledore was setting himself against him (and, by inference, the Ministry), but he was set straight. " 'The only one against whom I intend to work,' said Dumbledore, 'is Lord Voldemort. If

you are against him, then we remain, Cornelius, on the same side'"
(Book Four, p. 709).

Even though Dumbledore was open to all and accepted those
whose loyalties were questionable while Voldemort was in hiding,
there came a time when all had to declare their allegiance. There
was no longer middle ground, no wiggle room with regard to
which side one was on. This is similar to the progression of Jesus'
ministry. He called the crowds to him, including those who were
questionable or uncertain of their position with regard to God and
himself. However, a time came when everyone had to declare
whether they were with Jesus or against him:

> John said to him, "Teacher, we saw someone casting out
> demons in your name, and we tried to stop him, because he
> was not following us." But Jesus said, "Do not stop him; for
> no one who does a deed of power in my name will be able
> soon afterward to speak evil of me. Whoever is not against us
> is for us. For truly I tell you, whoever gives you a cup of water
> to drink because you bear the name of Christ will by no
> means lose the reward." (Mark 9:38–41)

At another time Jesus was being accused by the religious leaders of casting out demons by the power of Satan (aka: Beelzebul).
Jesus countered with this:

> If Satan also is divided against himself, how will his kingdom
> stand?—for you say that I cast out the demons by Beelzebul.
> Now if I cast out the demons by Beelzebul, by whom do your
> exorcists cast them out? Therefore they will be your judges.
> But if it is by the finger of God that I cast out the demons,
> then the kingdom of God has come to you. . . . Whoever is
> not with me is against me, and whoever does not gather with
> me scatters. (Luke 11:18–23)

Jesus and the religious leaders who refused to believe in him had
reached a parting of the ways. Not unlike Cornelius Fudge, the religious leaders Jesus confronted had a lot to lose if Jesus were truly

what he proclaimed himself to be—Son of God, Son of Man, Son of David, "I Am"—which adds up to Messiah. They had worked their whole lives to attain the positions he could make obsolete. Besides, his claims were sure to create conflict with their Roman governors, which would cause an uprising that might rightly be feared. The Roman way of dealing with such uprisings was brutal, and many would surely die. Besides, their entire political and religious establishment would be destroyed. They opted to shut their eyes because of the implications the truth could have for their own lives.

There will be a parting of the ways when everyone will have to choose sides. Jesus stated it this way: "Everyone therefore who acknowledges me before others, I also will acknowledge before my Father in heaven; but whoever denies me before others, I also will deny before my Father in heaven" (Matt. 10:32–33). Before we arrive at that parting of the ways, we would do well to see where we stand and whether any determination to shut our eyes might have more to do with the implications of what we might see rather than the reliability of the evidence and testimony of eye-witnesses recorded in the Bible.

We Are Only as Strong as We Are United

"Time is short, and unless the few of us who know the truth . . . stand united, there is no hope for any of us."
—Dumbledore to Professor Snape and
Sirius Black, Book Four, p. 712

As Professor Dumbledore sought to consolidate the ranks of those ready to oppose Voldemort, he had to bring together some who were openly hostile to each other. Sirius Black and Severus Snape were called on to lay aside their old differences, or at least call a truce, as Dumbledore pronounced them to be on the same side. If they did not stand together, they would not be able to stand at all. In the Great Hall, Dumbledore told the assembly,

> I say to you all, once again—in the light of Lord Voldemort's return, we are only as strong as we are united, as weak as we are divided. Lord Voldemort's gift for spreading discord and enmity is very great. We can fight it only by showing an equally strong bond of friendship and trust. Differences of habit and language are nothing at all if our aims are identical and our hearts are open. (Book Four, p. 723)

Unity is at the heart of the gospel, although this is often not apparent in the ranks of those who share a belief in the Bible, even among those who have a shared faith in Jesus as their Messiah. This is not unlike what we see in the ranks of those Dumbledore is assembling. Jesus made it clear that this call for unity was not something new, but was at the heart of the Old Testament declaration of the very nature of God:

> One of the scribes came near and heard them disputing with one another, and seeing that he answered them well, he asked him, "Which commandment is the first of all?" Jesus answered, "The first is, 'Hear, O Israel: the Lord our God, *the Lord is one;* you shall love the Lord your God with all your heart, and with all your soul, and with all your mind, and with all your strength.' The second is this, 'You shall love your neighbor as yourself.' There is no other commandment greater than these." (Mark 12:28–31)

Jesus' final prayer for his followers, in John 17:1–26, was a primarily a prayer for unity and protection from the evil one: "I ask you to protect them from the evil one. . . . I ask not only on behalf of these, but also on behalf of those who will believe in me through their word, that they may all be one" (John 17:15, 20–21). This prayer shows that unity among his followers was of utmost importance to Jesus.

The evil one warned against in the Bible has—as Dumbledore

phrased it—"a gift for spreading discord and enmity." Therefore, the Bible warns against the things that disrupt unity:

> Live by the Spirit, I say, and do not gratify the desires of the flesh. For what the flesh desires is opposed to the Spirit, and what the Spirit desires is opposed to the flesh. . . . Now the works of the flesh are obvious: fornication, impurity, licentiousness, idolatry, sorcery, enmities, strife, jealousy, anger, quarrels, dissensions, factions, envy, drunkenness, carousing, and things like these. I am warning you, as I warned you before: those who do such things will not inherit the kingdom of God. (Gal. 5:16–21)

In our world—as in Harry's—those who know the truth need to put aside old differences and stand united, thereby building up friendship and trust. When we do, we will act in unity with God and each other. Then the power of God can flow through us uninterrupted to accomplish God's will on earth as it is in heaven.

What Will Come, Will Come

> *"Known it fer years, Harry. Knew he was out there bidin'*
> *his time. It had ter happen. Well, now it has, an we'll jus'*
> *have ter get on with it. We'll fight. Migh' be able ter stop*
> *him before he gets a good hold."*
> —Hagrid to Harry, Ron, and Hermione,
> Book Four, p. 719

Although the coming battle is unwelcome, Hagrid knew it was inevitable. Voldemort is evil, and evil is aggressive. It seeks to overpower good, and therefore seeks to destroy all that is good. Dumbledore and those opposing Voldemort will not—dare not—step aside and let evil overtake their world. They knew that Voldemort had not been destroyed utterly. They had seen his schemes being worked out in various ways, through various willing and unwilling accomplices.

It was only a matter of time until there had to be an outright battle. Everyone will be forced to declare allegiance either to Voldemort's side or Dumbledore's side. Book Four ends with Harry thinking, "As Hagrid had said, what would come, would come . . . and he would have to meet it when it did" (Book Four, p. 734).

Anyone can look at our world and know that evil is still lurking out there. The Bible is quite clear in warning us that evil will not sit idle, but is biding its time.

The battle between good and evil is ongoing, in the everyday struggles of each human soul and as evidenced in any nightly news broadcast. However, beyond this, the Bible predicts a time when Satan (the evil one) and all the forces of evil will rise up to make a final challenge against God and those who align themselves on the side of good. History also teaches us that evil tyrants do not sit idle when they are out of power, although they may have to bide their time while awaiting an opportune moment to attack. Like Voldemort, evil tyrants, despots, terrorists, and would-be dictators all lie in wait, unseen, while planning their rise to power. They too resolve to destroy whoever gets in their way, with murderous intent and without remorse. Therefore, no matter how comfortable we feel, we would do well to bear in mind that evil-doers are always lurking out there somewhere in the world, planning, plotting, and biding their time. This awareness will help us not be caught unprepared.

As Dumbledore prepared his side for battle, Jesus similarly prepared his disciples to expect that there would be battles to be fought. But he also sought to ease their fears:

> "When you hear of wars and revolutions, do not be frightened. These things must happen first, but the end will not come right away."
> Then he said to them: "Nation will rise against nation, and kingdom against kingdom. There will be great earthquakes, famines and pestilences in various places, and fearful events and great signs from heaven." (Luke 21:9–11 NIV)

There are battles left to be fought: skirmishes in moral and political realms, "wars and rumors of wars," ethnic groups rising up to destroy other ethnic groups, nations rising up against nations. However, we are not to give in to fear, but rather to make sure that we take our stand on the side of good. In every battle between good and evil, within ourselves and in every earthly struggle, we too must choose sides carefully. With God's guidance, we can determine good from evil, dare to do that which is good, and bravely resist evil, regardless of the cost. But that is not the whole of the story.

The Bible gives us the advantage of knowing how to live intent on overcoming evil, but also assures us that the ultimate war between good and evil will be won by those on the side of good. In the face of the aggressive nature of evil, we are told, "Do not be overcome by evil, but overcome evil with good" (Rom. 12:21). The positive is to actively overcome the negative.

The Bible also tells us how:

> Be on guard so that your hearts are not weighed down with dissipation and drunkenness and the worries of this life, and that day catch you unexpectedly, like a trap. For it will come upon all who live on the face of the whole earth. Be alert at all times, praying that you may have the strength to escape all these things that will take place, and to stand before the Son of Man. (Luke 21:34–36)

In the Harry Potter series, Book Four ends in the middle of the larger story. As with most good stories, we are left hanging at a crisis point and do not know how the remaining battles will end. However, in our world, while acknowledging the ongoing battles between good and evil, the Bible tells us that we can look forward to a wonderful end. (I am expecting a positive outcome in Harry's world too.)

In Harry's world, Hagrid can face the battle to come with courage because he knows Dumbledore will be leading them: "Great man, Dumbledore. 'S long as we've got him, I'm not too worried" (Book Four, p. 719). God consoles us with the assurance that God is always with us, that the Holy Spirit is our comforter, and that whenever two or three gather in Jesus' name, he will be with us. So we have assurance that whatever battles we face, we are not alone and we are not helpless.

The Bible also gives us a "blessed hope" that a day will come when Jesus will return to earth physically to defeat the forces of evil in a final battle. It also tells us how to live until that day:

> For the grace of God that brings salvation has appeared to all men. It teaches us to say "No" to ungodliness and worldly passions, and to live self-controlled, upright and godly lives in this present age, while we wait for the blessed hope—the glorious appearing of our great God and Savior, Jesus Christ, who gave himself for us to redeem us from all wickedness and to purify for himself a people that are his very own, eager to do what is good. (Titus 2:11–14 NIV)

In our world—as in the wizarding world of Harry Potter—what is coming will come, and we will have to face it when it does. However, there is good news that counteracts the evil that remains active in our world. The Bible assures us that Jesus will come back. When he does, he will crush all the forces of evil and overcome evil with good forever! The promised return of Jesus, the Prince of Peace, is a bright opposite to the ominous expectation of the Dark Lord's return in Harry's world. Humanity does have to face the reality that there are battles left to be fought and won against evil in our world. While we must be vigilant, we can rest assured in "the blessed hope" that the One who is coming will come, and we can look forward to meeting him when he does.

Dumbledore Welcomes All Who Wish to Come

"Every guest in this Hall," said Dumbledore, and his eyes lingered upon the Durmstrang students, *"will be welcomed back here at any time, should they wish to come."*
—Book Four, p. 723

*B*ook Four ends with Voldemort having acquired human form, by force and dark magic. With the bone of the father he murdered, the flesh of one of his servants, and the blood of his enemy, the Dark Lord rose again. Dumbledore took his stand against him, and invited all to stand with him on the side of good. He called together the Hogwarts students and students who had been visiting from other wizarding schools for the Triwizard Tournament. He reminded them that they were always welcome in his banquet hall. His eyes lingered on the Durmstrang students, perhaps because Durmstrang was one of the schools that still taught some of the Dark Arts. Dumbledore wanted those students in particular to know that they could still choose good even if they had been schooled in evil.

Dumbledore had distinguished himself as one who extended open arms even to those others rejected. He excluded no one because of what they were, what had happened to them, what they were believed to be, or what they had done, if they were willing to turn away from evil. He had shown his open arms policy many times. He hired Professor Lupin, who was a werewolf. He hired Hagrid, even though he had been falsely convicted of opening the Chamber of Secrets and was obviously half-giant. He hired Professor Snape, even though he had once been a Death Eater. He invited schools to the Triwizard Tournament that had questionable leaders (Karkaroff had been a Death Eater, and Madam Maxime appeared to be part giant). He hired Filch, who was a squib (having magical parentage, but no apparent magical powers), and Gilderoy Lockhart, whose credentials were bogus. So Dumbledore's track-record of welcoming all who would come backed up his invitation.

The Bible lays out a panoramic battle between good and evil, God and Satan, and people are caught in the midst of this battle whether they like it or not. Such is the nature of human life. The battle began before we were born, and we each must end up on a side, whether by choice or default. But God sent us a message to let us know we are all welcome on his side under his protection, or—figuratively—in his banquet hall.

Jesus told a story about a fictional king who gave a wedding banquet for his son. But all the people originally invited refused to come. Again, the king sent out his servants to tell them that he had a wonderful feast planned for them, that they were wanted and welcome, but they made light of it and again declined his invitation to the banquet. Some simply went about their daily business, which they deemed more important, while others abused and killed the king's servants who delivered the invitation. So the king sent troops and killed those who had murdered his messengers. (Given the importance of the king and the villainous response of those invited, this was considered an appropriate response. Such a flagrant refusal to receive a king's hospitality was a dishonor to the royal family.) "Then he said to his slaves, 'The wedding is ready, but those invited were not worthy. Go therefore into the main streets, and invite everyone you find to the wedding banquet.' Those slaves went out into the streets and gathered all whom they found, both good and bad; so the wedding hall was filled with guests" (Matt. 22:8–10). This follows with a scene of the king arriving to find that one of the welcomed guests did not dress appropriately for the banquet and was therefore tossed out, but all the others—both good and bad— enjoyed the king's hospitality.

This parable was Jesus' way of speaking to the Jewish religious leaders of his day who knew the Scriptures and the prophecies of the Messiah. They had been the first to receive God's invitation to honor his Son. The religious elite were the ones represented as refusing the invitation and killing the king's messengers. They were the real villains of the story. Elsewhere, he accused them of masquerading as good, and referred to them as whitewashed tombs. So Jesus' story meant that God was done with them. They had come to a parting of the ways. Soon Roman troops would overthrow them and destroy the temple.

At the tail end of this sober warning for those who should have received the invitation but refused, there came good news for everybody else. God's banquet hall and lavish feast was now wide open to any and all who wished to come. Granted, those who did choose to come needed to dress appropriately, spiritually speaking (in the "robes of righteousness" provided for them) in order to stay.

In our world, we see the open arms of God when Jesus called for all who were weary and heavy laden to come to him, when he called for all who were thirsty to come to him, when all who were sick or possessed by demons came to him and were healed, when he called the little children to come to him and then picked them up in his arms and blessed them. God's arms were extended to everyone when Jesus sent his disciples out into all the world to preach the gospel of God's love.

John writes of Jesus,

> He was in the world, and the world came into being through him; yet the world did not know him. He came to what was his own, and his own people did not accept him. But *to all who received him,* who believed in his name, he gave power to become children of God, who were born, not of blood or of the will of the flesh or of the will of man, but of God. (John 1:10–13)

Peter extended this invitation to a crowd assembled in Jerusalem: "Repent, and be baptized *every one of you* in the name of Jesus Christ so that your sins may be forgiven; and you will receive the gift of the Holy Spirit. *For the promise is for you, for your children, and for all who are far away, everyone whom the Lord our God calls to him*" (Acts 2:38–39). God's invitation is not limited to a select guest list but is open to all: "For there is no distinction between Jew and Greek; the same Lord is Lord of all and is generous to all who call on him. For, 'Everyone who calls on the name of the Lord shall be saved'" (Rom. 10:12–13).

Albus Dumbledore's reminder to all the students, good and bad alike, that they are welcome back any time they wish to come reflects God's open arms and warm welcome to all who are willing to respond positively to his invitation.

Interlude

I began this book while looking at white clouds against a brilliant blue sky and reflecting on how they awakened my imagination and that of my kids. Metaphorically, this book goes from a bright sky on a spring day to a point midway through the Harry Potter series that might rightly be likened to dark clouds overshadowing the wizarding world. The end of Book Four leaves us at the darkest point, looking forward to an inevitable battle. We know there are three more books to follow, but we are left with much that is uncertain. We wonder where it will lead: What terrible things will happen? Who will live and who will die?

If this book simply looked at the themes of the Harry Potter stories, it might be appropriate to let it end under a darkened sky too. However, since this is a book about the gospel—God's *good news*—as it relates to Harry Potter, we do not have to end on a dark note. There is an appropriate gospel parallel that takes up where the story left off.

Imagine yourself as being alive during the time of Jesus. For this purpose, it makes little difference whether you would most aptly see yourself as a curious bystander, a skeptic, a seeker, a devoted disciple, or even an avowed enemy of Jesus. Imagine yourself in Jerusalem on the day of his crucifixion. You see him publicly condemned to death, beaten mercilessly, ridiculed, mocked, pushed along up that dusty hill that forms the shape of a skull. You hear the crack of wood and iron as the mallet pounds the nails through human flesh, and the attendant screams of the three men being crucified that day. The spectacle gets underway at about nine in the morning, then at noon an ominous darkness covers the entire sky. The Gospel of Luke describes it this way:

> It was now about the sixth hour, and darkness came over the whole land until the ninth hour, for the sun stopped shining. And the curtain of the temple was torn in two. Jesus called out with a loud voice, "Father, into your hands I commit my spirit." When he had said this, he breathed his last.

137

The centurion, seeing what had happened, praised God and said, "Surely this was a righteous man." When all the people who had gathered to witness this sight saw what took place, they beat their breasts and went away. But all those who knew him, including the women who had followed him from Galilee, stood at a distance, watching these things. (Luke 23:44–49)

The darkness at midday gave way to a hurried burial and to a dark night in which no one in Jerusalem could celebrate an untroubled Passover. However, they did not have to wait years for the rest of the story! At daybreak on the third day, the sun arose with a brilliance that was put to shame only by the brilliance of the angels who announced that Jesus had risen from the dead just as he promised. The curse was indeed broken! All who would believe in him, trusting that he had taken the curse of death in their place, would live eternally.

Before he died, Jesus had told his disciples that he must go up to Jerusalem, be given over into the hands of evil men, suffer many things, be crucified, die, and be buried. Then on the third day he would rise from the dead. Apparently his disciples thought this was some sort of literary metaphor. But the predictions Jesus made were not a flight of fantasy. His resurrection confirmed that he had foretold a glorious reality.

Everyone who heard the glad tidings and curious rumors about his resurrection had to decide what to believe about the stories he had told, the claims he had made, and the man who claimed to be the one and only Son of God. Even the disciples had to think it all through again in the fresh light of his resurrection. What did it all mean now? What about Jesus' warnings that some of them would die because of their testimony about him before kings and governors? What of all the other stories they may have taken as fantasy or metaphor—could those be real too? What of all his promises, predictions, warnings—what did all that he had taught mean for them and the future of the human race?

Jesus stayed with them for forty days, appearing and disappearing (or *disapparating,* as they would say in Harry's world). One time he appeared to over five hundred witnesses at once. He taught his disciples many things regarding the kingdom of God. That kingdom of God had arrived and they were part of it, although it was invisible to most. That kingdom had come, but it was also yet to come. Jesus was going away to prepare a place for them, but he would return to earth to fight one last battle when he would destroy the forces of evil entirely. The disciples were told to wait in Jerusalem until they received power from on high when the Holy Spirit would come upon them. Then they would use that power to be his witnesses to the ends of the earth and until the end of time. Then Jesus went back up into heaven, ascending before their eyes until the clouds obscured him from their sight.

I like the idea of leaving you looking up at the clouds, where we began. But I also want to reprise Albus Dumbledore's invitation. You may have picked up this book for any number of reasons, perhaps the least of which was to seek God or actually hear the gospel. I wrote this book for several reasons, but one was to extend God's welcoming invitation to you. I particularly hoped that some would really hear the gospel who had never heard it before, perhaps because they were turned off by the way it has been presented.

Another reason I wrote this book was to challenge my fellow Christians to think again about the Harry Potter books. Many non-Christians share my discomfort with the fact that many critics of Harry Potter have never read even one of the four books for themselves. It is hard to be adamant if you choose to remain personally ignorant by relying only on impressions and hearsay without reading the story in question for yourself.

I find it an interesting parallel that many who have neglected or rejected the gospel have done so without actually reading even one of the four Gospels for themselves. Whatever conclusions they have come to are also based on impressions, hearsay, and second-hand accounts. All seekers of truth owe it to themselves to read at least one of the four Gospels. (For a free copy of the Gospel of John, contact The Pocket Testament League at 1-800-636-8785 or www.readcarryshare.org.)

I hope you enjoyed this alternative look at Harry Potter. We live at a time when the battle between evil and good is growing intense; sides are being drawn up even still. As we face our own battles and dark days ahead, let us remember that good will triumph over evil and that God's arms are open wide, his banquet hall is open to us all, and he welcomes all who wish to come.

Glimmers of the Gospel in Book Five
Harry Potter and the Order of the Phoenix

Introduction to Book Five

This story opens on Privet Drive, with Harry frustrated at having heard nothing about what has happened since Voldemort's return to a physical form and the reinstatement of his band of Death Eaters. When Harry and Dudley are attacked by dementors, Harry uses the Patronus Charm to protect himself and rescue Dudley's soul from the dementor's kiss—an example of Christ's command to love one's enemy. In response to this act of heroism, Harry is expelled from Hogwarts, then is temporarily reinstated pending a disciplinary hearing before the Wizengamot at the Ministry of Magic—an example of bureaucratic injustice that must be opposed courageously and with truth.

At 12 Grimmauld Place Harry is introduced to the Order of the Phoenix, a secret society committed to opposing Voldemort. The strategy of those on the side of evil is to pretend that evil does not exist, that Voldemort has not returned. The campaign of silence about that which truly endangers the Wizarding world and the Muggle world is accompanied by a whispering campaign to bring Harry and Dumbledore into disrepute. They are ridiculed by the *Daily Prophet,* and Dumbledore has been demoted from the Wizengamot and otherwise been discredited. In the face of such lies, the truth must be brought to light.

The hearing is obviously an attempt to expel Harry from Hogwarts; however, Mr. Weasley and Dumbledore manage to get Harry to the hearing despite a last-minute time change, provide credible witnesses, and thwart the attempt to further discredit him. Among the Ministry of Magic officials is one Delores Jane Umbridge: sugarcoated evil in a pink dress. When school resumes and Umbridge is introduced as the new Defense Against the Dark Arts teacher, it becomes obvious that the Ministry of Magic is attempting to interfere with the education at Hogwarts. Professor Umbridge blatantly denies that Voldemort has returned, accuses Harry of lying about this, and punishes him by having him use her "special quill" to write in his own blood *I must not tell lies.* As Umbridge's tyrannical grip on the school expands, freedoms are restricted, the practice of defensive magic is forbidden, spying and reporting on fellow students is rewarded, and torture is threatened.

Thus, the need for an effective (although covert) response is called for, and the students decide the way to fight back is to continue to practice—actively practice—Defense Against the Dark Arts. The resulting secret meetings of the D.A., alternately known as the "Defense Association" or "Dumbledore's Army," allow interested students to learn Defense Against the Dark Arts directly from Harry. This aspect of the story might be used to illustrate the need for active spiritual warfare against invisible forces of evil.

Meanwhile, Harry is troubled by dreams and dark thoughts that lead him to a locked door within the Ministry of Magic, and finally toward the Hall of Prophecy that he did not previously know existed. The Order of the Phoenix remains secretive toward the underage wizards and witches who attend Hogwarts, with only whispers—sometimes overheard with "extendable ears"—that indicate that the Dark Lord has a mysterious hold on Harry's thoughts and that those in the Order must be on duty to protect something, perhaps a weapon Voldemort might use. Harry worries that he may be that weapon, and so he withdraws from his friends. During one of Harry's disturbing dreams, he sees Mr. Weasley being attacked by a giant snake at the Ministry of Magic. He awakes to alert those in the Order that Mr. Weasley has been attacked, shielding the fact that he saw the attack through the eyes of the snake, as though *he were* the snake. While being hailed the hero for sending the help that saved Mr. Weasley's life, Harry is deeply troubled by his connection with the evil foe who has infiltrated his thoughts and allowed him insight into the attack. All attempts to close Harry's mind to these unbidden dreams and visions seem to fail.

Meanwhile, Hagrid returns from his prolonged absence on a mission for the Order. He is badly injured, without sufficient explanation, and continues receiving injuries. He resumes his position as Care of Magical Creatures teacher at the same time Professor Umbridge, now elevated to Hogwarts High Inquisitor, is examining all teachers. It soon becomes clear that Professor Trelawney and Hagrid are both in danger of losing their posts. Ultimately it is revealed that Hagrid's injuries come from his half-brother, Grawp, a "small" giant who does not know his own strength. Hagrid has relocated him to the Forbidden Forest and is trying to civilize him, thus upsetting the centaurs. When it becomes apparent that Hagrid will soon lose his position, he enlists the help of Harry, Hermione, and Ron to care for Grawp in his absence. Hagrid's love for his brother demonstrated in practical care resounds of Christian charity.

Amid Ron's triumphs in Quidditch (after Fred, George, and Harry have been banned) and the fifth-years' studying for their O.W.L.s—getting career advice as they look toward what life may hold for them—the D.A. is discovered. Dumbledore takes the fall for the group and escapes before he can be sent—unjustly—to Azkaban. Fred and George manage to create havoc for Umbridge, while testing out and demonstrating their joke shop fare before making a memorable departure from Hogwarts.

Hermione decides it's time for the truth to be told about Voldemort's return, so she uses her influence over Rita Skeeter to get her to write the true story of what happened between Harry, Voldemort, and the Death Eaters on the night Cedric Diggory died and Voldemort regained the use of a human body (with the help of the bone of his father, the flesh of his servant, and the blood of his enemy). Hermione practices the diplomatic skill of a peacemaker by getting Luna Lovegood's father (the editor of *The Quibbler*) to publish the piece. Umbridge's banning of the paper ensures that everyone will read it (perhaps those who support banning the *Harry Potter* books could learn from this). Boldly speaking truth to power like Hermione does here is reminiscent of what Jesus' disciples did after his resurrection when they confronted the religious elite of their day with the truth that the Jesus they had condemned to death, crucified, buried, and whose tomb their soldiers had guarded had risen from the dead.

The dreams of the door, which have been luring Harry closer and closer to the Ministry of Magic, take a decisive turn when Harry sees his godfather, Sirius, being tortured by Voldemort in the Hall of Prophecies. Against Hermione's better judgment, with misdirection from Kreacher, and only after escaping Professor Umbridge (who was delightfully carried away by a herd of centaurs she had enraged with her bigotry), Harry, Ron, Hermione, Luna, Neville, and Ginny set off for the Ministry of Magic on a rescue mission. They soon discover that this is a trick to lure Harry to pick up the prophecy about himself and Voldemort, which Voldemort wants in order to understand how to destroy Harry. A battle ensues between the Death Eaters, led by Lucius Malfoy, and the members of the D.A., who are joined by members of the Order of the Phoenix. The battle takes them through the Department of Mysteries and into the Death Chamber, where a veil hangs in an archway on a raised dais. During the battle, Bellatrix Lestrange hits Sirius with a curse that sends him falling though the veil of death. Harry is left bereft, struggling with his guilt over being lured into Voldemort's trap and his anger at Sirius's death, much of which is vented at Dumbledore (who appears at the Ministry to battle Voldemort). In those final throes of the battle, Harry is momentarily possessed by Voldemort in Voldemort's attempt to get Dumbledore to kill Harry in an attempt to kill Voldemort. However, the love that Harry has for Sirius, which he feels so keenly in his grief, makes it impossible for Voldemort to remain inside Harry. As the battle comes to an end, Harry is released from Voldemort's hold, the Death Eaters are rounded up, and Voldemort disappears, but not before being recognized by many employees of the Ministry, including the Minister himself. Thus, Harry and Dumbledore are proved to have been telling the truth all along.

Dumbledore allows Harry to vent his anger at the death of Sirius and at having succumbed to the trickery of the evil one. Dumbledore confesses that he feels partly responsible for Sirius's death, because he did not previously tell Harry about the prophecy, which is what prompted Voldemort to lure them all to the battle. Dumbledore then reveals his recollection of the prophecy—delivered by Professor Trelawney—to Harry: "Either must die at the hand of the other for neither can live while the other survives."

The Christian themes most prominent in this book are the need for truth and courage to stand against oppression and tyranny, the power of spiritual warfare that must be practiced and not just understood in theory, the strategy on the part of evil to pretend that evil does not exist, the danger of officials (whether political or religious) seeking to rule over people rather than empowering them, and the power of love that alone can defeat evil.

EXPECTO PATRONUM!

"EXPECTO PATRONUM!" An enormous silver stag erupted from the tip of Harry's wand; its antlers caught the dementor in the place where its heart should have been; it was thrown backward, weightless as darkness, and as the stag charged, the dementor swooped away, bat-like and defeated.

—Book Five, p. 18

*A*t the moment when Harry and Dudley were attacked by the dementors, Harry called on his stag Patronus to protect them both. Even though Dudley blamed Harry for what was happening, even though Harry could have escaped and saved himself, leaving Dudley to the dementor's kiss, he chose not to. Harry chose to protect Dudley.

The word "Patronus" comes from the Latin word *pater,* or "father." The idea of a fatherly protector is reinforced because Harry's Patronus takes the form of a stag, like that of James Potter. As Harry thinks a happy thought and calls out, "Expecto Patronum!" it is as if he is calling out to his father for protection.

Similarly, most Christians pray the prayer that Jesus taught his disciples to pray:

Our Father in heaven,
hallowed be your name,
your kingdom come,

your will be done
   on earth as it is in heaven.
Give us today our daily bread.
Forgive us our debts,
   as we also have forgiven our debtors.
And lead us not into temptation,
but deliver us from the evil one.
                  (Matt. 6:9–13 NIV)

In this prayer we are given the privilege of calling God in heaven our Father and are invited to call out to him for help when we need earthly provision or forgiveness. At the same time, we are reminded of our obligation to forgive those who have hurt us. We are taught here to ask for supernatural help to deliver us from evil—as Harry needed supernatural help to fend off the dementors—and told to seek God's help in avoiding temptation. No matter how tempting it may have been for Harry to leave Dudley while protecting himself, he did not. Rather, he used his privilege of supernatural help to cover them both. The Bible explains one reason our prayers might not be answered: "When you ask, you do not receive, because you ask with wrong motives, that you may spend what you get on your pleasures" (Jas. 4:3 NIV). Harry didn't do that. In a moment of frightful and terrible danger, he called out for rescue, not just for himself but also for his enemy.

"Wands Away!" Theory without Practice Is Useless

"I repeat, as long as you have studied the theory hard enough—"

"And what good's theory going to be in the real world?" said Harry loudly, his fist in the air again.

                        —Book Five, p. 244

*T*he Minister of Magic, who fears Dumbledore might raise up a private army with which to overthrow him, puts Professor Umbridge in Hogwarts. The Ministry has already demonstrated its corruption, as evidenced by Harry's unjust disciplinary hearing. Now, Umbridge seeks to implement a theory-only course of study that forbids actually practicing Defense Against the Dark Arts. It's not that Professor Umbridge disbelieves in the power of defensive magic; she simply believes that such power might be used against the Ministry (since it has shifted its allegiances from good and toward evil). She is determined to squash the development of practices that would lead the students to actually become powerful out of fear that that power might not benefit the Ministry.

If the Ministry of Magic were likened to an official religious body, Professor Umbridge's approach would promote right teaching (orthodoxy) while forbidding right practice (orthopraxy). According to Jesus, right teaching without right practice brings destruction. He told a story comparing a person who built his house on solid rock to one who built on sand. What did this symbolize? Jesus explained:

> Therefore everyone who hears these words of mine and puts them into practice is like a wise man who built his house on the rock. The rain came down, the streams rose, and the winds blew and beat against that house; yet it did not fall, because it had its foundation on the rock. But everyone who hears these words of mine and does not put them into practice is like a foolish man who built his house on sand. The rain came down, the streams rose, and the winds blew and beat against that house, and it fell with a great crash. (Matt. 7:24–27 NIV)

Harry and his friends understood that just learning the theory without applying it could lead to their destruction, and they were right.

Besides, Professor Umbridge was a "teacher" who might have had a form of right teaching, but she didn't uphold what was right in her own life. She was a hypocrite. She was the one who sent the dementors after Harry, then sat in judgment over him seeking to punish him for the reaction she had prompted. While promoting a lie, she forced Harry to carve *I must not tell lies* into his hand. Second Timothy describes the corruption to come about in the last days, including those "having a form of godliness but denying its power," and warns, "Have nothing to do with them" (2 Tim. 3:1–5 NIV). So Harry and his friends' instincts were right about her.

Judging from the way Jesus reprimanded the hypocritical teachers in a corrupt system in his day, we might suppose Umbridge would warrant similarly harsh comments, as when Jesus said:

> Woe to you, teachers of the law and Pharisees, you hypocrites! You give a tenth of your spices—mint, dill and cummin. But you have neglected the more important matters of the law—justice, mercy and faithfulness. You should have practiced the latter, without neglecting the former. You blind guides! You strain out a gnat but swallow a camel. (Matt. 23:23–24 NIV)

While Professor Umbridge was straining out any attempt to practice Defense Against the Dark Arts, she was fully engaged in injustice and showed no mercy. Just as Harry understood the vital importance of actually being prepared to fight against the evil lurking in his world, we too need to put the Bible's teachings into practice. We need theory and practice to keep our lives free of hypocrisy and powerful against evil.

The Order of the Phoenix: Preparing Ourselves for Combat

"I was thinking that—maybe the time has come when we should just—just do it ourselves."
"Do what ourselves?" said Harry suspiciously. . . .
"Well—learn Defense Against the Dark Arts ourselves," said Hermione. . . .

"It's about preparing ourselves, like Harry said in Umbridge's first lesson, for what's waiting out there. It's about making sure we really can defend ourselves."
—Book Five, p. 325

*H*ermione realized that it was vitally important for the students to actually learn to defend themselves against Voldemort and the Death Eaters. She believed Harry when he told her Voldemort had returned with murderous intent. Given this, she understood that she and the other students would have to prepare themselves for battle. And that would take practice of specific skills to fight evil in the Wizarding world.

The Bible tells us we too have a spiritual foe. First Peter warns, "Be self-controlled and alert. Your enemy the devil prowls around like a roaring lion looking for someone to devour" (1 Pet. 5:8–9 NIV). So we are to prepare ourselves for spiritual warfare. The Letter to the Ephesians says, "Be strong in the Lord and in his mighty power. Put on the full armor of God so that you can take your stand against the devil's schemes" (Eph. 6:10–11 NIV). Just as Voldemort had not revealed himself physically yet, the evil we are dealing with is not manifest as a flesh-and-blood person:

> For our struggle is not against flesh and blood, but against the rulers, against the authorities, against the powers of this dark world and against the spiritual forces of evil in the heavenly realms. Therefore put on the full armor of God, so that when the day of evil comes, you may be able to stand your ground, and after you have done everything, to stand. (Eph. 6:12–13 NIV)

Cornelius Fudge was afraid that Dumbledore was having the students trained in combat. Later, when Harry and the other members of the D.A. were facing the Death Eaters, Bellatrix Lestrange was incredulous:

> "You hear him? *You hear him?* Giving instructions to the other children as though he thinks of fighting us!"

"Oh, you don't know Potter as I do, Bellatrix," said Malfoy softly. "He has a great weakness for heroics; the Dark Lord understands this about him." (Book Five, p. 782)

What Mr. Malfoy called "a great weakness for heroics" was really a wise and practical determination to fight actively against evil, using the weapons of the Wizarding world. When we relate this fighting evil to our world, this does not necessarily mean that we should take up weapons of warfare like guns or bombs to fight in an army. Rather, we should think of this in spiritual terms. Second Corinthians describes it this way: "For though we live in the world, we do not wage war as the world does. The weapons we fight with are not the weapons of the world. On the contrary, they have divine power to demolish strongholds. We demolish arguments and every pretension that sets itself up against the knowledge of God, and we take captive every thought to make it obedient to Christ" (2 Cor. 10:3–5 NIV). The training and preparation the Bible describes is internal preparation for engaging thoughts, ideas, and arguments that would mislead people with regard to a true understanding of God and the good life he calls us to live.

The "Come and Go Room" and the Power of Prayer

"It is a most amazing room, sir," [said Dobby].

"How many people know about it?" said Harry, sitting up straighter in his chair.

"Very few, sir. Mostly people stumbles across it when they needs it, sir, but often they never finds it again, for they do not know that it is always there waiting to be called into service, sir."

—Book Five, p. 387

*W*hen Harry was in need of a place for the D.A. to meet secretly, Dobby told him about the Room of Requirement, also known as the Come and Go Room because it would come and go according to need. If Dumbledore needed a chamber pot, it was filled with chamber pots; if Dobby needed a place for Winky to sober up with some privacy and comfort, such a place appeared for her; if Harry and friends needed a place to practice Defense Against the Dark Arts, it supplied itself with books on defensive magic, pillows to fall on after being stunned, and even a whistle when Harry needed it. The room seemed to be no respecter of persons, providing a hiding place for those seeking to cover wrongdoing or a place to keep their secrets. Later in the stories we learn that "you've got to ask it for *exactly* what you need," as Neville did (Book Seven, p. 578).

What is striking about Dobby's description of the Room of Requirement is that even though people stumbled upon it when they were in dire need, they did not realize that it was always there for them. Therefore, they did not make full use of it. This reminds me of how almost everyone will pray while in desperate need and perhaps be surprised by unexpected provision that they receive. However, as a matter of course most people neglect prayer if the need is not desperate.

Jesus taught his disciples, "Therefore I tell you, whatever you ask for in prayer, believe that you have received it, and it will be yours" (Mark 11:24 NIV). Another time he encouraged them, "Ask and it will be given to you; seek and you will find; knock and the door will be opened to you. For everyone who asks receives; he who seeks finds; and to him who knocks, the door will be opened" (Matt. 7:7–8 NIV). Granted, seeking God's help in prayer is not magical manipulation. There are certain requirements regarding motives and the purpose of our prayers being worthy of God's help. Certainly we could not expect God to make provision for evil or for things that would be harmful to us in the long run. However, if we were to limit ourselves to just thinking of the Come and Go Room as it might relate to praying for worthy needs, I'm still inclined to think that we have much in common with the students of Hogwarts who ran across it when they were in dire need but did not return to it regularly to find those things they needed on a regular basis.

Dirty, Contaminated, and Unworthy: Voldemort's Taint and Harry's Self-Loathing

He felt dirty, contaminated, as though he were carrying some deadly germ, unworthy to sit on the underground train back from the hospital with innocent, clean people whose minds and bodies were free of the taint of Voldemort. . . . He had not merely seen the snake, he had been the snake, he knew it now.

—Book Five, p. 492

*W*hen Harry realized the strange perspective from which he had seen Mr. Weasley attacked by the snake, he was rightfully troubled. His conscience was not and could not be clean. Somehow, although he didn't understand fully why, the evil he loathed seemed to be inside him, or at least he was enveloped in evil. He hated what the snake had done. Inwardly he wanted to protect Mr. Weasley, and yet he saw that he was somehow bound up with the very evil he hated. This is reminiscent of when he had feared that he might have been the Heir of Slytherin at the end of his second year. He saw strange likenesses between himself and Voldemort, which Dumbledore acknowledged and the Sorting Hat intimated meant he would have done well in Slytherin House.

This wrestling with evil—not just battling external evil but discovering to our chagrin that evil is within us—is a foundational tenet of the Bible's message.

Before we can discover good news (which is what the word *gospel* means) we must come to the traumatic realization that even when we want to do that which is good, even when we recoil at the thought of evil, the evil we hate isn't "out there" somewhere. Evil is somehow bound up within our physical being. The apostle Paul describes it like this:

> So I find this law at work: When I want to do good, evil is right there with me. For in my inner being I delight in God's law; but I see another law at work in the members of my body, waging war against the law of my mind and making me a prisoner of the law of sin at work within my members. What a wretched man I am! Who will rescue me from this body of death? (Rom. 7:21–24 NIV)

It would not be until much later in the story that Harry would discover the precise reason that he was able to see through the eyes of the snake. However, Dumbledore's clue that Voldemort had put a little of himself into Harry when he gave him his scar is instructive here. Our problem is much like Harry's: the "evil one" in our world put sin within our physical nature when humanity was hit with the curse. At this point in the story, Harry seemed to be rightfully self-condemned. How would he break free from the evil with which he had been united through the curse? For those of us considering our predicament being bound up in sin, even when we are struggling against it, there is only one answer. It is not about self-improvement. The only answer is to have the sin within us put to death, somehow without it killing us and the part of us that truly wants to do good. That took place by transferring our sins to a sinless person (Jesus Christ), who was put to death in an act of self-sacrifice and substitution. This had taken place for the apostle Paul, and the answer for him, and for us, when we are feeling rightfully dirty, contaminated, and unworthy is this: "Thanks be to God—through Jesus Christ our Lord!" (Rom. 7:25 NIV).

I Couldn't Leave Him—
He's My Brother

*"Hermione, I couldn' leave him," said Hagrid, tears now
trickling down his bruised face into his beard. "See—he's
my brother!"*

—Book Five, p. 691

*H*agrid's mysterious injuries turn out to be the result of his trying to care for his half-brother, Grawp. It seemed so simple to
Hagrid. He couldn't leave him. He was his brother, and because
he was his brother, he had to love him.

He loved Grawp in a thoroughly biblical way. The Bible says that
love "always protects, always trusts, always hopes, always per-
severes. Love never fails" (1 Cor. 13:7–8 NIV). Hagrid simply
loved his brother. He protected him by bringing him away from
the larger giants, who surely would have killed him eventually.
He trusted that his friends would help him. He hoped that Grawp
could be civilized. He persevered even though he was continually being hurt, even though his friends thought he was crazy to
do this, even though he had to defend himself against the centaurs
and no one else had hope for Grawp.

Loving our brother (or sister) is not just a fond sentiment; it's a
command: "And he has given us this command: Whoever loves
God must also love his brother" (1 John 4:21 NIV). We would do
well to consider how Hagrid showed love for his brother and to do
likewise. As the story plays out, Hagrid's efforts do not fail. We
will see that Grawp becomes more civilized and even becomes a
powerful ally on the side of good.

Incarcerous Yourself!
The Comeuppance of
Delores Umbridge

"Filthy half-breeds!" she screamed, her hands still tight
over her head. "Beasts! Uncontrolled animals!"
   "Be quiet!" shouted Hermione, but it was too late—
Umbridge pointed her wand at Magorian and screamed,
"Incarcerous!"

—Book Five, p. 755

*T*he end of Book Five shows Umbridge being carried away by a
herd of enraged centaurs after revealing her bigotry against them.
She got was she deserved, but I wasn't quite satisfied. Dumbledore
showed great compassion when he went into the forest alone to
retrieve her. I tended more toward Hermione's reaction after
Umbridge tried to sneak up on Hagrid in the dead of night: "'That
evil woman!' gasped Hermione, who seemed to be having diffi-
culty talking due to rage" (Book Five p. 722). So I was quite
pleased to learn from a post-series interview with J. K. Rowling
that Delores Umbridge ended up being incarcerated in Nurmen-
gard. Even though this was beyond the scope of the book, it
seemed to me that such blatant evil needed just retribution.

This is in keeping with what the Bible says: "Do not be deceived:
God cannot be mocked. A man reaps what he sows. The one who
sows to please his sinful nature, from that nature will reap destruction" (Gal. 6:7 NIV) She who tried to incarcerate the centaurs ended up incarcerated. This also reminds me of an evil character in the
book of Esther. Haman, a similarly power-hungry administrator in
the court of the king of Persia, laid plans to have all the Jews killed.
He particularly hated Mordecai who, unbeknownst to Haman, was
a close relative to Queen Esther (who had kept her Jewish heritage

a secret). By manipulating the justice system, Haman planned to have Mordecai condemned to death; he even prepared the gallows. However, in a satisfying turn of events, Haman ended up being the one condemned to death and was hung on the gallows he had built for Mordecai. Similarly, Delores Umbridge paved the way to her own incarceration by seeking to incarcerate anyone who could not prove they were of pure blood.

Manipulated and Misdirected Thoughts

"You see," continued Dumbledore heavily, "I believed it could not be long before Voldemort attempted to force his way into your mind, to manipulate and misdirect your thoughts, and I was not eager to give him more incentives to do so."

—Book Five, pp. 827–28

*O*ne of Harry's greatest weaknesses was that Voldemort had a way to influence his thoughts, to suggest points of view, to confuse, condemn, and misdirect him within his mind. Although Dumbledore tried to help Harry learn occlumency, this did nothing to remedy the hold the evil one had on his mind. Ron was in a similar state of danger when he was attacked in the Department of Mysteries by the brains with tentacles of thought that bound him. Even after his escape and his stay in the hospital, "there were still deep welts on his forearms where the brain's tentacles had wrapped around him. According to Madam Pomfrey, thoughts could leave deeper scarring than almost anything else, though since she had started applying copious amounts of Dr. Ubbly's Oblivious Unction, there seemed to be some improvement" (Book Five, p. 847).

A similar kind of mental torment is noted in Psalm 13:2: "How long must I wrestle with my thoughts and every day have sorrow in my heart? How long will my enemy triumph over me?" (NIV). The apostle Paul described a kind of aggressive guarding of our thoughts when he said, "We take captive every thought to make it obedient to Christ." (2 Cor. 10:5 NIV). The most blatant example of someone's having the enemy get hold on his mind came when Jesus was explaining to his disciples that he would soon be arrested, die, be buried, and then rise from the dead on the third day. Peter, one of Jesus' three closest friends and a leader among the disciples, reacted strongly to Jesus' plainspoken description of his coming suffering: "Peter took him aside and began to rebuke him. But when Jesus turned and looked at his disciples, he rebuked Peter. 'Get behind me, Satan!' he said. 'You do not have in mind the things of God, but the things of men'" (Mark 8:33 NIV)

So Dumbledore's warnings about the evil one seeking to manipulate and misdirect Harry's thoughts is a good reminder that even in our world, one of the most powerful ways the evil one will attempt to hurt us is to get hold of our thoughts and turn them away from the things of God.

Trusting in the Sacrificial Blood

"You would be protected by an ancient magic of which he knows, which he despises, and which he has always, therefore, underestimated—to his cost. I am speaking, of course, of the fact that your mother died to save you. She gave you a lingering protection he never expected, a protection that flows in your veins to this day. I put my trust therefore in your mother's blood."
—Dumbledore to Harry, Book Five, pp. 835–36

*D*umbledore revealed that because of Lily's self-sacrifice, her blood provided a special protection for Harry. Within her family of blood relatives (her sister, her only living relative) Harry would remain safe because of the blood of the one who gave herself to die to save him.

The need for a blood sacrifice is a recurrent theme throughout the Bible, first the blood of animals to cover sin temporarily, then the blood of Jesus Christ, who is likened to a sacrificial animal, namely, the Passover lamb. The curse we have to overcome is the curse of sin, which gives the evil one the right to our death. In order to be protected from death, we need righteousness imputed to us, which was done through the blood of the one who sacrificed himself for us:

> But now a righteousness from God, apart from law, has been made known, to which the Law and the Prophets testify. This righteousness from God comes through faith in Jesus Christ to all who believe. There is no difference, for all have sinned and fall short of the glory of God, and are justified freely by his grace through the redemption that came by Christ Jesus. God presented him as a sacrifice of atonement, through faith in his blood. (Rom. 3:21–25 NIV)

Any who trust in the blood of Jesus Christ are called into a family of faith. Within that family, united by the blood of Jesus Christ, we are promised protection akin to that which Harry had while living with his mother's sister.

Fulfilling the Terms of the Prophecy

"Voldemort tried to kill you as a baby because of a prophecy made shortly before your birth. He knew the prophecy had been made, though he did not know its full contents. He set out to kill you when you were still a baby,

believing he was fulfilling the terms of the prophecy. He
found out, to his cost, that he was mistaken, when the
curse intended to kill you backfired."

—Dumbledore to Harry, Book Five, p. 839

Voldemort knew enough about the prophecy to realize that Harry might be a threat to him and his plans to rule the Wizarding world. Therefore, seeking to head off any future confrontation, he tried to kill Harry when the boy was still a baby, but failed.

There is a striking similarity between Voldemort's attempt to kill Harry as a baby and the reaction the king in Jerusalem had when he heard rumblings that there had been a baby boy born who had been prophesied as a coming king of the Jews. This tyrant also sought to solve his problem with an attempt on the baby's life. The Gospel of Matthew recounts it this way:

> After Jesus was born in Bethlehem in Judea, during the time of King Herod, Magi from the east came to Jerusalem and asked, "Where is the one who has been born king of the Jews? We saw his star in the east and have come to worship him."
>
> When King Herod heard this he was disturbed, and all Jerusalem with him. When he had called together all the people's chief priests and teachers of the law, he asked them where the Christ was to be born. "In Bethlehem in Judea," they replied, "for this is what the prophet has written:
>
> > "'But you, Bethlehem, in the land of Judah,
> >   are by no means least among the rulers of Judah;
> > for out of you will come a ruler
> >   who will be the shepherd of my people Israel.'"
>
> (Matt. 2:1–6 NIV)

So King Herod sent the Magi to seek the child, pretending also to want to worship him but secretly planning to kill the child. God warned the Magi, and they went home by another route after offering their gifts to the baby, who was prophesied to one day become the King of all Kings.

When Herod realized that he had been outwitted by the Magi, he was furious, and he gave orders to kill all the boys in Bethlehem and its vicinity who were two years old and under, in accordance with the time he had learned from the Magi. Then what was said through the prophet Jeremiah was fulfilled:

"A voice is heard in Ramah,
   weeping and great mourning,
Rachel weeping for her children
   and refusing to be comforted,
because they are no more."

(2:16–18 NIV)

In trying to kill the prophesied "king of the Jews" as a baby, King Herod missed killing Jesus—because God warned Joseph in a dream to take him away to Egypt—but fulfilled another prophecy through what is known as the "slaughter of the innocents." King Herod was just as ruthless and heartless as Voldemort in his attempt to destroy anyone who threatened his power and likewise unable to thwart the destiny of the one who came to overthrow evil with good.

Real Prophecies
versus Doubtful Divination

"Bet Dumbledore wishes he could've got rid of Trelawney for good," said Ron, now munching on his fourteenth Frog. "Mind you, the whole subject's useless if you ask me, Firenze isn't a lot better. . . .

"How can you say that?" Hermione demanded. "After we've just found out that there are real prophecies?"

—Book Five, p. 849

*H*ere we see an acknowledgment that there is a difference between doubtful divination and real prophecy. Indeed, Professor Trelawney's inability to actually predict the future (consistently) helped convince Ron and Harry of that which Hermione declared early on—that divination was not to be trusted. However, the stories make a distinction. Here we come to see that even in the Wizarding world there is such a thing as a true prophecy.

There were rare occasions when Professor Trelawney was a conduit for a true prophecy, since she was the one who gave the prophecy about Harry and the Dark Lord. However, another of her accurate predictions—that Peter Pettigrew would escape and return to be Voldemort's servant—served the evil side.

The Bible has much to say about foretelling the future, divination, and prophecies. It warns people to be very careful when encountering anyone who claims to know the future. It declares that there are some prophecies written in the Bible that come from God through people, saying:

> And we have the word of the prophets made more certain, and you will do well to pay attention to it, as to a light shining in a dark place, until the day dawns and the morning star rises in your hearts. Above all, you must understand that no prophecy of Scripture came about by the prophet's own interpretation. For prophecy never had its origin in the will of man, but men spoke from God as they were carried along by the Holy Spirit. (2 Pet. 1:19–21 NIV)

Jesus himself warned people to

> watch out for false prophets. They come to you in sheep's clothing, but inwardly they are ferocious wolves. By their fruit you will recognize them. Do people pick grapes from thornbushes, or figs from thistles? Likewise every good tree bears good fruit, but a bad tree bears bad fruit. A good tree cannot bear bad fruit, and a bad tree cannot bear good fruit.

Every tree that does not bear good fruit is cut down and thrown into the fire. Thus, by their fruit you will recognize them. (Matt. 7:15–20 NIV)

As those who are opposed to the Harry Potter stories remind us, the Bible forbids divination while upholding true God-given prophecy. The passage they cite is, "Let no one be found among you who sacrifices his son or daughter in the fire, who practices divination or sorcery, interprets omens, engages in witchcraft, or casts spells, or who is a medium or spiritist or who consults the dead. Anyone who does these things is detestable to the LORD" (Deut. 18:10–13 NIV).

We too need to be careful not to rely on unreliable divination, not to turn to messages channeled through a medium, but only to seek true prophecies that are from God and are proven in Scripture as well as by the life and consistent accuracy of the prophet. On the whole, it seems that Professor Trelawney was most useful with her crystal balls when she was chucking them over the banister onto the heads of invading Death Eaters.

Beyond the Veil of Death

It seemed to take Sirius an age to fall. His body curved in a graceful arc as he sank backward through the ragged veil hanging from the arch. . . .

And Harry saw the look of mingled fear and surprise on his godfather's wasted, once-handsome face as he fell through the ancient doorway and disappeared behind the veil, which fluttered for a moment as though in a high wind and then fell back into place.

Harry heard Bellatrix Lestrange's triumphant scream, but knew it meant nothing—Sirius had only just fallen through the archway, he would reappear from the other side any second. . . .

But Sirius did not reappear.

—Book Five, p. 806

*T*he Department of Mysteries held rooms where time could be manipulated, where the universe and minds could be studied, where prophecies collected dust on shelf after numbered shelf. There was also a room called the Death Chamber, featuring an ancient archway on a raised dais that attracted Harry's attention, drawing him to it and frightening Hermione so that she urged him away from it. Hermione's instincts again proved reliable. When the battle ensued, it led to the Death Chamber and this is where Sirius fell through the veil and was separated from the living. Harry could not go to him and he could not return to Harry. Those who understood this aspect of the mystery of death restrained Harry in his grief.

Back in the castle, Harry sought out Nearly Headless Nick, thinking that perhaps Sirius could come back as a ghost, but he was disappointed. Nick explained that not everyone comes back as a ghost—only those who, like himself, are afraid of death and choose not to go on. He was sure Sirius would have "gone on." Harry pelted him with questions about death that most people have when a loved one has died but Nick could not sufficiently answer these profound questions.

Such questions are addressed and answered in the Bible, with confidence. Jesus told a story about a rich man and a poor beggar named Lazarus. Both died but ended up in very different circumstances. Here is Jesus' account:

> The time came when the beggar died and the angels carried him to Abraham's side. The rich man also died and was buried. In hell, where he was in torment, he looked up and saw Abraham far away, with Lazarus by his side. So he called to him, "Father Abraham, have pity on me and send Lazarus to dip the tip of his finger in water and cool my tongue, because I am in agony in this fire."
>
> But Abraham replied, "Son, remember that in your lifetime you received your good things, while Lazarus received bad things, but now he is comforted here and you are in agony. And besides all this, between us and you a great chasm has been fixed, so that those who want to go

from here to you cannot, nor can anyone cross over from there to us."

He answered, "Then I beg you, father, send Lazarus to my father's house, for I have five brothers. Let him warn them, so that they will not also come to this place of torment."

Abraham replied, "They have Moses and the Prophets; let them listen to them."

"No, father Abraham," he said, "but if someone from the dead goes to them, they will repent."

He said to him, "If they do not listen to Moses and the Prophets, they will not be convinced even if someone rises from the dead." (Luke 16:22–31 NIV)

There is "a great chasm" fixed between the living and the dead, a place of paradise and a place of torment which goes beyond what Nearly Headless Nick understood. By telling this story, Jesus showed that he cared about those who have questions about death. He let us know *before* we go on so we could take our choices into account while we are still living. His last comment about people not being convinced "even if someone rises from the dead" strikes me as sad, since it seems that he was looking forward to his own death and resurrection, already knowing that even that would not be enough to keep some people from going to that place of torment. Perhaps something like this is what Dumbledore meant when he spoke of there being things much worse than death. Happily, we will later see that a much happier afterlife awaited Sirius.

Luna Believed
So Many Extraordinary Things

"Yes, it was rather horrible," said Luna conversationally. "I still feel very sad about it sometimes. But I've still got Dad. And anyway, it's not as though I will never see Mum again, is it?"

"Er—isn't it?" said Harry uncertainly.

She shook her head in disbelief. "Oh, come on. You heard them, just behind the veil, didn't you?"

"You mean . . ."

"In that room with the archway. They were just lurking out of sight, that's all. You heard them."

They looked at each other. Luna was smiling slightly. Harry did not know what to say, or to think. Luna believed so many extraordinary things . . . yet he had been sure he had heard voices behind the veil too.

—Book Five, p. 863

*I*n the Death Chamber, Harry and Luna heard whispering coming from behind the veil. Harry demanded to know if anyone else could hear it. " 'I can hear them too,' breathed Luna, joining them around the side of the archway and gazing at the swaying veil. 'There are people *in there*' " (Book Five, p. 774). Hermione, who heard nothing, became upset, demanding to know what they meant by "in there," since according to her natural senses there was no "in there" only a veil in an archway that was beginning to frighten her. So she urged Harry away from the veil.

Later, after they had all learned that there was more to the veil than the human eye could see—that is, after Sirius had fallen through and could not return—Harry was left to wonder. Back at Hogwarts, as the school year was about to conclude, Harry had opportunity to talk with Luna about what they had shared when they were near the veil of death. She confided that her mother had died, but she had a confident assurance that she would see her again, whereas Harry did not have that confidence. Luna reassured Harry that they would be reunited with their loved ones who had died. She pointed out that they had both heard the voices on the other side of the veil. She believed simply; Harry was still seeking and struggling with his doubts, bearing in mind that "Luna believed so many extraordinary things."

The Bible notes that there are those who grieve without hope of being reunited after death and that there are those who grieve with confident hope similar to Luna Lovegood's. This hope comes from Jesus himself initially. Just before he was going to die, Jesus offered assurance about life after death to his disciples. After he told them what was about to happen to him, they became very sad and troubled. So he said to them, "Let not your hearts be troubled; believe in God, believe also in Me. In My Father's house are many dwelling places; if it were not so, I would have told you; for I go to prepare a place for you. And if I go to prepare a place for you, I will come again, and receive you to Myself; that where I am, there you may be also" (John 14:1–2 NASB). In a letter to one of the first-century churches this question came up again and was answered like this: "Brothers, we do not want you to be ignorant about those who fall asleep, or to grieve like the rest of men, who have no hope. We believe that Jesus died and rose again and so we believe that God will bring with Jesus those who have fallen asleep in him. . . . Therefore encourage each other with these words" (1 Thess. 4:13–18 NIV). Those who have this kind of confident hope can use it to encourage others, as Luna was able to encourage Harry in his time of grief over the death of a loved one.

It is true that Luna did believe extraordinary things, but just because they were extraordinary did not mean they were not true. Just because Hermione could not see them with her natural senses did not mean that they were not real. Those of us who love the Harry Potter stories surely have an appetite for that which is extraordinary. Perhaps our longing for the extraordinary indicates that we were made for life beyond this one. Listen carefully and maybe you will be able to hear someone whispering.

Glimmers of the Gospel in Book Six

Harry Potter and the Half-Blood Prince

Introduction to Book Six

The story begins with a revelation that there is a curious connection between the Muggle world and the Wizarding world. Cornelius Fudge, dubbed "the Other Minister," briefs the Prime Minister of Britain on occurrences in the Wizarding world that have impacted events in the Muggle world. This picture of overlapping worlds—one material and nonmagical being influenced by one where powers of good and evil battle unseen behind the scenes to cause catastrophes in the ordinary world—is in keeping with biblical ideas. There are references to angelic beings and demonic beings, usually unseen but involved in human events, battling behind the scenes of our world. This dual reality frames the story.

Headmaster Dumbledore has decided that it is time to take a more direct role in Harry's training, so he picks him up from the Dursleys personally. They take a detour to find Horace Slughorn and persuade him to rejoin the faculty of Hogwarts. Slughorn's inclination to be impressed by those who have wealth, fame, or power draws him to Harry, whom he would love to have in his "Slug Club" as one of the favored students. It turns out that Professor Slughorn has an altered memory of an encounter with Tom Riddle that is essential to have revealed truthfully in order to complete Dumbledore's plans for Harry's education. In the character of Slughorn we see a soft, self-serving person who finds a way to gain enough courage to do what is right even at great risk to himself.

Harry's previous hatred of Potions class diminishes with a new teacher and an old book. He is given the book once belonging to someone called "the Half-Blood Prince," whose marginal notes make Harry the best in his class. Of course, this use of another's knowledge to gain good marks offends Hermione's sense of what's right, but Harry ignores this. He is caught up in the wonder of finally being able to excel in Potions class. Thus, he grows to trust one whom he does not know, who speaks to him from a very old book. After what happened to Ginny Weasley in Book Two, we understand this danger, but Harry resists all warnings and even uses spells the Half-Blood Prince made up. Some are amusing, while others will prove to be very dangerous.

Much of the story line revolves around Harry's lessons with Dumbledore in which he is taken on a guided tour of everything Dumbledore knows about Voldemort's history, his inclinations, and his descent into evil. He introduces Harry to the idea of Horcruxes and his theory that Voldemort has splintered his soul into at least six Horcruxes, with the last shred of humanity remaining in his mutated body, which has taken on snakelike characteristics. In these lessons we see Tom Riddle's disconnection from everything that would make him human or connect him to others; we see him become less and less human with every murder he commits. His becoming snakelike in appearance denotes his affiliation with Slytherin but also reminds anyone with minimal knowledge of the Bible of the serpent in the garden of Eden and the imagery of the "Serpent of Old," which is the devil. The more we learn about Voldemort's nature, the better example we have of biblical evil.

The new Minister of Magic, Rufus Scrimgeour, tries to get Harry to pretend to be working for the Ministry, but Harry wants nothing to do with this ruse. He calls on Scrimgeour to release Stan Shunpike, who has been arrested as a Death Eater, when it is clear that the arrest is bogus and was done to give the illusion that the Ministry was making some progress against the Death Eaters. When Scrimgeour refuses to effect justice for Stan Shunpike, Harry rebuffs him.

Meanwhile, Harry suspects that Draco Malfoy may have become a Death Eater, or at least that he is up to no good during the times when he disappears repeatedly. It turns out that Draco is indeed up to no good, plotting Dumbledore's murder on Voldemort's orders. In a coerced attempt on Dumbledore's life, he accidentally causes Katie Bell's near death from touching a cursed necklace, and he almost kills Ron with poisoned mead. Disaster is averted by a combination of luck and quick thinking on the part of Harry and friends. Luck also plays a crucial part in Harry's being able to extract the truthfully recounted memory from Professor

Slughorn. It turns out that Slughorn's shame over giving Tom Riddle information about Horcruxes has caused him not only to lie to others but to alter his own memory. Harry's use of Felix Felicis aids him in persuading Slughorn to tell him the truth, out of respect for Harry's mother, Lily Evans (who was one of Slughorn's favorite students). So luck and love work together to reveal the truth that Tom Riddle was indeed seeking a way to split his soul into many parts, perhaps as many as seven.

When Harry presses to know what Draco is doing, he happens upon him crying in the bathroom, where he is talking to Moaning Myrtle. Using a spell the Half-Blood Prince designated "for enemies," Harry almost kills Draco, who is rescued by Professor Snape. Harry is punished, but seemingly not as much as attempted murder on another student might warrant. In seeking to hide the source of his spell, Harry hides the book from which he got the spell in the Room of Hidden Things and substitutes it with Ron's book for Snape's inspection.

Dumbledore offers to take Harry with him to destroy one of the Horcruxes, which takes them into the cave where Voldemort has hidden a locket that Dumbledore suspects contains a shred of his shattered soul. While they retrieve the locket, enduring the curses and evading the protections set to keep intruders from getting it, Dumbledore is seriously weakened. As they return to Hogwarts they see the Dark Mark over the Astronomy Tower. Rushing to the tower, they discover they have been lured into a trap. Draco Malfoy has allowed Death Eaters into the castle. Dumbledore is trapped by Draco and by Amycus and Alecto Carrow (a Death Eater, brother and sister duo), who are accompanied by Fenrir Greyback, a vicious werewolf. Draco hesitates at killing Dumbledore, but Snape arrives to deliver the death curse, *Avada Kedavra*. Dumbledore is blown from the tower. Snape, Draco, and the Death Eaters escape. Harry finds the locket they had retrieved from the cave, only to discover that it is not the Horcrux but that the real Horcrux was taken by one R. A. B., who plans to destroy it. The story ends with Dumbledore's funeral and Fawkes the phoenix leaving the school while piping his sad song of lament.

The Worlds to Which Harry Belonged

"What a week, what a week..."
"Had a bad one too, have you?" asked the Prime Minister stiffly....
"Yes, of course," said Fudge, rubbing his eyes wearily and looking morosely at the Prime Minister. "I've been having the same week you have, Prime Minister"...
"You—er—your—I mean to say, some of your people were—were involved in those—those things, were they?"
—Book Six, p. 4

He could not return to living full-time with the Dursleys, not now that he knew the other world, the one to which he really belonged.
—Book Five, p. 44

*H*arry Potter lived in two worlds, the Muggle world and the Wizarding world, where an intense war between good and evil was carrying on. Once he realized that there were dual realms, he could not accept a world without the extraordinary dimension he had discovered in the Wizarding world. He knew that one world impacted the other, even if the Muggles were unaware of the source of their sufferings. Going back as far as the deaths of the Riddle family that had never been solved, we see that the battle between good and evil seeped into the lives of people who didn't even believe in it.

In Book Seven Kingsley Shacklebolt explained that "Muggles remain ignorant of the source of their suffering as they continue to sustain heavy casualties." He went on to tell of inspirational stories of those in the Wizarding world taking risks to protect Muggle friends and neighbors, even though the Muggles didn't even realize the dangers that threatened them. Kingsley called on all in the Wizarding world to do their part to protect unsuspecting Muggles by "casting a protective charm over any Muggle dwellings in your street. Many lives could be saved if such simple measures are taken" (Book Seven, p. 440).

The Bible also shows us that there is a natural world surrounded by a supernatural world, and there are some who live in both realms and know how to provide protection for those who only have eyes to see that which is in the natural realm. Many times in the Bible something takes place in the spiritual realm that has a direct impact on the natural world. On the third day after Jesus had been crucified, residents of Jerusalem were awakened shortly after dawn by a strong earthquake:

> After the Sabbath, at dawn on the first day of the week, Mary Magdalene and the other Mary went to look at the tomb. There was a violent earthquake, for an angel of the Lord came down from heaven and, going to the tomb, rolled back the stone and sat on it. His appearance was like lightning, and his clothes were white as snow. The guards were so afraid of him that they shook and became like dead men. (Matt. 28:1–4 NIV)

The disciples of Jesus were acting like the equivalent of Muggles at that point: the women ran back to tell them that the earthquake had been associated with the angels they had seen and the message that Jesus had risen from the dead, but the men didn't believe them. It was only after they had seen Jesus in the flesh, seen his wounds from the execution and even ate with him to make sure he was not a ghost, that their lives took a dramatic turn. Like Harry, they too could not return to living full-time in the non-supernatural world, not now that they knew the real world to which they belonged. Every one of them spent the remainder of his life telling others of the supernatural occurrences that had happened that morning in Jerusalem and what it meant about the spiritual realm surrounding and impacting the natural realm. Not unlike those in the Wizarding world who cast a protective charm even over those who do not believe or have any experience with the supernatural realm, those who live in both worlds in our reality often send up a prayer on behalf of those who are unaware of what lies beyond the reach of our natural senses.

The Danger of Obsessive "Love"

"Amortentia doesn't really create love, of course. It is impossible to manufacture or imitate love. No, this will simply cause a powerful infatuation or obsession. It is probably the most dangerous and powerful potion in this room—oh, yes," [Slughorn] said, nodding gravely at Malfoy and Nott, both of whom were smirking skeptically. "When you have seen as much of life as I have, you will not underestimate the power of obsessive love."

—Book Six, p.186

*T*he danger of obsessive love is shown through Ron's contamination with the love potion from Romilda Vane that was intended for Harry. Indeed, it is that obsession and Harry's attempt to find a remedy for Ron's powerful infatuation that led to them being in Slughorn's office, where Ron was offered the poisoned mead that almost killed him. However, there is a darker scenario that is not highlighted, which shows the danger of creating obsessive love and taking that "love" against the will of the intended. While retracing Voldemort's ancestry and conception, Harry learned that his mother probably used a love potion to make Tom Riddle Sr.—Voldemort's Muggle father—marry her. So the one who would grow up to be the most evil and powerful Dark Wizard of all time, was conceived of coerced obsessive infatuation. Apparently such mandated "love" was not satisfying, because eventually Merope, Voldemort's mother, withdrew that which caused the infatuation, hoping for true love. When that hope was dashed, she wandered without love to an orphanage, where she gave birth to Tom Marvolo Riddle and then died. One is left to ponder what the absence of any real love and the use of forced obsession had to do with the loveless evil being Voldemort would become.

The Bible does not shy away from stories that show the dangers of obsessive "love" that amounts to lust and domination for self-satisfaction. There is even a story in the family of King David where the consequences of such an obsessive infatuation are portrayed tragically:

> Amnon son of David fell in love with Tamar, the beautiful sister of Absalom son of David.
>
> Amnon became frustrated to the point of illness on account of his sister Tamar, for she was a virgin, and it seemed impossible for him to do anything to her.
>
> Now Amnon had a friend named Jonadab. . . . Jonadab was a very shrewd man. He asked Amnon, "Why do you, the king's son, look so haggard morning after morning. Won't you tell me?"
>
> Amnon said to him, "I'm in love with Tamar, my brother Absalom's sister."
>
> "Go to bed and pretend to be ill," Jonadab said. "When your father comes to see you, say to him, 'I would like my sister Tamar to come and give me something to eat. Let her prepare the food in my sight so I may watch her and then eat it from her hand.'"
>
> So Amnon lay down and pretended to be ill. When the king came to see him, Amnon said to him, "I would like my sister Tamar to come and make some special bread in my sight, so I may eat from her hand."
>
> David sent word to Tamar at the palace: "Go to the house of your brother Amnon and prepare some food for him." So Tamar went to the house of her brother Amnon, who was lying down. She took some dough, kneaded it, made the bread in his sight and baked it. Then she took the pan and served him the bread, but he refused to eat.
>
> "Send everyone out of here," Amnon said. So everyone left him. Then Amnon said to Tamar, "Bring the food here into my bedroom so I may eat from your hand." And Tamar took the bread she had prepared and brought it to her brother Amnon in his bedroom. But when she took it to him to eat, he grabbed her and said, "Come to bed with me, my sister."

"Don't, my brother!" she said to him. "Don't force me. Such a thing should not be done in Israel! Don't do this wicked thing. What about me? Where could I get rid of my disgrace? And what about you? You would be like one of the wicked fools in Israel. Please speak to the king; he will not keep me from being married to you." But he refused to listen to her, and since he was stronger than she, he raped her.

Then Amnon hated her with intense hatred. In fact, he hated her more than he had loved her. Amnon said to her, "Get up and get out!"

"No!" she said to him. "Sending me away would be a greater wrong than what you have already done to me."

But he refused to listen to her. He called his personal servant and said, "Get this woman out of here and bolt the door after her." So his servant put her out and bolted the door after her. She was wearing a richly ornamented robe, for this was the kind of garment the virgin daughters of the king wore. Tamar put ashes on her head and tore the ornamented robe she was wearing. She put her hand on her head and went away, weeping aloud as she went. (2 Sam. 13:1–19 NIV)

Tamar was disgraced and went to live with her brother, Absalom, a desolate woman. Absalom's anger at the lack of justice for his sister led to his rebellion against his father. He seized his father's throne, publicly had sex with his father's concubines, then raised an army to fight against his father's forces. However, in the course of the battle, Absalom's long hair caught in the branches of a tree, leaving him a helpless dangling target for the warriors who came to kill him. King David was now left desolate as well because he grieved the loss of one of his sons, knowing that he bore partial responsibility because he had not come to the rescue of his daughter Tamar, who had fallen victim to the power of an obsessive infatuation. It seems that in our world, as well as in the Wizarding world, Professor Slughorn's assessment of the danger of such an obsession holds true.

The Chosen One

"People believe you are 'the Chosen One,' you see," said Scrimgeour. "They think you quite the hero—which, of course, you are, Harry, chosen or not! How many times have you faced He-Who-Must-Not-Be-Named now? Well, anyway," he pressed on, without waiting for a reply, "the point is, you are a symbol of hope for many, Harry. The idea that there is somebody out there who might be able, who might even be destined, to destroy He-Who-Must-Not-Be-Named—well, naturally, it gives people a lift."

—Book Six, p. 344–45

*H*arry was believed to be "the Chosen One" because the prophecy identified him as the one who had the power to defeat the Dark Lord. This was confirmed by the amount of interest he elicited from Voldemort, causing him to "mark him as his equal," which also fulfilled part of the prophecy. Add to that the fact that Harry had faced Voldemort several times and lived, and it's no wonder that those in the Wizarding world set their hopes on him.

Some people have called Harry a Christ figure. Yes, there are some things that happen to Harry that are similar to events in the life of Jesus Christ but quite different from various Old Testament prophecies of the Messiah, such as this one from Isaiah:

> Look at my servant, whom I strengthen. He is my chosen one, and I am pleased with him. I have put my Spirit upon him. He will reveal justice to the nations. He will be gentle—he will not shout or raise his voice in public. He will not crush those who are weak or quench the smallest hope. He will bring full justice to all who have been wronged. He will not stop until truth and righteousness prevail throughout the earth. Even distant lands beyond the sea will wait for his instruction. (Isa. 42:1–4 NLT)

I don't see Harry's designation as "the Chosen One" being up to this level. The universal quality of the prophecy here "revealing justice to the nations" and not stopping until "truth and righteousness prevail throughout the earth" seems out of his league, given his tendency to lie when it serves his purposes and his penchant for rule breaking. The term "chosen one" or "anointed one" is used throughout the Bible not just to refer to the Messiah but also to people chosen by God to defeat a particular enemy or to accomplish a specific purpose. The book of Judges is full of stories of people God designated as a "chosen one" to accomplish a specific purpose. There is even an account where God predicted that a man named Cyrus would be his chosen one to rebuild Jerusalem and help the exiles return after being taken captive to Babylon (Isa. 45) Those prophecies about Cyrus were written over one-hundred-fifty years before Cyrus, king of Persia overthrew the Babylonian kingdom, returned the Jewish exiles, and helped rebuild Jerusalem. This fulfilled the role of "chosen one" in the Bible—and Cyrus didn't even acknowledge the God of Israel (which was also mentioned in the prophecies of Isaiah).

The reason I make this distinction is that Harry Potter displays some characteristics that are definitely not Christlike (even though he qualifies as a "chosen one" to defeat a particular enemy). Jesus Christ, the Chosen One who came to fulfill the universal prophecy of the Messiah, lived his life without sin. This point is vital, because the only way his sacrifice on the cross could have paid for the sins of the world would be if he had had no sins of his own that had to be paid. On that count alone, Harry's wrongdoings would disqualify him as Christ material. However, if you were to compare Harry to one of the judges, such as Gideon, there are numerous similarities. In the case of Gideon a young man is stuck in a frustrating situation where his people are being oppressed and attacked by the Midianites. He is appointed by God to lead the battle against them. This is confirmed with supernatural signs supplied by "the angel of the Lord" (Judg. 6–8).

If we look at Harry Potter as one "chosen" by Providence to defeat Voldemort, then the parallel with that one chosen by God for a particular task is an apt fit. Scrimgeour was right about a few things: the sense that there is a superior power—the Author of our world—who knows the outcome of the story and has predestined a specific character or person to defeat the evil of our day does give people a lift.

A Bit of a Saving-People-Thing

"You . . . This isn't a criticism, Harry! But you do . . . sort of . . . I mean—don't you think you've got a bit of a—a— saving-people-thing?" [Hermione] said.

He glared at her. "And what's that supposed to mean, a 'saving-people-thing'?"

—Book Five, p. 733

Mrs. Weasley seized hold of Harry and hugged him very tightly. "Dumbledore's told us how you saved [Ron] with the bezoar," she sobbed. "Oh, Harry, what can we say? You saved Ginny . . . you saved Arthur . . . now you've saved Ron . . ."

"Don't be . . . I didn't . . ." muttered Harry awkwardly.

"Half our family does seem to owe you their lives, now I stop and think about it,'" Mr. Weasley said in a constricted voice.

—Book Six, p. 403

*E*ven though Harry's list of sins and unrighteous deeds disqualifies him from being likened in every way to the Christ, he does have some Christlike qualities and experiences that reflect an understanding of biblical themes throughout the books. One of the most striking is his tendency to save people. After Mrs. Weasley thanked him, the phrase "Harry Saves" would seem to have been in order. Indeed, these were not the last people, elves, and goblins Harry will save as the stories continue. Hermione got it right when she said that he had a "sort of—a—a—*saving-people-thing.*"

This was such a part of Harry's character that his enemy could count on him coming to rescue anyone he loved who might be in danger.

Here Harry is like Jesus. The Bible says that Jesus "came to seek and save that which was lost" (Luke 19:10). He loves all people the way Harry loved Sirius. Thinking of Jesus' story in that way, one might describe what Jesus did as if he had been lured to earth into a human body so that he could try to save us. One might see his death as allowing himself to "fall into the trap" of his enemy Satan, set through the sham trial where he was convicted even though no one could convict him of sin. This is where Harry and Jesus have similar characters, in the matter of loving so much they put themselves in peril to save the ones they love. In Harry's story the enemy thought he could trap him and kill him, but the tables were turned. In Jesus' story his death on the cross that looked like a victory for his enemy became the means for our salvation. Think about the similarities between that outcome for Jesus and the outcome of Harry's final showdown with Voldemort when it comes. In the life of Jesus, the cross became a double-cross defeating the aims of the evil one; in Harry's we shall see that his inclination toward "a-saving-people-thing" will play a role in good overcoming evil.

A Horcrux? Death Would Be Preferable

> *"A Horcrux is the word used for an object in which a person has concealed part of their soul."*
>
> *"I don't quite understand how that works, though, sir,"* said Riddle.
>
> *His voice was carefully controlled, but Harry could sense his excitement.*
>
> *"Well, you split your soul, you see," said Slughorn, "and hide part of it in an object outside the body. Then,*

*even if one's body is attacked or destroyed, one cannot die,
for part of the soul remains earthbound and undamaged.
But of course, existence in such a form . . . few would want
it, Tom, very few. Death would be preferable."
But Riddle's hunger was now apparent; his expression
was greedy, he could no longer hide his longing.*
—Book Six, p. 497

*T*he idea that there is something far worse than death has been woven through the entire Harry Potter series. Going all the way back to Book One when Dumbledore explained that Nicolas Flamel and his wife opted to give up the Philosopher's Stone (or the Sorcerer's Stone, as it is known in the American edition) rather than risk its falling into the wrong hands, there are some characters who—while loving life—do not fear death. We see this in the courage of the members of the Order of the Phoenix as well. Voldemort's downfall had its source in his compelling fear of his own death, which led him to opt to destroy his soul while seeking to evade death. This disregard for the proper care of his eternal soul was the weakness Dumbledore referred to when they battled at the Ministry of Magic at the end of Book Five.

"You do not seek to kill me, Dumbledore?" called Voldemort, his scarlet eyes narrowed over the top of his shield. "Above such brutality, are you?"

"We both know that there are other ways of destroying a man, Tom," Dumbledore said calmly, continuing to walk toward Voldemort as though he had not a fear in the world, as though nothing had happened to interrupt his stroll up the hall. "Merely taking your life would not satisfy me, I admit—"

"There is nothing worse than death, Dumbledore!" snarled Voldemort.

"You are quite wrong," said Dumbledore, still closing in upon Voldemort and speaking as lightly as though they were discussing the matter over drinks. . . . "Indeed, your failure to understand that there are things worse than death has always been your greatest weakness." (Book Five, p. 814)

This idea that Dumbledore advanced repeatedly is one put forward by Jesus when he said to his disciples, "Don't be afraid of those who want to kill you. They can only kill your body; they cannot touch your soul. Fear only God, who can destroy both soul and body in hell" (Matt. 10:28 NLT). So Voldemort's rabid fear of those who wanted to kill his body was his weakness. It led him to commit evil acts that showed total disregard for the lives of others and dishonor to his own eternal soul. This truly was his greatest weakness. Death would have been preferable.

The Power the Dark Lord Knows Not

> *"So when the prophecy says that I'll have 'power the Dark Lord knows not,' it just means—love?' asked Harry, feeling a little let down.*
> *"Yes—just love," said Dumbledore.*
>
> —Book Six, p. 509

*L*ove. Just love—that power that protected Harry as a baby when his mother died to save him. Love, the most mysterious of the many subjects studied in the Department of Mysteries, where can be found, said Dumbledore, a room containing it "that is kept locked at all times. It contains a force that is at once more wonderful and more terrible than death, than human intelligence, than forces of nature" (Book Five, p. 843). It was love that caused Harry to try to rescue Sirius, that protected him from the lure of the Dark Arts. It was love that filled his heart and mind so as to drive out Voldemort when he sought to possess Harry. Love made all the difference.

Some of the most well-known lines in the Bible also show us that love is the virtue above all virtues. As the apostle Paul wrote to the Corinthians:

If I speak in the tongues of men and of angels, but have not love, I am only a resounding gong or a clanging cymbal. If I have the gift of prophecy and can fathom all mysteries and all knowledge, and if I have a faith that can move mountains, but have not love, I am nothing. If I give all I possess to the poor and surrender my body to the flames, but have not love, I gain nothing. (1 Cor. 13:1–3 NIV)

After recounting the qualities of love, the passage concludes, "And now these three remain: faith, hope and love. But the greatest of these is love" (1 Cor. 13:13).

Voldemort did not love. He had not loved his parents or his grand-parents. He had never loved a friend or any of his caretakers at the orphanage. He did not love any of the Death Eaters or even his own soul. Indeed, perhaps if Tom Riddle had known love there may never have been a Voldemort. In the same passage from 1 Corinthians, Paul says that "love does not delight in evil but rejoices with the truth." Tom Riddle's absence of love made a way for him to take delight in evil, but that lack of love made him no match for Harry.

Harry may or may not have had uncommon skill, but he did have the power of love, that power Voldemort had never had. It was Harry's love for his parents, godfather, teachers, and friends that empowered him to drive Voldemort out of him during the battle at the Ministry. Although Harry long underestimated the power of love, his love for others that exceeded his love for himself proved to be his greatest power and greatest weapon against evil. Yes—just love.

The Incomparable Power
of an Untarnished Soul

You have flitted into Lord Voldemort's mind without damage to yourself, but he cannot possess you without enduring mortal agony, as he discovered in the Ministry. I do not think he understands why, Harry, but then, he was in such a hurry to mutilate his own soul, he never paused to understand the incomparable power of a soul that is untarnished and whole.

—Dumbledore, Book Six, p. 511

Voldemort was in a hurry, urgently trying to create more Horcruxes than any evil wizard before him. He never paused to understand the *incomparable* power of a soul that is untarnished and whole. Perhaps we should pause to do just that.

The Letter to Titus says, "To the pure, all things are pure, but to those who are corrupted and do not believe, nothing is pure. In fact, both their minds and consciences are corrupted" (Titus 1:15 NIV). With every act of evil committed, with every murder, with every Horcrux, Tom Riddle became more and more corrupt, and less and less truly human. With this devolution into evil, Voldemort's mind and conscience were corrupted. He had no pangs of guilt at the evil he committed or the pain he caused. He also lost the ability to understand that which might have saved his soul.

In their early years Tom Riddle and Harry Potter had much in common. Both were raised by Muggles, both were outsiders to the magical world, both were inclined to break the rules. However, Tom Riddle became more and more selfish, more corrupt, more murderous, and his conscience hardened to the point of being useless; the opposite progression occurred in Harry's life.

Harry developed a good conscience and recognized, even worried about, his inclination to do things that are wrong. He displayed a lust for vengeance against Sirius when he thought Sirius was the one who had betrayed his parents. Then when he discovered that the betrayer was really Peter Pettigrew, Harry was tempted to let Lupin and Sirius kill Pettigrew. But his conscience prevented him from standing aside, and so he stopped the murder. When he thought he might be the Heir of Slytherin, he was troubled by his likeness to Tom Riddle. When he was being attacked by Death Eaters while trying to make his escape from the Dursleys just before coming of age, he gave himself away with the Expelliarmus Charm rather than risk killing Stan Shunpike, whom he assumed to be under the Imperius Curse. As Harry grows into a man, he exercises his conscience so as to make it more sensitive and receptive to doing that which is good. Harry is certainly not perfect, nor is he without sin, but he grows in goodness to the point where he is able to choose that which is good for others over his own self-preservation.

Contrary to what many opponents of the Harry Potter stories have insisted, the Bible does not present flawless characters who model moral perfection. Indeed, every Bible hero's story records misdeeds and sins, even—for some—murders, adultery, and rebellion against God. The story of the Bible is like the Harry Potter stories in this regard: some characters harden themselves to the point that they have no conscience and end up being destroyed, while other characters recognize their sinfulness, respond to their pangs of conscience, and are transformed into the heroes they become in the end.

King David is one of the best examples of the second category. While his army was out on the battlefield, he committed adultery with the wife of one of his most faithful warriors. When she later told David that she was pregnant, he tried to trick her husband into coming home from battle to sleep with her so that he would think the baby was his. When that ruse failed, he had the husband put on the front lines, where he was sure to be killed. This plan worked, and David thought he had gotten away with murder. But a prophet confronted him with the truth. At that point David's conscience was put to the test. Psalm 51 records his response:

> Surely I was sinful at birth,
>   sinful from the time my mother conceived me.
> . . . .
> Cleanse me with hyssop, and I will be clean;
>   wash me, and I will be whiter than snow.
> . . . .
> Hide your face from my sins
>   and blot out all my iniquity.
> Create in me a pure heart, O God,
>   and renew a steadfast spirit within me.
>   (Ps. 51:5, 7, 9–10 NIV)

Harry Potter was as sinful as the next person at birth too. He even had the added burden of having a part of Voldemort attached to him when he was struck with the curse. But Harry was very different from Tom Riddle. When he sat on the stool awaiting the pronouncement of the Sorting Hat, he said, "Not Slytherin! Not Slytherin!" When he thought he might be the Heir of Slytherin, this troubled him. When he was on the verge of vengeance, he stopped himself. Over and over and over again Harry makes choices that show he is responding to his conscience. When he does wrong and is caught, Harry bears his rightful punishment. He is very different from Voldemort in that he pauses to consider that which would be damaging to his soul and chooses to resist it.

The Letter of James says, "Religion that God our Father accepts as pure and faultless is this: to look after orphans and widows in their distress and to keep oneself from being polluted by the world" (Jas. 1:27 NIV). In the final analysis, if we were to judge Harry by this standard, by his care for the oppressed and his persistent efforts to keep himself from being polluted by the evil in his world, I would say he comes out very well.

Drinking the Cup of Suffering

"No . . ." he groaned, as Harry lowered the goblet back into the basin and refilled it for him. "I don't want to. . . . I don't want to. . . . Let me go. . . ."

"It's all right, Professor," said Harry, his hand shaking. "It's all right, I'm here. . . . Take this, now, take this. . . ."

And obediently, Dumbledore drank, as though it was an antidote Harry offered him, but upon draining the goblet, he sank to his knees, shaking uncontrollably.

—Book Six, pp. 571–72

When Harry and Dumbledore went into the cave to retrieve and destroy one of Voldemort's Horcruxes, they knew they would face powerful protection around it. Dumbledore was prepared to do whatever was required to stop Voldemort. When they made it to the island and saw the locket at the bottom of the basin covered with a potion put there by Voldemort, Dumbledore knew what he would have to do. He told Harry to make him drink it all and not to let him stop no matter what he said or did. As Dumbledore drank the contents of the cursed basin it caused him to suffer terribly with recollections of his complicity in his sister's death. But Harry obeyed Dumbledore's previous command, and Dumbledore obeyed Harry's insistence that he drink the contents of the cup entirely.

Jesus came to earth knowing that he was destined to suffer and die a terrible death; he understood that for the "greater good" of the whole world he would have to take on himself the sins of all humanity and endure temporary separation from God the Father. He knew all of this and agreed to it before his incarnation in human flesh. However, once he was human like us he was prone to the same feelings and fears, the same trepidation in the face of imminent suffering.

When the time came for Jesus to be arrested, he knew very well what was coming, and it affected him deeply:

> Then Jesus went with his disciples to a place called Gethsemane, and he said to them, "Sit here while I go over there and pray." He took Peter and the two sons of Zebedee along with him, and he began to be sorrowful and troubled. Then he said to them, "My soul is overwhelmed with sorrow to the point of death. Stay here and keep watch with me."
>
> Going a little farther, he fell with his face to the ground and prayed, "My Father, if it is possible, may this cup be taken from me. Yet not as I will, but as you will" . . .
>
> He went away a second time and prayed, "My Father, if it is not possible for this cup to be taken away unless I drink it, may your will be done."
>
> . . . So he left them and went away once more and prayed the third time, saying the same thing. (Matt. 26:36–44 NIV)

The Letter to the Hebrews gives some more details:

> During the days of Jesus' life on earth, he offered up prayers and petitions with loud cries and tears to the one who could save him from death, and he was heard because of his reverent submission. Although he was a son, he learned obedience from what he suffered and, once made perfect, he became the source of eternal salvation for all who obey him. (Heb. 5:7–9 NIV)

The common theme here is that both Dumbledore and Jesus faced drinking a cup that they anticipated would hold suffering for them. Dumbledore's cup held suffering that came from his own sins and failures in life brought back to him by Voldemort's cursed potion; Jesus' cup held suffering that came to him as the result of taking on our sins. Nevertheless, both of them had the very human reaction of wanting the suffering to stop. Yet both of them chose to obey and accept the suffering that would contribute to overcoming evil. Dumbledore became a part of the plan that would save the Wizarding world from Voldemort. Jesus' obedient acceptance of suffering offers eternal salvation to any who will respond to him with obedience. So by drinking the cup of suffering both helped to bring the cup of salvation for others.

Please Do Not Use That Offensive Word in Front of Me

"I got the idea of poisoning the mead from the Mudblood Granger as well. I heard her talking in the library about Filch not recognizing potions."

"Please do not use that offensive word in front of me," said Dumbledore.

Malfoy gave a harsh laugh. "You care about me saying 'Mudblood' when I'm about to kill you?"

"Yes, I do," said Dumbledore."

—Book Six, p. 589

*F*rom the first time Draco Malfoy calls Hermione a Mudblood, back in Book Two, it is apparent that it is a word laced with shame. The racial prejudice and even hatred toward those of mixed blood is an undercurrent to the pervasive evil of these stories. As the power of Voldemort takes hold after he regains his body, the use of the word *Mudblood* is bantered about more openly, until we see open derision directed toward anyone of mixed blood, escalating to the point of hunting such people down to incarcerate them, or worse.

Allusions to racial hatred and "ethnic cleansing" in the history of our world are obvious. In the Harry Potter stories we see various characters wrestle with their own prejudices. Even Professor Snape has a moment of conviction after recalling the way his use of the word *Mudblood* caused a break in his relationship with Lily Evans when they were students at Hogwarts.

Dumbledore would not be party to such bigotry. Even as he knew he was about to die, he asked Draco not to use the word *Mudblood* in his presence. This rejection of bigotry was a hallmark of Albus Dumbledore's character to the very end.

Likewise, one of the most revolutionary aspects of the ministry of Jesus was that he broke down barriers of race, gender, religion, and anything else that caused one group of people to elevate themselves over another in their own minds. Jesus was very sensitive to covering the shame of those being looked down on or condemned by others.

In the spirit of Jesus, the apostle Paul also strove to overcome barriers: "As the Scripture says, 'Anyone who trusts in him will never be put to shame.' For there is no difference between Jew and Gentile—the same Lord is Lord of all and richly blesses all who call on him, for, 'Everyone who calls on the name of the Lord will be saved'" (Rom. 10:11–13 NIV). Albus Dumbledore welcomed anyone and everyone who wanted to join the good side, while rejecting bigotry. Likewise Jesus opened the way for anyone and everyone who wants to come to him to be saved, even welcoming a despised thief on the cross next to him as he was dying. Both Dumbledore and Jesus rejected the bigotry of their day, even at the moment of their impending deaths.

He Cannot Kill You
if You Are Already Dead

> *"I can help you, Draco," [said Dumbledore].*
>
> *"No, you can't," said Malfoy, his wand hand shaking very badly indeed. "Nobody can. He told me to do it or he'll kill me. I've got no choice."*
>
> *"He cannot kill you if you are already dead. Come over to the right side, Draco, and we can hide you more completely than you can possibly imagine. What is more, I can send members of the Order to your mother tonight to hide her likewise. Nobody would be surprised that you had died in your attempt to kill me—forgive me, but Lord Voldemort probably expects it. Nor would the Death Eaters be surprised that we had captured and killed your mother—it is what they would do themselves, after all. Your father is safe at the moment in Azkaban. . . . When the times comes, we can protect him too. Come over to the right side, Draco . . . you are not a killer."*
>
> —Book Six, 591–92

Although Draco Malfoy was marked for death by Voldemort from the moment he commanded him to kill Albus Dumbledore, there was a way out. Dumbledore understood the Death Eaters. He knew that they would expect the same murderous brutality that characterized them from their enemies. Therefore, if Draco would choose to abdicate from the evil side and join the good side, there was hope for him. He could feign his death with the help of the Order of the Phoenix, and then hide along with any members of his family who were willing to become dead to their previous association with evil.

This is a biblical idea. When someone chose to follow Jesus in the New Testament narrative, they were commanded to be baptized. Baptism—as practiced in the New Testament, showed new believers being immersed under water and raised back up. This is a symbol of dying to one's old life, being buried (under the water), and being raised to live a new life. Although Christians of various denominations and traditions now baptize in various ways, the symbolism of death to one's old life and resurrection to new life remains. In Romans, Paul gives these instructions to believers:

> In the same way, count yourselves dead to sin but alive to God in Christ Jesus. Therefore do not let sin reign in your mortal body so that you obey its evil desires. Do not offer the parts of your body to sin, as instruments of wickedness, but rather offer yourselves to God, as those who have been brought from death to life; and offer the parts of your body to him as instruments of righteousness. (Rom. 6:11–13 NIV)

Draco had offered himself as an instrument of wickedness and found himself trapped. The only way out was death—either he was to kill Dumbledore or Voldemort would kill him. He overlooked a better option. Had he changed allegiances he could have pretended to be dead and started a new life under the protection of those on the side of good. Then Voldemort could not have killed him because, in essence, he would have already reckoned himself dead and escaped into a new life.

Never Again Would Dumbledore Speak to Him—or Would He?

Dumbledore's eyes were closed; but for the strange angle
of his arms and legs, he might have been sleeping. Harry
reached out, straightened the half-moon spectacles upon
the crooked nose, and wiped a trickle of blood from the
mouth with his own sleeve. Then he gazed down at the wise
old face and tried to absorb the enormous and incompre-
hensible truth: that never again would Dumbledore speak
to him, never again could he help.

—Book Six, pp. 608–9

*D*umbledore's death was a traumatic blow to Harry. He believed
that Dumbledore would never again speak to him. Harry had been
seeking to understand much about life, but he had little to trust in
that would cause him to believe in life after death. Surely the Dursleys had not taught him anything from the Bible that might have
given him that assurance. So when Dumbledore died, Harry was
understandably devastated.

Similarly, there was a time after the death of Jesus when his disciples had lost all hope. On the third day after Jesus had been crucified, rumors flew about that some women had seen angels at the
tomb saying he was risen from the dead. But most of Jesus' followers thought this was nonsense, as did two on their way to Emmaus:

> Now that same day two of them were going to a village called
> Emmaus, about seven miles from Jerusalem. They were talk-
> ing with each other about everything that had happened. As
> they talked and discussed these things with each other, Jesus
> himself came up and walked along with them; but they were
> kept from recognizing him.
>   He asked them, "What are you discussing together as you
> walk along?"

They stood still, their faces downcast. One of them, named Cleopas, asked him, "Are you only a visitor to Jerusalem and do not know the things that have happened there in these days?"

"What things?" he asked.

"About Jesus of Nazareth," they replied. "He was a prophet, powerful in word and deed before God and all the people. The chief priests and our rulers handed him over to be sentenced to death, and they crucified him; but we had hoped that he was the one who was going to redeem Israel. And what is more, it is the third day since all this took place." (Luke 24:13–21 NIV)

These two devastated and disappointed disciples of Jesus had hoped that Jesus was the promised messiah. But when he died on the cross, they thought he was dead and gone. Like Harry with Dumbledore, they thought Jesus would never speak to them again. They were oblivious to the fact that the man accompanying them was the risen Jesus, disguised to them. Those who know the rest of this story, may feel a sense of giddy anticipation, knowing that for the remainder of their walk, this "stranger" will explain to them how the Christ had to suffer and die in order for his mission to be fulfilled; knowing that when they sit down to dinner in Emmaus he will give thanks, break the bread, reveal himself as the living Jesus, then disappear. In that instance, their grief would turn to incredulous joy and exhilaration. Those who thought Jesus would never speak to them again had been listening to his voice all afternoon. Similarly, those of us who have read the rest of Harry's story may have a sense of anticipation that counters Harry's devastation as he thinks Dumbledore will never speak to him again. Perhaps death is not the end.

Before Jesus died, he affirmed his willingness to accept death; before Dumbledore died he had assured Harry that "to the well-organized mind, death is but the next great adventure" (Book One, p. 297). Jesus had even been so specific as to tell his disciples that they would mourn his death while the world rejoiced but that their sorrow would be turned to joy when he rose from the dead. Even with these assurances, Jesus' disciples didn't get it. They were devastated at his death, similar to the way Harry was devastated at Dumbledore's death. Thank God that in both cases that was not the end of the story.

Evil Is a Strong Word

"I should've shown the book to Dumbledore," said Harry.
"All that time he was showing me how Voldemort was evil
even when he was at school, and I had proof Snape was
too—"
  " 'Evil' is a strong word," said Hermione quietly.
                                        —Book Six, p. 638

*H*arry Potter and the Half-Blood Prince might aptly be described as a study in the nature of evil. Much of the story covers Dumbledore's lessons on Voldemort's descent into evil.

In Book Five Harry, Hermione, and Ron grew to hate Professor Umbridge. After detention with Umbridge, Harry found himself weighing whom he hated more, Umbridge or Snape. Even Hermione, who usually defended any teacher, concluded Umbridge was evil when she tried to oust Hagrid from his teaching position in the dead of night. But it turns out that understanding evil was more complex than Harry and his friends first supposed, a lesson they learned when they suggested to Sirius that Professor Umbridge might have been a Death Eater:

"I know her by reputation and I'm sure she's no Death Eater—"
    "She's foul enough to be one," said Harry darkly and Ron and Hermione nodded vigorously in agreement.
    "Yes, but the world isn't split into good people and Death Eaters," said Sirius with a wry smile. (Book Five, p. 302)

As Harry and his friends tried to work out how to deal with people who were far from good, they wrestled with issues of love and hate.

As Paul says in Romans, "Love must be sincere. Hate what is evil; cling to what is good" (Rom. 12:9 NIV). But when we are dealing with imperfect people it seems that Sirius had a more mature view. He realized that human beings cannot quickly be labeled as good or evil. The Psalms also remind us that "no one living is righteous before [God]" (Ps. 143:2).

As these stories unfold, we discover that we should be very careful before we deem a person good or evil. Going all the way back to choosing between Professor Quirrell and Professor Snape, or watching Ron defend Scabbers, or watching people recoil at the wanted posters of the fugitive "murderer" Sirius Black, we have seen time and again that these characters are complex and that what may appear to be true about a character at first turns out not to be so. We still should be sure to hate what is evil and to cling to what is good, but when we are dealing with who someone is, it is best to postpone applying a label of good or evil until we know the whole story.

Phoenix Song and Jesus' Stricken Lament

Somewhere out in the darkness, a phoenix was singing in a way Harry had never heard before: a stricken lament of terrible beauty. And Harry felt, as he had felt about phoenix song before, that the music was inside him, not without: It was his own grief turned magically to song that echoed across the grounds and through the castle windows.

—Book Six, pp. 614–15

*T*he phoenix is a symbol of resurrection. Through its living, dying, and rising again from the ashes, it gives hope of life after death. Yet at the death of Dumbledore, his faithful phoenix Fawkes sings a song of stricken lament. Even though there is assurance of life after death, it seems that death itself calls for a solemn lament.

This sad theme is also seen in an episode from the life of Jesus as he prepared to demonstrate his power over death. He knew that his good friend Lazarus was sick to the point of death, and he purposely stayed away until after Lazarus died. Four days after Lazarus's funeral, Jesus went to his sisters, Mary and Martha. Both said, "If you had been here, he would not have died." Jesus knew this; he had plans that were beyond their wildest dreams. However, before Jesus showed them that he really is the resurrection and the life, he stopped by the tomb of Lazarus and wept. He too felt the pain of death and loss:

> Jesus, once more deeply moved, came to the tomb. It was a cave with a stone laid across the entrance. "Take away the stone," he said.
>
> "But, Lord," said Martha, the sister of the dead man, "by this time there is a bad odor, for he has been there four days."
>
> Then Jesus said, "Did I not tell you that if you believed, you would see the glory of God?"
>
> So they took away the stone. Then Jesus looked up and said, "Father, I thank you that you have heard me. I knew that you always hear me, but I said this for the benefit of the people standing here, that they may believe that you sent me."
>
> When he had said this, Jesus called in a loud voice, "Lazarus, come out!" The dead man came out, his hands and feet wrapped with strips of linen, and a cloth around his face.
>
> Jesus said to them, "Take off the grave clothes and let him go." (John 11:38–44 NIV)

Even though the phoenix is a symbol of resurrection and life after death, Fawkes cried with a stricken lament at Dumbledore's death and left the grounds of Hogwarts during his funeral. Even though Jesus Christ is the resurrection and the life, he cared enough to share our sorrow by weeping at his friend's grave before he raised him back to life to demonstrate the glory of God. Here too, as Harry came to discover, grief over the loss of a loved one is a poignant expression of love.

Rest in Peace, Dumbledore

Gryffindor's sword in its glass case [lay] gleaming in the moonlight, the Sorting Hat on a shelf behind the desk. But Fawkes's perch stood empty, he was still crying his lament to the grounds. And a new portrait had joined the ranks of the dead headmasters and headmistresses of Hogwarts: Dumbledore was slumbering in a golden frame over the desk, his half-moon spectacles perched upon his crooked nose, looking peaceful and untroubled.

—Book Six, p. 626

Albus Dumbledore had not feared death, yet his passing from this life into the next was deeply sorrowful and troubling to all who loved him. Even though in the Wizarding world Dumbledore was able to remain within limited reach through the magical portraits in the headmaster's office, the reality of death and loss raised many questions for those who loved him and to whom he had become the dearly departed.

J. K. Rowling does not get into any theological pronouncements about life after death, but a few verses from Isaiah would no doubt have been comforting to those mourning the passing of Albus Dumbledore, a man who came as close to a "righteous" person in his actions and attitudes toward others as any literary character:

> The righteous perish,
>   and no one ponders it in his heart;
> devout men are taken away,
>   and no one understands
> that the righteous are taken away
>   to be spared from evil.
> Those who walk uprightly
>   enter into peace;

they find rest as they lie in death.
(Isa. 57:1–2 NIV)

Rest in peace, Dumbledore. Rest in peace.

Fight, and Fight Again, and Keep Fighting

It was important, Dumbledore said, to fight, and fight again, and keep fighting, for only then could evil be kept at bay, though never quite eradicated.
—Book Six, pp. 644–45

*E*vil is relentless and aggressive. Dumbledore understood this and spent most of his life fighting evil. He fought his own personal battles against evil and his temptations toward it. He fought the evils in his society and in the magical realm. He fought, and fought again, and kept fighting until the end of his life. Even his death took place in the context of the fight against evil. Before he died, he taught his protégé to fight, and fight again, and keep fighting, which Harry did. It was only the relentless determination of those on the side of good to do so that had any chance of eradicating evil in their time.

In the first century a man named Saul of Tarsus started out fighting against Jesus and his followers, even approving of the stoning of one of Jesus' followers named Stephen shortly after Jesus' death. After having a radical encounter with the risen Jesus, Saul became Paul and spent the rest of his life fighting evil. Not only did he fight evil as best he could, but he also raised up a protégé by the name of Timothy whom he taught to continue in what he called "the good fight":

> Timothy, my son, I give you this instruction in keeping with the prophecies once made about you, so that by following them you may fight the good fight, holding on to faith and a good conscience. (1 Tim. 1:18–19 NIV)

> But you, man of God, flee from all this, and pursue righteousness, godliness, faith, love, endurance and gentleness. Fight the good fight of the faith. Take hold of the eternal life to which you were called when you made your good confession in the presence of many witnesses. (1 Tim. 6:11–12 NIV)

As Paul faced death in a Roman prison, he had these reflections on his own life: "For I am already being poured out like a drink offering, and the time has come for my departure. I have fought the good fight, I have finished the race, I have kept the faith" (2 Tim. 4:6–7 NIV). Like Dumbledore and Harry, and like Paul and Timothy, let us too continue to fight the good fight against evil. May we fight, and fight again, and keep fighting to keep evil at bay as long as we live.

Glimmers of the Gospel in Book Seven

Harry Potter and the Deathly Hallows

Introduction to Book Seven

Several themes in the final volume of the Harry Potter stories are in keeping with Christianity. Throughout *Harry Potter and the Deathly Hallows*, Harry repeatedly shows love for his enemies and does good to those who have despitefully used him (as Jesus commanded). Harry makes sure the Dursleys are hidden from danger. He risks exposing himself among the decoys by using the Expelliarmus Charm rather than a spell that would have endangered Stan Shunpike. He even goes back into the fire to try and rescue Draco Malfoy, Crabbe, and Goyle (although it was too late for Crabbe). Later when Draco is being assaulted by Death Eaters in the castle, Harry protects him again—although Ron lets Draco know he isn't pleased about it. Harry isn't the only one who shows love to an enemy. During the Battle of Hogwarts, Hermione protects Lavender Brown, who was her former romantic rival for Ron's affections. So those on the good side distinguish themselves by demonstrating love for their enemies throughout this concluding volume.

We also see a sweeping climax to the racial hatreds and prejudices that have been seething under the surface all along. What had been mistrust and dislike of those of mixed blood by some in the Wizarding world becomes full-blown persecution and threatens to become organized incarceration and genocide. Harry, his friends, members of the Order of the Phoenix, and others who stand for what is right and good oppose those who would oppress and destroy those deemed "impure" ethnically. They risk their lives and freedom to rescue and save others whose lives and freedoms are at risk. They even look out for unsuspecting Muggles. This is not exclusively a Christian virtue but a virtue shared by all decent human beings. It is certainly in keeping with the Christian concern for lifting up those who are oppressed.

The last major Christian theme in this volume has to do with tearing down idols. Throughout the previous six books Harry has grown to idolize Albus Dumbledore. As Harry's quest proceeds he must face the reality that Albus Dumbledore was a man who had made mistakes, disappointed those he loved, and shared the human frailty common to all. As Harry comes to see that Dumbledore too has feet of clay, he is shaken, but he manages to trust Dumbledore's wisdom in spite of the flaws and secrets that are revealed. Once Dumbledore is no longer an idol in Harry's mind, he can realize that even flawed people who make wrong choices and give in to their desire for power can choose to turn their lives around to fight evil and make significant contributions in the world.

Before we focus on specific glimmers of the gospel in this very complex novel, this summary may help you recall the overview of the story. It begins with the Dark Lord ascending in power, torturing and murdering the Muggles Studies teacher who was kidnapped from Hogwarts. Snape, the Malfoys, and other Death Eaters watch passively, highlighting that it is not only those who actively commit evil deeds who are responsible but those who sit idly by and allow it to happen.

Harry and the Order manage to get the Dursleys out of harm's way. The Order gets Harry away from Privet Drive with an elaborately planned decoy operation in which George Weasley loses an ear and the Order loses a seasoned warrior when Mad-Eye Moody is killed. Harry's seventeenth birthday celebration is interrupted by a visit from Rufus Scrimgeour, the Minister of Magic, who comes to deliver the items Dumbledore has left in his will to Harry, Hermione, and Ron—and to interrogate them in hopes of finding out why they were the only students remembered.

Bill and Fleur's wedding is lovely except for a minor disturbance when Viktor Krum accuses Mr. Lovegood of wearing Grindelwald's symbol and Ron's Aunt Muriel speaks ill of Dumbledore. The wedding is broken up suddenly when Kingsley Shacklebolt's Patronus appears to warn everyone to flee. The Ministry has fallen, Scrimgeour is dead, and the Death Eaters are in charge. Everyone disperses, including Harry, Hermione, and Ron, who were already prepared to leave on their quest to find and destroy Voldemort's remaining Horcruxes.

After disapparating to a Muggle street, where Death Eaters

quickly follow them, the three take up hiding at 12 Grimmauld Place. While there Harry discovers that R. A. B.—who took the locket Horcrux from Voldemort's hiding place in the cave—was Sirius's brother, Regulus. Kreacher obeys Harry's command and tells what happened to Regulus, revealing that, although once a Death Eater, Regulus was also a good seeker. He sought and discovered what Voldemort was doing with the Horcruxes and gave his life in his attempt to stop him.

After discovering that the locket is now in the possession of Delores Umbridge, Undersecretary to the Minister of Magic, the three determine to get it even though the Ministry is no longer safe. The new Minister of Magic, Pius Thickness, is under the control of the Death Eaters. (Given that J. K. Rowling is not one to choose names haphazardly, I wonder whether this name with religious overtones might suggest a similarity between the corruption of the Ministry of Magic and the way organized religion has been corrupted at times throughout history. I asked Arthur A. Levine, publisher of the Scholastic books, but he didn't know her intentions in giving the Minister of Magic such a suggestive name.) The Ministry of Magic has authorized the rounding up and incarceration of those deemed not to be pureblood or who are of questionable heritage. The Ministry also disseminates a propaganda campaign led by Umbridge.

Harry, Hermione, and Ron sneak into the Ministry looking for the Horcrux. They discover the plight of the Muggle-borns, find Mad-Eye Moody's magical eye being used by Umbridge to spy on her workers, and manage to retrieve both the magical eye and the Horcrux while also releasing terrified Muggle-borns awaiting interrogation.

Hogwarts has also fallen under a dark shadow. Severus Snape has been appointed Headmaster, with Death Eaters assigned as his deputies. Neville, Ginny, Luna and other remaining members of the D.A. form a resistance force in hopes that Harry will return to overthrow the corrupt administration.

Meanwhile Harry, Hermione, and Ron have taken to hiding out in the forests and fields; they take the locket Horcrux with them in hopes of finding a way to destroy it. Harry discovers that Voldemort is abroad seeking out a famed wandmaker. The three friends are worn down by difficult conditions, confusion, and the dark influence of the Horcrux. Ron abandons the quest, leaving Harry and Hermione upset but determined to press on.

Harry and Hermione go to Godric's Hollow in search of the sword of Gryffindor, which can destroy Horcruxes, arriving on Christmas Eve. There they discover a memorial to the Potters, the home where Voldemort gave Harry his scar, a graveyard where Dumbledore's mother and sister are buried near Harry's parents, and the grave of Ignotius Peverell, which bears the strange symbol Mr. Lovegood was wearing at the wedding and which is in the book Dumbledore left Hermione. They are met by an old woman they believe to be Bathilda Bagshot. Following her to her home in hopes of finding the sword, Harry is lured away from Hermione and Bathilda becomes Voldemort's snake, Nagini. Harry and Hermione narrowly escape before Voldemort arrives, but Harry's wand is broken beyond repair.

Back in the forest, devastated by the loss of his wand, Harry and Hermione skim the contents of Rita Skeeter's book *The Life and Lies of Albus Dumbledore*, which accuses the young Dumbledore of befriending the notorious wizard Grindelwald and of complicity in his tyrannical plot to take over the world by subjecting Muggles to Wizard domination. It also accuses Dumbledore of being party to his young sister's captivity and mysterious death. Harry is wracked by unanswered questions and doubts.

In his darkness, a bright light appears in the form of a doe Patronus. Harry follows the Patronus, which leads him to a frozen pool where a "great cross"—the sword of Gryffindor—lies submerged at the bottom. Harry strips off and goes in to get the sword, but the Horcrux around his neck begins to choke him. As Harry begins to die, Ron returns and jumps in to rescue Harry and retrieve the sword. Before Ron can destroy the Horcrux, he is taunted by the evil within it and momentarily caused to waver, but at Harry's urging, Ron destroys the Horcrux.

Hermione's anger and worry over Ron's leaving them comes out when he returns, but she is subdued by Ron's tales of how the Deluminator led him back to them and of what is happening in the rest of the Wizarding world. They decide their next move is to decipher the strange symbol that keeps recurring, so they set off for the home of Luna Lovegood and her father, Xenophilius. There they are detained by Mr. Lovegood under the pretense that Luna will be along shortly while he explains about the Deathly Hallows: the Resurrection Stone, the Elder Wand, and the Invisibility Cloak. Death Eaters turn up, but Harry, Hermione, and Ron escape.

Shortly thereafter, they are captured and taken to Malfoy Manor, Voldemort's headquarters. Harry and Ron are held in the cellar along with Luna, Dean, Griphook the Goblin, and Mr. Ollivander, while Bellatrix Lestrange tortures Hermione to find out where they got the sword. She demands to know if they have been in her vault at Gringotts. Peter Pettigrew is sent to look in on the hostages, but Harry and Ron attack him. While trying to subdue and kill Harry, he hesitates—recalling at Harry's suggestion the debt he owes Harry for his life—and is strangled by his own magical hand given him by the Dark Lord, reaping what he has sown. Dobby the house-elf arrives to rescue Harry and friends, but he is mortally wounded by Bellatrix during their escape from Malfoy Manor.

Harry and friends give Dobby a proper burial near Shell Cottage. While digging the grave by hand, Harry resolves to seek the Horcruxes rather than the Hallows, choosing a path of faith and obedience even though he has doubts. Harry seeks out Ollivander to gain better knowledge of wand lore, and asks Griphook to help him break into Bellatrix Lestrange's vault at Gringotts. While at Shell Cottage, Remus Lupin arrives to announce the birth of Teddy, asking Harry to be the child's godfather, an honor Harry accepts.

Harry, Hermione, and Ron break into Gringotts and the Lestrange vault with Griphook's help. Protection charms reveal the break-in, but they manage to get the Horcrux (the cup of Helga Hufflepuff) and escape astride a dragon. In the midst of the heist, Griphook turns on them and takes the sword of Gryffindor. They are left with the Horcrux but no way to destroy it.

Looking into Voldemort's mind, Harry sees that he has realized Harry is hunting Horcruxes. Voldemort decides to check his hiding places to make sure that the fragments of his soul are still safe. When he discovers that they are not, he is enraged. The race is on for Harry to get to the final Horcrux before Voldemort manages to get the Elder Wand, which might give him the power to destroy Harry before Harry is able to destroy him.

Helped along by a shard of the mirror Sirius had given him (which revealed a piercing blue eye reminiscent of Albus Dumbledore's eyes), Harry, Hermione, and Ron make their way to Hogsmead. There they narrowly escape Death Eaters and dementors with the help of Aberforth Dumbledore, proprietor of the Hog's Head and Albus Dumbledore's brother. He tells them more about his brother's youth and corroborates some of the accusations made by Rita Skeeter. Then he agrees to help them get into Hogwarts, where Harry is sure he will find one of the hidden Horcruxes. A tunnel leads them to a reunion with Neville and other members of the D.A., who have holed up in the Room of Requirement.

The resistance fighters are delighted to see their old friends and leader but are disappointed to learn that Harry's mission is not the same as theirs. They persuade him to let them help him find the object he is seeking. Deciding that the Horcrux is most likely the lost diadem of Rowena Ravenclaw, they set out to find it. The Death Eaters try to stop Harry, but with the help of the professors who have not succumbed to the Dark Lord, Harry and friends figure out where the diadem is hidden.

Meanwhile, the teachers and staff try to evacuate the school because Voldemort is already on the grounds and seething with murderous rage. Snape runs away as the battle is about to begin. Harry, Hermione, and Ron make their way to the Room of Hidden Things to retrieve the diadem. There they are accosted by Draco Malfoy, Crabbe, and Goyle. Crabbe sends cursed fire ablaze in the room but cannot control or stop it. Harry and friends manage to get the Horcrux while rescuing Malfoy and Goyle, but Crabbe is destroyed by the cursed fire he called up. That fire also destroys the Horcrux in the diadem.

The Battle of Hogwarts is fierce, with Death Eaters invading the grounds. Percy Weasley shows up, fully repentant, in time to join the good side with his family, fighting the Ministry and Death

Eaters. In the battle, Fred Weasley is killed along with others. Hagrid is carried off by giant spiders while Harry, Hermione, and Ron press on to get close enough to Nagini to destroy what they think is the final Horcrux.

They hide in the tunnel outside the Shrieking Shack, where Voldemort and Nagini await Severus Snape, whom Voldemort has summoned. Voldemort has (wrongly) concluded that the reason the Elder Wand, stolen from Dumbledore's tomb, isn't working as hoped is because its true master must be Snape, who killed Dumbledore. The three watch as Voldemort sends Nagini to kill Snape, and the great snake pierces Snape's neck. After Voldemort leaves the room, Harry enters and looks into the eyes of the dying man. Snape gives Harry his memories that contain that which Harry needs to know.

Harry takes the vial containing Snape's memories to the Pensive alone. There he discovers that Snape had sent the doe Patronus to lead him to the sword of Gryffindor and that Snape had loved his mother from childhood. Therefore Snape had agreed to protect Harry at Hogwarts. Snape's memory reveals that Dumbledore wanted Harry to know that Voldemort had accidentally turned Harry into the final Horcrux and that the only way Voldemort could become mortal would be for Harry to willingly die at his hands. Harry is devastated but determined to fulfill his destiny. He makes his choice to die willingly.

Hidden under the Invisibility Cloak, Harry makes his way through the castle. Seeing those who have died, including Tonks and Lupin, he finds Neville and tells him to kill Nagini if he gets the chance, then heads toward the forest where he knows Voldemort and death await him. Realizing that this is the end—his end—he turns to the Snitch, which "opens at the close," and discovers the Resurrection Stone. He turns it three times and is accompanied by Lily, James, Sirius, and Lupin, who comfort and encourage him as he willingly walks toward his own death.

Harry reveals himself bravely to Voldemort, who casts the Killing Curse once more. The Boy Who Lived goes down, but so does Voldemort. Harry awakens in a place like King's Cross, but he does not need his glasses, as his vision is perfect there. He sees

Albus Dumbledore, dead but very much alive. He also sees the remaining fragment of Voldemort's soul, which has been blasted from him with the force of the curse. Harry's soul is free of the Horcrux; his scar is finally only a scar. Dumbledore also explains himself, going from sublime happiness to sadness and regret as he tells Harry about the errors of his youth and how he sought to make up for them. He explains that Harry is not dead because of the protective power of his mother's blood, which still flows in Voldemort (who stole it from Harry), and that Harry can choose to go on or go back. Harry is disturbed by the creature, the shriveled remnant of Voldemort's soul, but Dumbledore declares that it is beyond their help.

Harry chooses to return, being assured by Dumbledore that their good-bye is only for the present. Harry returns to consciousness in his body and sees Voldemort being helped up. He plays dead and is carried by Hagrid out of the forest and back to the castle, where Voldemort displays him as a trophy, seeking to cause all to surrender. Neville Longbottom stands up to Voldemort, but—with Harry's help from under the Invisibility Cloak—is protected from Voldemort's spells. The resistance rises, inspired by Neville's bravery. Voldemort puts the Sorting Hat on Neville's head and sets it aflame, but out of the flaming hat, Neville pulls the Sword of Gryffindor and strikes off the head of Nagini, destroying the final Horcrux.

Harry reveals himself—apparently risen from the dead—and squares off with Voldemort. Harry pleads with Voldemort to try for some remorse, still offering him one last chance to save what is left of his soul, but Voldemort will not or cannot. Harry reveals the secrets he knows about the Elder Wand and whose authority it is under, about the Horcruxes that have all been destroyed. The final spells are cast: Avada Kedavra versus Expelliarmus. Voldemort is disarmed by Harry and killed by his own rebounding spell.

Celebration breaks out. Harry receives applause from the portraits of the former headmasters, but basks in Dumbledore's approval most of all. Friends and families are reunited. The prisoners are set free. In the epilogue, set nineteen years later, we learn that Harry and Ginny got married and have a family, as did Ron and Hermione. They raise their children and send them off to Hogwarts when the time comes. Evil has been restrained; good has triumphed. Harry's scar has not pained him in nineteen years. Love has conquered death. All was well.

Your Life or Your Soul?

Again Dudley appeared to grapple with thoughts too unwieldy for expression before mumbling, "You saved my life."

"Not really," said Harry. "It was your soul the dementor would have taken."

—Book Seven, p. 40

*T*he idea of the life of the soul as distinct from physical life is repeated throughout these stories. Voldemort underestimated the value of his soul while going to terrible lengths to protect his physical life. In the above dialogue Dudley is confused, thinking Harry had saved his life, but Harry clarifies that it was actually his soul that had been saved. Later in the story, when the Death Eaters threaten to loose the dementors on Harry, he knows it would be better to die than to lose his soul:

"What about dementors?" called another Death Eater. "Let 'em have free rein, they'd find him quick enough!"

"The Dark Lord wants Potter dead by no hand but his—"

"—an dementors won't kill him! The Dark Lord wants Potter's life, not his soul. He'll be easier to kill if he's been Kissed first!"

There were noises of agreement. Dread filled Harry. (Book Seven, p. 555)

Harry's reaction proved that he was more afraid of losing his soul than of losing his physical life. He had the good sense to know

his soul was of greater value than his life. This distinction was reinforced when Hermione explained the nature of a Horcrux:

> "Because a Horcrux is the complete opposite of a human
> being."
> Seeing that Harry and Ron looked thoroughly confused,
> Hermione hurried on. "Look, if I picked up a sword right
> now, Ron, and ran you through with it, I wouldn't damage
> your soul at all."
> "Which would be a real comfort to me, I'm sure," said
> Ron. Harry laughed.
> "It should be, actually! But my point is that whatever hap-
> pens to your body, your soul will survive, untouched," said
> Hermione. (Book Seven, p. 104)

This is the same kind of distinction Jesus made when he said,
"What good will it be for a man if he gains the whole world, yet
forfeits his soul? Or what can a man give in exchange for his soul?"
(Matt. 16:26 NIV). These are clearly rhetorical questions. Your life
or your soul? There is nothing equal in value to one's eternal soul.
This is a point on which one dare not be wrong or confused.

Thank God! Thank God! Thank God!

> *"He's alive."*
> *"Yeah," said Harry. "Thank God."*
> —Mrs. Weasley to Harry, Book Seven, pp. 73–74

*B*y the time the final book in the Harry Potter series was about to
be released, a commentator for an influential news magazine made
a statement that the only one who would die in Book Seven was
God, since there was no mention of him anywhere.

It was fun, therefore, to note that Book Seven was dotted with positive references to God as well as a well-timed prayer Harry uttered when he was trying to escape from the terrible flames in the Room of Hidden Things. Here are a few of these comments:

Harry saw a clean, gaping hole where George's ear had been. "How is he?"

Mrs. Weasley looked around and said, "I can't make it grow back, not when it's been removed by Dark Magic. But it could have been so much worse. . . . He's alive."

"Yeah," said Harry. "Thank God." (Book Seven, pp. 73–74)

During Jesus' arrest, one of his disciples cut off the ear of a servant of the high priest in a futile attempt to stop Jesus from being arrested. While the source of this injury was different than George Weasley being struck by dark magic, Jesus was able to heal the severed ear before allowing himself to be arrested (see Luke 22:50–51).

"Ah, God bless 'em" (Ted Tonks, spoken after hearing how Ginny, Neville, and Luna tried to retrieve the sword of Godric Gryffindor). (Book Seven, p.298)

When Bill and Fleur were late from transporting their appointed Harry replicas, everyone was anxiously awaiting them.

Mrs. Weasley's sentence was drowned in a general outcry: A thestral had just soared into sight and landed a few feet from them. Bill and Fleur slid from its back, windswept but unhurt.

"Bill! Thank God, thank God" (Book Seven, pp. 77–78).

Even Ron made sure to thank God, even though he did so while putting down the family of Draco Malfoy.

"So that's little Scorpius," said Ron under his breath. "Make sure you beat him in every test, Rosie. Thank God you inherited your mother's brains."

"Ron, for heaven's sake," said Hermione, half stern, half amused. (Book Seven, p.756)

So, let it not be said that there is no acknowledgment of God in the Wizarding world. J. K. Rowling put that to rest with her final volume. Thank God!

Kreacher's Conversion

Nothing in the room, however, was more dramatically different than the house-elf who now came hurrying toward Harry, dressed in a snowy-white towel, his ear hair as clean and fluffy as cotton wool, Regulus's locket bouncing on his thin chest.

—Book Seven, p. 225

Arguably, the most dramatic character conversion in the entire Harry Potter series is that of Kreacher, the Black family house-elf. Kreacher, the old and apparently demented creature who prowled the halls of 12 Grimmauld Place muttering about Mudbloods and blood traitors under his breath, was the one who deceived Harry on the night Sirius died. Everything about him, from his filthy loin-cloth and even filthier nest, reflected his soiled attitude. Dumbledore attributed some of this to the way Kreacher had been mistreated by wizards, among them Sirius Black. Few would have held out any hope for Kreacher's conversion.

But something amazing happened. Harry, Kreacher's new master after the Black family died out, took Dumbledore's words to heart and began to treat Kreacher as "a being with feelings as acute as a human's." While still acknowledging Kreacher's position as his slave, Harry spoke to him with kindness and respect:

"Kreacher," said Harry after a while, "when you feel up to it, er . . . please sit up."

It was several minutes before Kreacher hiccupped himself into silence. Then he pushed himself into a sitting position again, rubbing his knuckles into his eyes like a small child.

"Kreacher, I am going to ask you to do something," said Harry. He glanced at Hermione for assistance. He wanted to give the order kindly, but at the same time he could not pretend that it was not an order. However, the change in his tone seemed to have gained her approval: She smiled encouragingly.

"Kreacher, I want you, please, to go and find Mundungus Fletcher. We need to find out where the locket—where Master Regulus's locket is. It's really important. We want to finish the work Master Regulus started, we want to—er—ensure that he didn't die in vain."

Kreacher dropped his fists and looked up at Harry.

"Find Mundungus Fletcher?" he croaked.

"And bring him here, to Grimmauld Place," said Harry. "Do you think you could do that for us?" (Book Seven, pp. 198–99)

Harry spoke to him kindly and even gave him a gift, the locket R. A. B. had left in the basin in the cave. He offered it to him as a token of gratitude. Harry's act of kindness combined with his kindly attitude toward this continually rejected creature overwhelmed him. Kreacher changed from a mere creature to a new creation.

The kind of dramatic conversion we see in Kreacher is like how Paul describes what happens when someone trusts Christ and comes into his family: "Therefore, if anyone is in Christ, he is a new creation; the old has gone, the new has come!" (2 Cor. 5:17 NIV). That sounds great in theory, but even in the Bible some people mistreated others, especially those who were of lower rank than them or considered to be property. Therefore, Scripture reminds us that in God's kingdom all are brothers and God commands us to treat one another kindly.

During the time the New Testament was written, slavery was commonplace. So those who became believers in Jesus had to learn how to treat their slaves differently (until slavery could be abolished, which, sadly, still has not happened worldwide). So the New Testament has instructions for masters:

> Masters, provide your slaves with what is right and fair, because you know that you also have a Master in heaven. (Col. 4:1 NIV)

> You masters, act on the same [principle] toward them and give up threatening and using violent and abusive words, knowing that He Who is both their Master and yours is in heaven, and that there is no respect of persons (no partiality) with Him. (Eph. 6:9 AMP)

It also has encouragement for slaves, assuring them that "whatever good anyone does, he will receive his reward from the Lord, whether he is slave or free" (Eph. 6:8 AMP).

As with Kreacher, who was converted so as to be almost unrecognizable from his original state, a slave in the Bible experienced a dramatic conversion, not only in his personal or spiritual life but in his relationship with his earthly master. The slave's name was Onesimus; his master was Philemon, a Christian convert who held church meetings in his home, where Onesimus served. We don't know if Onesimus muttered under his breath like Kreacher did or not.

However, Onesimus became so disgruntled that he ran away from his master, but after encountering Paul he came to trust Jesus Christ as his Savior. Even though he was not Paul's slave, he was his "son in the faith," so he began to serve Paul out of love not out of compulsion. However, eventually Onesimus had a pang of conscience over having run away from his master, Philemon. So Paul wrote a letter pleading with Philemon to accept Onesimus back, but even though he was his slave, to treat him as a brother: "Perhaps the reason he was separated from you for a little while was that you might have him back for good—no longer as a slave, but better than a slave, as a dear brother. He is very dear to me but even dearer to you, both as a man and as a brother in the Lord" (Phlm. 15–16 NIV).

While acknowledging the role of slaves in that culture, the Bible also seeks to shift the slave-owner's attitude. Like Sirius with Kreacher, first-century masters did not think of their slaves as people with feelings as keen as their own. To call this master to receive his runaway slave "both as a man and as a brother in the Lord" was revolutionary.

Matthew Henry comments on one of Paul's arguments for Philemon's accepting Onesimus back as a brother as well as a servant: "What happy changes conversion makes—of evil good! of unprofitable useful! Religious servants are a treasure in a family. Such will make conscience of their time and trusts, promoting the interests of those whom they serve, and managing all they can for the best."[7]

This is a great description of what happened to Kreacher when Harry began to treat him with kindness and respect. The conversion of Kreacher's heart resulted in a conversion in the way he served his master:

> The kitchen was almost unrecognizable. Every surface now shone: Copper pots and pans had been burnished to a rosy glow; the wooden tabletop gleamed; the goblets and plates already laid for dinner glinted in the light from a merrily blazing fire, on which a cauldron was simmering. Nothing in the room, however, was more dramatically different than the house-elf who now came hurrying toward Harry, dressed in a snowy-white towel, his ear hair as clean and fluffy as cotton wool, Regulus's locket bouncing on his thin chest. (Book Seven, p. 225)

Not only did Kreacher become a better house-elf, he actually became an ally to Harry in the battle against evil. When the Battle of Hogwarts was underway and the house-elves had been freed, Kreacher did not slink away; rather, he led the charge of the house-elves, who were effective in distracting the Death Eaters and helping to turn the tide of the battle: "The house-elves of Hogwarts swarmed into the entrance hall, screaming and waving carving knives and cleavers, and at their head, the locket of Regulus Black bouncing on his chest, was Kreacher, his bullfrog's voice audible even above this din: 'Fight! Fight! Fight for my Master, defender of house-elves! Fight the Dark Lord, in the name of brave Regulus! Fight!'" (Book Seven, p. 734).

So we see in Kreacher's conversion a powerful example of the kind of conversion heralded in the Letter to Philemon. Both were a conversion not only of a slave but of a master; both instances demonstrate becoming a "new creation." As a result, in Kreacher's fantasy story and the Bible's true story of Onesimus, the overall battle against evil was advanced by a converted slave and master working together for the greater good.

Christmas Time Supersedes Halloween's Curse

They heard a snatch of laughter and pop music as the pub door opened and closed; then they heard a carol start up inside the little church.
   "Harry, I think it's Christmas Eve!" said Hermione.
   "Is it?"
   He had lost track of the date; they had not seen a newspaper for weeks.
   "I'm sure it is," said Hermione, her eyes upon the church."

—Book Seven, p. 323

*A*lthough not much attention is brought to this point, it is worth noting that Voldemort's curse that killed Harry's family and left Harry scarred took place in Godric's Hollow on Halloween, a holiday often associated with dark spiritual forces and evil. Harry's escape from the snake Voldemort sent, and from Voldemort himself, took place in Godric's Hollow on Christmas Eve and as the bells rang in Christmas Day.

There are many references to Christmas as Harry and Hermione head back to Godric's Hollow to find Harry's parents' grave and to seek the sword of Godric Gryffindor:

★   As Harry realized it was time to go to Godric's Hollow, they spotted "Christmas trees twinkling from several sitting room windows" (p. 315).
★   They got the hairs for their Polyjuice Potion from "Muggles who were Christmas shopping" (p. 321).

★ Their first sight of Godric's Hollow showed "cottages stood on either side of the narrow road, Christmas decorations twinkling in their windows" (p. 322).

★ The memorial to the Potter family was "partly obscured by a windblown Christmas tree" not far from "a little church whose stained-glass windows were glowing jewel-bright across the square" (p. 323).

★ They found the graves of Harry's parents and Dumbledore's family on Christmas Eve.

★ The influence of the Christmas carols is noted twice from the church and once from the pub, reminding Harry of Christmas memories at Hogwarts.

★ When Harry and Hermione found his parents' grave, Harry realized, "He should have brought something to give them, and he had not thought of it, and every plant in the grave-yard was leafless and frozen. But Hermione raised her wand, moved it in a circle through the air, and a wreath of Christmas roses blossomed before them. Harry caught it and laid it on his parents' grave" (p. 329).

★ The snake attacked on Christmas Eve but Harry and Hermione escaped.

★ Voldemort raced to catch Harry in Godric's Hollow, but Voldemort was too late: "He screamed with rage, a scream that mingled with the girl's, that echoed across the dark gardens over the church bells ringing in Christmas Day" (p. 342).

★ Ron heard Hermione's voice early on Christmas Day and found the light to lead him back to his friends.

What Voldemort began on a Halloween night began to be undone during Christmas time, the commemoration of the birth of the Savior, the coming of the light of the world that will eventually defeat darkness and evil. I think it significant that the tide began to turn against the evil one with the coming of Christmas. True, there were still battles to be fought, but Christmas had brought with it the hope of the final defeat. As in Harry's world, so too in ours.

Where Your Treasure Is, There Will Your Heart Be Also

She pointed to the dark stone. Harry stooped down and saw upon the frozen, lichen-spotted granite, the words KENDRA DUMBLEDORE *and, a short way below her dates of birth and death,* AND HER DAUGHTER ARIANA. *There was also a quotation:*
Where your treasure is, there will your heart be also.
—Book Seven, p. 325

*T*wo prominent Bible verses are used on tombstones in *Harry Potter and the Deathly Hallows.* During a Los Angeles press conference, J. K. Rowling said that she thought these two quotations could sum up the entire series. This first one is from the Gospel of Matthew (and is repeated in the Gospel of Luke). In context, it reads:

Lay not up for yourselves treasures upon earth, where moth and rust doth corrupt, and where thieves break through and steal:
But lay up for yourselves treasures in heaven, where neither moth nor rust doth corrupt, and where thieves do not break through nor steal:
For where your treasure is, there will your heart be also.
(Matt. 6:19–21 KJV)

What was Voldemort's downfall? He tried to lay up for himself treasures on earth that could contain fragments of his soul. He valued the precious treasures of the ring, the locket, the cup, and the diadem more than he valued his eternal soul. He thought that he was so clever that he could find hiding places that no thief could break into. But he was wrong: Dumbledore broke into the shack where Marvolo Gaunt's ring was hidden. Regulus Black broke into the basin in the cave where the locket was hidden. Harry and friends broke into the Lestrange vault in Gringotts to destroy the cup. And again Harry was able to break into the Room of Hidden

Things at Hogwarts to retrieve the diadem of Ravenclaw. Even though Voldemort had taken monumental precautions and went to great lengths to protect his treasures in the two most secure places in the Wizarding world, thieves broke in and stole them, which contributed to his soul's ultimate destruction.

The part of the verse that made its way onto the Dumbledore tombstone highlights an additional reason for putting our treasures in heaven, beyond just the assurance that if our treasures are in heaven they remain safe from the corruption of this temporal world. Kendra Dumbledore's heart was devoted to her family, particularly her daughter Ariana. She ended up giving her life in her efforts to protect Ariana. At the time, Albus Dumbledore had allowed his heart to stray away from his family to a quest for world domination. So the selection of this verse by Albus would have been a way to commemorate that his mother's had been in the right place. Etched in stone, it is also a reminder to all who read it that there are consequences for trying to store up treasures on earth while not laying up treasures in heaven.

With the death of his sister, Albus Dumbledore learned the cost of seeking earthly treasures above treasuring people and relationships. At that time, his quest to find the Elder Wand, the Resurrection Stone, and the Invisibility Cloak that made up the Deathly Hallows took his heart away from his sister, who depended on him for protection. Perhaps the selection of this particular Bible verse was Albus Dumbledore's first act of contrition for violating this verse's command.

When we meet him during Harry's stay at Hogwarts we see that Dumbledore has given up his quest for material things. Indeed, when Harry is breaking Dumbledore's things after Sirius's death, Dumbledore comments that he probably has too many possessions anyway. Rather than spending his life seeking material treasures, Dumbledore's new quest is to seek and find those objects that Voldemort has treasured over his own soul, over the other human beings whose lives he has snuffed out to make Horcruxes. This contrast between the materialism of Voldemort and the value system of those who treasure helping the oppressed, who treasure goodness and fighting evil—all things that allow us to lay up treasures in heaven—is woven throughout the series. The final outcome shows us the consequences of a shattered soul that trusted in this world, as compared to the happy, contented souls of those who have laid up their treasures in heaven.

The Last Enemy That Shall Be Destroyed Is Death

Harry read the words slowly, as though he would have only one chance to take in their meaning, and he read the last of them aloud.

" 'The last enemy that shall be destroyed is death' . . ."
A horrible thought came to him, and with it a kind of panic. "Isn't that a Death Eater idea? Why is that there?"

"It doesn't mean defeating death in the way the Death Eaters mean it, Harry," said Hermione, her voice gentle. "It means . . . you know . . . living beyond death. Living after death."

—Book Seven, p. 328

When Harry and Hermione finally found the grave of Harry's parents they also found another Bible verse, "The last enemy that shall be destroyed is death" (1 Cor. 15:26 KJV), although neither seemed to know the precise origins of the quotation. Harry noticed that the idea had something in common with the ideology that drove the Death Eaters. They too were seeking a way to eliminate the problem of death. Those seeking the Deathly Hallows sought to become "masters, conquerors, vanquishers" of death. The various factions within the Harry Potter stories needed a way to deal with death. How they went about it made all the difference.

Harry's cluelessness about the quotation was understandable, given that he was raised by the Dursleys. Hermione understood the essential difference between the Death Eaters' approach and that referred to on the Potters' gravestone. However, even her explanation was vague. She had the right idea but was missing the foundational basis for confidence that one day death would be destroyed.

The quotation on Harry's parents' gravestone comes at the end of a passage in Corinthians where the apostle Paul is seeking to correct a false teaching that was spreading in the church in Corinth—namely, that there was no resurrection of the dead. His carefully reasoned argument fills the fifteenth chapter of 1 Corinthians. First, he reminded them of the basis for their faith in life after death, the death and resurrection of Jesus Christ, which was witnessed by the twelve disciples, more than five hundred people at one time and James, and by Paul himself in a vision (see 1 Cor. 15:1–8).

Paul then connects Christ's resurrection with the assurance that the last enemy that shall be destroyed is death, using carefully reasoned arguments:

> But if it is preached that Christ has been raised from the dead, how can some of you say that there is no resurrection of the dead? If there is no resurrection of the dead, then not even Christ has been raised. And if Christ has not been raised, our preaching is useless and so is your faith. More than that, we are then found to be false witnesses about God, for we have testified about God that he raised Christ from the dead. But he did not raise him if in fact the dead are not raised. For if the dead are not raised, then Christ has not been raised either. And if Christ has not been raised, your faith is futile; you are still in your sins. Then those also who have fallen asleep in Christ are lost. If only for this life we have hope in Christ, we are to be pitied more than all men.
>
> But Christ has indeed been raised from the dead, the firstfruits of those who have fallen asleep. For since death came through a man, the resurrection of the dead comes also through a man. For as in Adam all die, so in Christ all will be made alive. But each in his own turn: Christ, the firstfruits; then, when he comes, those who belong to him. Then the end will come, when he hands over the kingdom to God the

Father after he has destroyed all dominion, authority and power. For he must reign until he has put all his enemies under his feet. The last enemy to be destroyed is death. (15:11–26 NIV)

Those familiar with this Bible passage may have foreseen how the story would end before the seventh Harry Potter book was written. J. K. Rowling gave a nod in this direction in 2000 when she told a reporter for *The Vancouver Sun*, "Every time I've been asked if I believe in God, I've said yes, because I do, but no one ever really has gone any more deeply into it than that, and I have to say that does suit me, because if I talk too freely about that I think the intelligent reader, whether 10 or 60, will be able to guess what's coming in the books."[8]

I alluded to the essence of the quote on the Potters' grave in the first half of this book, published in 2003, saying,

In our world, as in Harry's world, though some are safe, the Killing Curse still threatens many people. The Bible points us to a day when the curse of death will be destroyed entirely. We will have to wait and see what becomes of it in Harry's story.

In another book I wrote, *Wizards, Wardrobes, and Wookiees* (InterVarsity Press 2007), published before the final volume of the Harry Potter series revealed this verse on the gravestone, I actually quoted the verse on page 126 of that book, showing its centrality to the themes in the Harry Potter story. I had no idea that it would be chosen by J. K. Rowling as the inscription on the grave of Harry's parents but did see it as a central theme to the novels.

Since the Bible says that death is the wages of sin, the way Christ was able to defeat death was to live a sinless life. Then when he willingly gave himself to die as a sacrifice for the world, without defending himself, his body died and was buried, but once the deal was done, he rose back to life. This offered the world proof that death–the last enemy–could be defeated. Since Jesus never died again but ascended into heaven in his resurrected body, this gives hope to everyone who trusts in him that they too will be able to defeat death. Which, as Hermione so haltingly put it "means. . . you know . . . living beyond death. Living after death." So even though Hermione didn't know the details—unusual for her—she had the right idea.

Growing Doubts and Groping in the Darkness

Out of sheer desperation they had talked themselves into believing that Godric's Hollow had answers, convinced themselves that they were supposed to go back, that it was all part of some secret path laid out for them by Dumbledore; but there was no map, no plan. Dumbledore had left them to grope in the darkness, to wrestle with unknown and undreamed-of terrors, alone and unaided: Nothing was explained, nothing was given freely, they had no sword, and now, Harry had no wand.
—Book Seven, p. 351

The subtitle of this book dubs Harry "the World's Greatest Seeker," and that doesn't just refer to his skill on the Quidditch pitch. I also see Harry as a seeker in the larger sense of the word. In this passage we see him groping in the dark, but he is still groping. At this point he *felt* abandoned and misled, yet he did not stop seeking. Here he felt sure there was no secret path (there was) and no map or plan (there was), but the story does not end here. Harry had to use the perseverance and skill Dumbledore mentioned in his will to discover the path and the plan he could not see. These steps were taken by faith, not by sight.

This persistence is attested to further in the story after Harry decides to seek the Horcruxes rather than the Hallows (which was a part of the plan that Dumbledore had revealed to him clearly before his death). When he was questioning this decision, Hermione reminded him,

> "You could never have broken into Dumbledore's grave."
> But the idea of Dumbledore's corpse frightened Harry much less than the possibility that he might have misunderstood the living Dumbledore's intentions. He felt that he was still groping in the dark; he had chosen his path but kept looking back, wondering whether he had misread the signs, whether he should have taken the other way. (Book Seven, p. 503)

This is what makes Harry such a great seeker. Even though he doubted himself, he pressed on. He felt he was groping in the dark, but he followed the little light he had and pressed on to obey the clear instructions Dumbledore had left him. Later he will realize that the path he had chosen was the right path, and that the difficulties he encountered on that path were part of a larger plan.

This correlates to something in the Judeo-Christian faith. One way we can find encouragement when we feel like we are groping in the dark is to recall stories of biblical characters who held on to their faith in God even though they felt alone and confused. The book of Job describes the prolonged struggle of one man who felt left in the dark as he faced monumental losses and pain. Here's some of what he said while he was groping in the dark:

> Why then did you bring me out of the womb?
>   I wish I had died before any eye saw me.
> If only I had never come into being,
>   or had been carried straight from the womb to the grave!
> Are not my few days almost over?
>   Turn away from me so I can have a moment's joy
> before I go to the place of no return,
>   to the land of gloom and deep shadow,
> to the land of deepest night,
>   of deep shadow and disorder,

where even the light is like darkness.

(Job 10:18–22 NIV)

Much later in Job's story, when things have gone from bad to worse, he says, "Yet when I hoped for good, evil came; when I looked for light, then came darkness" (Job 30:26 NIV).

But Job did not stop seeking, and he refused to curse God regardless of the darkness in which he was groping to understand the course of his life. In the end his life turned around and he became a source of inspiration for everyone who feels like they are groping in the darkness, and like Harry felt in the passages quoted above.

Job's story ended in this way:

> The LORD made him prosperous again and gave him twice as much as he had before. All his brothers and sisters and everyone who had known him before came and ate with him in his house. They comforted and consoled him over all the trouble the LORD had brought upon him, and each one gave him a piece of silver and a gold ring.
>
> The LORD blessed the latter part of Job's life more than the first. (42:10–12 NIV)

Some people try to turn Harry into a Christ figure, which doesn't really hold up (although there are some experiences Harry goes through that are similar to some of the events in the life of Christ). I think Harry's most consistent role that we can learn from and emulate is that of a seeker. All people who have ever wondered whether there is a path laid out for them, whether there is some greater plan, whether they should be looking for a map to guide them, can be encouraged by Harry's perseverance in pursuit of the right path in life. As he pressed on and did not give up, he was rewarded in the end. He continued to seek, and he found far more than he had dared to hope for. Those who worry that perhaps they have taken a wrong turn and that they should give up can draw strength and hope from Harry's example.

The Bright Silver Doe
and the Great Silver Cross

Caution murmured it could be a trick, a lure, a trap. But instinct, overwhelming instinct, told him that this was not Dark Magic. He set off in pursuit.

Snow crunched beneath his feet, but the doe made no noise as she passed through the trees, for she was nothing but light. Deeper and deeper into the forest she led him, and Harry walked quickly. . . .

He moved forward rather cautiously and looked down. The ice reflected his distorted shadow and the beam of wandlight, but deep below the thick, misted gray carapace, something else glinted. A great silver cross . . .

His heart skipped into his mouth: He dropped to his knees at the pool's edge and angled the wand so as to flood the bottom of the pool with as much light as possible. A glint of deep red . . . It was a sword with glittering rubies in its hilt. . . . The sword of Gryffindor was lying at the bottom of the forest pool.

—Book Seven, pp. 366–67

*T*he bright silver doe, the Patronus and symbol of his mother who sacrificed her life for his, leads Harry to a "great silver cross." This sword of Gryffindor is the instrument of death with which Harry killed the basilisk, the king of snakes, to rescue Ginny. It is the same sword that will be used by Neville to behead the snake Nagini, destroying the final Horcrux, to make way for Voldemort's destruction.

The Bible makes the cross—a cruel means of execution—the center point of God's plan to save humanity while defeating evil and death in our world. Symbolically, the cross is the sword with which God beheaded the "king of snakes" in our world, Satan, in order to destroy his power of death over humanity. Any who trust in the cross of Christ have their sins forgiven, are deemed "not guilty" and therefore no longer worthy of death. In the cross of Christ believers are empowered to defeat death and Satan. The apostle Paul wrote, "May I never boast except in the cross of our Lord Jesus Christ, through which the world has been crucified to me, and I to the world" (Gal. 6:14 NIV). That symbol of death holds the promise of life. It signified a death to self, but also assurance of forgiveness of sins and the promise of eternal life. The cross must have held some such significance for Harry since he etched it on the tree under which he buried Alastor Moody's "Mad-Eye"—the only part of his remains to be recovered (see Book Seven p. 284).

The bright silver doe—Harry's mother's love projected in light—leads him to a great silver cross; surely this potent symbolism was not lost on such an astute author as J. K. Rowling. The one who died that Harry might live was reflected in the light that directed him to the cross. This also directs readers to the symbol of the cross, pointing to the One who died in our world so that whoever believes in him may not perish but have eternal life.

The Moment of Total Submersion: Harry's Baptism?

"Diffindo."
It cracked with a sound like a bullet in the silence: The surface of the pool broke and chunks of dark ice rocked on the ruffled water. As far as Harry could judge, it was not deep, but to retrieve the sword he would have to submerge himself completely.
—Book Seven, p. 369

*H*arry's total submersion in the pool to retrieve the sword of Gryffindor is akin to a baptism.

In New Testament times baptism was a total submersion in water, an act with deep religious significance. The baptism practiced by John the Baptist was a baptism of repentance, symbolic of washing a guilty conscience. Jesus was baptized by John, but not because he had anything on his conscience to feel guilty about. Jesus said he was being baptized to "fulfill all righteousness." In a sense, Jesus was being immersed in the same way as every sinner for whom he would die. He was identifying with us through water baptism. After Christ's death and resurrection, baptism took on added meaning. It also became symbolic of dying (going under the water completely being likened to burial) and resurrection (being brought up out of the water being likened to being raised from death to life).

The Letter to the Romans explains baptism in this way:

> Don't you know that all of us who were baptized into Christ Jesus were baptized into his death? We were therefore buried with him through baptism into death in order that, just as Christ was raised from the dead through the glory of the Father, we too may live a new life.
>
> If we have been united with him like this in his death, we will certainly also be united with him in his resurrection. For we know that our old self was crucified with him so that the body of sin might be done away with, that we should no longer be slaves to sin—because anyone who has died has been freed from sin.
>
> Now if we died with Christ, we believe that we will also live with him. For we know that since Christ was raised from the dead, he cannot die again; death no longer has mastery over him. The death he died, he died to sin once for all; but the life he lives, he lives to God. (Rom. 6:3–10 NIV)

This passage can help us understand how significant it is that Harry knew he would have to be completely submerged in order to retrieve the sword. The symbolic struggle with death in the water furthers this understanding. This is also true of Jesus' challenge to his disciples, "If anyone would come after me, he must deny himself and take up his cross and follow me" (Matt. 16:24 NIV), Before Harry could go into the pool, he had to make a conscious decision to deny himself all physical comforts. He also laid aside all his earthly treasures, even his clothes, to "take up the cross" at the bottom of the pool:

> He was shivering now, his teeth chattering horribly, and yet he continued to strip off until at last he stood there in his underwear, barefooted in the snow. He placed the pouch containing his wand, his mother's letter, the shard of Sirius's mirror, and the old Snitch on top of his clothes, then he pointed Hermione's wand at the ice.
>
> "*Diffindo.*"
>
> It cracked with a sound like a bullet in the silence: The surface of the pool broke and chunks of dark ice rocked on the ruffled water. As far as Harry could judge, it was not deep, but to retrieve the sword he would have to submerge himself completely.
>
> Contemplating the task ahead would not make it easier or the water warmer. He stepped to the pool's edge and placed Hermione's wand on the ground, still lit. Then, trying not to imagine how much colder he was about to become or how violently he would soon be shivering, he jumped. (Book Seven, p. 369)

When Jesus told his disciples that in order to follow him they would have to take up their own cross, they weren't thinking of a decorative piece of jewelry. They were thinking of a humiliating march toward execution. This was and is the kind of total commitment disciples of Jesus are called to, and it was this kind of total commitment Harry displayed in his willingness to go into that pool as part of his quest to destroy Voldemort. In that pool, Harry came to the end of himself. He was as good as dead if it were not for someone else in the water who lifted him up to life again:

> Harry had no strength to lift his head and see his savior's identity. All he could do was raise a shaking hand to his throat

and feel the place where the locket had cut tightly into his flesh. It was gone. Someone had cut him free. . . .

There before him stood Ron, fully dressed but drenched to the skin, his hair plastered to his face, the sword of Gryffindor in one hand and the Horcrux dangling from its broken chain in the other. (pp. 370–71)

Given that Ron was the one who raised Harry back up out of the pool, Dr. James Thomas, who teaches a class on Harry Potter at Pepperdine University (my alma mater) has quipped, "What do we have here, *Ron* the Baptist?"[9]

The Eyes in the Locket

The contents of the locket rattled like a trapped cockroach. It would have been easy to pity it, except that the cut around Harry's neck still burned.

"One . . . two . . . three . . . open" . . .

Behind both of the glass windows within blinked a living eye, dark and handsome as Tom Riddle's eyes had been before he turned them scarlet and slit-pupiled.

"Stab," said Harry holding the locket steady on the rock.

Ron raised the sword in his shaking hands: The point dangled over the frantically swiveling eyes. . . .

Then a voice hissed from out of the Horcrux.

"I have seen your heart, and it is mine."

"Don't listen to it!" Harry said harshly. "Stab it!"

—Book Seven, p. 375

*V*oldemort had bad eyes! Think of all the mistakes he made because he could not see or understand that which was right in front of his eyes. In the "King's Cross" chapter of Book Seven Dumbledore explains, "His knowledge remained woefully incomplete, Harry! That which Voldemort does not value, he takes no trouble to comprehend. Of house-elves and children's tales, of love, loyalty, and innocence, Voldemort knows and understands nothing. Nothing. That they all have a power beyond his own, a power beyond the reach of any magic, is a truth he has never grasped" (pp. 709–10). Voldemort's perception was full of darkness, and that great darkness was his downfall.

The Bible has much to say about those who have eyes but cannot see, those who are blind to essential spiritual truths. Immediately following the quote that appears on Kendra and Ariana Dumbledore's gravestone, "For where your treasure is, there your heart will be also," is this: "The eye is the lamp of the body. If your eyes are good, your whole body will be full of light. But if your eyes are bad, your whole body will be full of darkness. If then the light within you is darkness, how great is that darkness!" (Matt. 6:22–23 NIV)

There was also a voice that came out of the locket. It was a voice Harry warned Ron not to listen to. That voice brought Ron's deepest fears and magnified that which was destructive to his friendships and his mission. Tom Riddle had no concern for Ron, but he may have known a thing or two about Ron's heart. The voice said, "I have seen your heart, and it is mine." The prophet Jeremiah says, "The human heart is most deceitful and desperately wicked. Who really knows how bad it is?" (Jer. 17:9 NLT). Knowing all about wickedness, Voldemort knew the dark shadows of Ron's heart, which were projected out of the locket. Jesus taught his followers to distinguish between God, who loves us and wants the best for us, and Satan, whom he called "the thief" who "comes only to kill and steal and destroy" (see John 10:10). We are to listen to the voice of the one who loves us and reject the voice of evil. As long as Ron was listening to the voice of evil, he was in danger; when Ron listened to Harry's voice, the voice of someone who truly loved him, he was able to resist evil and break free of its destructive hold on him.

This battle with the Horcrux in the locket serves to remind us of the importance of our spiritual senses. It is vital that we not allow ourselves to be enveloped in the darkness projected by evil, nor to listen to the condemnation hurled at us by the evil one or the fears that lurk in the dark places of our hearts. Contrary to Voldemort's eyes being darkened by evil, those who seek the light can experience the opposite aspect of this spiritual principle: "The eye is the lamp of the body. If your eyes are good, your whole body will be full of light" (Matt. 6:22 NIV). Harry had good eyes in this battle and was able to see the truth and persuade Ron to strike back against evil. That ability and Ron's willingness to resist evil saved the day and destroyed the Horcrux in the eyes of the locket.

Ron's Repentance and Reinstatement

"I'm sorry," [Ron] said in a thick voice. "I'm sorry I left. I know I was a—a—"

He looked around at the darkness, as if hoping a bad enough word would swoop down upon him and claim him.

"You've sort of made up for it tonight," said Harry. "Getting the sword. Finishing off the Horcrux. Saving my life."

—Book Seven, pp. 378–79

"[Dumbledore] knew what he was doing when he gave me the Deluminator, didn't he? He—well," Ron's ears turned bright red and he became engrossed in a tuft of grass at his feet, which he prodded with his toe, "he must've known I'd run out on you."

"No," Harry corrected him. "He must've known you'd always want to come back."

—Book Seven, p. 391

*R*epentance is a change of mind and heart that causes one to turn around and go in another direction. After abandoning Harry and Hermione, Ron quickly had a change of mind and heart and wanted to go back, but it wasn't easy. Ron needed the light of the

Deluminator that he had inherited from Dumbledore to show him the way. His repentance was accompanied with sincere remorse, which Harry met with forgiveness. Ron had given considerable thought to why Dumbledore had given him the Deluminator, concluding that Dumbledore knew he would run out on his friends. Harry had a different take on it, insisting that Dumbledore must have also known that Ron would want to come back.

Dumbledore's foreknowledge of Ron's running away, his provision for him to come back, and Harry's reassurance that Ron still had an important part to play are all reminiscent of what happened to Simon Peter, one of Jesus' disciples. Peter had followed Jesus for three years and was one of his three closest disciples. On the last night they were together, Jesus told Peter, "Simon, Simon, Satan has asked to sift you as wheat. But I have prayed for you, Simon, that your faith may not fail. And when you have turned back, strengthen your brothers." When you have turned back. That implied that Simon Peter would run away and leave Jesus, prompting him to reply, "Lord, I am ready to go with you to prison and to death." Jesus answered with that devastating prediction: "I tell you, Peter, before the rooster crows today, you will deny three times that you know me" (Luke 22:31–34 NIV).

The story played out as Jesus had predicted. When he was arrested all of his disciples, including Peter, ran away. Peter deserves at least some credit for trying to put up a fight: he managed to slice off the ear of one of the arresting officers (which Jesus promptly healed). The last we see of Peter on the night Jesus was arrested he is weeping bitterly after denying three times that he knew Jesus. Peter then went into hiding. He dared not show his face at the foot of the cross. He only heard tales of the gruesome crucifixion. He was not there to help move Jesus' body to the borrowed tomb. He had run away and was hiding in disgrace.

On the morning of the third day after Jesus died, some women went to the tomb and were greeted by an angel at the empty tomb. "'Don't be alarmed,' he said. 'You are looking for Jesus the

Nazarene, who was crucified. He has risen! He is not here. See the place where they laid him. But go, tell his disciples and Peter, "He is going ahead of you into Galilee. There you will see him, just as he told you"'" (Mark 16:6–7 NIV). The angel was a messenger of God. He carried a message for the disciples; however, knowing that Peter felt he had disqualified himself as a disciple, the angel made it clear that Peter was still included.

As the days passed and tales of seeing the risen Jesus spread rapidly, Peter must have wrestled with his standing much as Ron did. As Harry went out of his way to reassure Ron that Dumbledore must have known that he would want to come back, Jesus went out of his way to reinstate Peter. When he finally revealed himself to his disciples, Jesus had a reassuring conversation with Peter:

> When they had finished eating, Jesus said to Simon Peter, "Simon son of John, do you truly love me more than these?"
> "Yes, Lord," he said, "you know that I love you."
> Jesus said, "Feed my lambs."
> Again Jesus said, "Simon son of John, do you truly love me?"
> He answered, "Yes, Lord, you know that I love you."
> Jesus said, "Take care of my sheep."
> The third time he said to him, "Simon son of John, do you love me?"
> Peter was hurt because Jesus asked him the third time, "Do you love me?" He said, "Lord, you know all things; you know that I love you." (John 21:15–17 NIV)

Three times Peter denied Jesus; three times Jesus gave Peter the opportunity to reaffirm his devotion to him and to the work they were doing together. Simon Peter went on to be a great apostle and leader of the early church. In both of these stories we can see that sincere repentance is met with reinstatement. With Ron Weasley we see that his repentance was sincere. He went on to prove himself. Not only did he come back to the cause, but his deep change of heart was evidenced during the Battle of Hogwarts:

> "Hang on a moment!" said Ron sharply. "We've forgotten someone!"
> "Who?" asked Hermione.

"The house-elves, they'll all be down in the kitchens, won't they?"

"You mean we ought to get them fighting?" asked Harry.

"No," said Ron seriously, "I mean we should tell them to get out. We don't want any more Dobbies, do we? We can't order them to die for us—" (Book Seven, p. 625)

A follower who turns away is only a failure if he or she does not repent and return to the fellowship of friends and the work of fighting evil. Both Ron Weasley, as a fictional character and Simon Peter, a biblical character model the kind of success that can follow sincere repentance and reinstatement.

Following the Light

"The little ball of light was hovering there, waiting for me, and when I came out it bobbed along a bit and I followed it behind the shed and then it . . . well, it went inside me."
—Ron, Book Seven, p. 383

*R*on explains to Harry and Hermione how the Deluminator projected her voice and guided him by a light he was supposed to follow:

"So I took it out," Ron went on, looking at the Deluminator, "and it didn't seem different or anything, but I was sure I'd heard you. So I clicked it. And the light went out in my room, but another light appeared outside the window."

Ron raised his empty hand and pointed in front of him, his eyes focused on something neither Harry nor Hermione could see.

"The little ball of light was hovering there, waiting for me, and when I came out it bobbed along a bit and I followed it behind the shed and then it . . . well, it went inside me. . . .

"It was here," he touched a point close to his heart, "I could feel it, it was hot. And once it was inside me I knew what I was supposed to do, I knew it would take me where I needed to go. So I Disapparated and came out on the side of a hill." (Book Seven, p. 383)

This imagery of following the light of God within is found throughout the Bible. In the King James Version of the Bible, which J. K. Rowling used for the Bible verses she quoted, Paul says, "For we walk by faith, not by sight" (2 Cor. 5:7). Psalm 119:105 says, "Thy word *is* a lamp unto my feet, and a light unto my path." By internalizing the word of God and putting faith in God's word, one will have enough illumination to know how to take the next step.

Jesus said of himself, "I am the light of the world. Whoever follows me will never walk in darkness, but will have the light of life" (John 8:12 NIV). After defining himself as the light, Jesus later told his followers he would be in them:

"If you love me, you will obey what I command. And I will ask the Father, and he will give you another Counselor to be with you forever—the Spirit of truth. The world cannot accept him, because it neither sees him nor knows him. But you know him, for he lives with you and will be in you. I will not leave you as orphans; I will come to you. Before long, the world will not see me anymore, but you will see me. Because I live, you also will live. On that day you will realize that I am in my Father, and you are in me, and I am in you." (John 14:15–20 NIV)

Later, John wrote to the church:

This is the message we have heard from him and declare to you: God is light; in him there is no darkness at all. If we claim to have fellowship with him yet walk in the darkness, we lie and do not live by the truth. But if we walk in the light, as he is in the light, we have fellowship with one another, and the blood of Jesus, his Son, purifies us from all sin. (1 John 1:5–7 NIV)

So the idea of following a light or having a light inside ourselves that will guide us as we seek to do the right thing is a biblical idea beautifully described through Rowling's character Ron Weasley.

Ron's obedience in following that light—which was a matter of choice, as it is for us with regard to following the light of God in our world—was essential in his finding his way back to Harry and Hermione, back to the mission, and ultimately back to the good future the author had in mind for him all along.

Master, Conqueror, Vanquisher of Death

"Those of us who understand these matters, however, recognize that the ancient story refers to three objects, or Hallows, which, if united, will make the possessor master of Death" . . .
    "When you say 'master of Death'—" said Ron.
    "Master," said Xenophilius, waving an airy hand.
"Conqueror. Vanquisher. Whichever term you prefer."
                           —Book Seven, p. 410

*T*hroughout the Harry Potter stories the unspoken enemy is death, not Voldemort. Voldemort is more frightened of death than are any on the side of good. Dumbledore, Harry's parents, the members of the Order of the Phoenix, and, in the end, Harry all faced death with courage. Most of them gave their lives as a sacrifice to protect someone else. The Deathly Hallows have one object that represents power (the Elder Wand), one that can protect others as well as oneself (the Invisibility Cloak), and one that can bring back the dead (the Resurrection Stone). All three of these elements are in Harry's possession at the end of his story.

Similarly, power, protection for others, and resurrection power are present in the finished work of Jesus Christ. Indeed, the Bible proclaims him the one who conquers death and over whom death has no mastery. That would make him the master of death. Jesus Christ *through* his own death vanquished death for all of us. By laying down his power temporarily, he gave us the power to live forever. By taking our sins on himself he has made our sins invisible and protected us against the wrath of God. By dying and being resurrected bodily three days later, never to die again, he has proven himself the true master, conqueror, and vanquisher of death.

The Bible asserts this in several places. For example, the apostle Peter told the people of Jerusalem:

> Men of Israel, listen to this: Jesus of Nazareth was a man accredited by God to you by miracles, wonders and signs, which God did among you through him, as you yourselves know. This man was handed over to you by God's set purpose and foreknowledge; and you, with the help of wicked men, put him to death by nailing him to the cross. But God raised him from the dead, freeing him from the agony of death, because it was impossible for death to keep its hold on him. (Acts 2:22–24 NIV)

Likewise, the Letter to the Romans says:

> Now if we died with Christ, we believe that we will also live with him. For we know that since Christ was raised from the dead, he cannot die again; death no longer has mastery over him. (Rom. 6:8–9 NIV)

Looking forward to the final conquest, when all of those who trust in Jesus will receive eternal life, Paul describes it as a victory over death:

> When the perishable has been clothed with the imperishable, and the mortal with immortality, then the saying that is written will come true: "Death has been swallowed up in victory."
>
>> "Where, O death, is your victory?
>> Where, O death, is your sting?"
>>   (1 Cor. 15:54–55 NIV)

Paul's letter to Timothy asserts that Jesus Christ has "destroyed death":

This grace was given us in Christ Jesus before the beginning of time, but it has now been revealed through the appearing of our Savior, Christ Jesus, who has destroyed death and has brought life and immortality to light through the gospel. (2 Tim. 1:9–11 NIV)

In the book of Revelation, John sees this vision of the risen Jesus in heaven:

His face was like the sun shining in all its brilliance. When I saw him, I fell at his feet as though dead. Then he placed his right hand on me and said: "Do not be afraid. I am the First and the Last. I am the Living one; I was dead, and behold I am alive for ever and ever! And I hold the keys of death and Hades. (Rev. 1:16b–18 NIV)

The ideas of the Deathly Hallows and of one who could be the master of Death are thoroughly biblical ideas that were fulfilled in the life, death, and resurrection of Jesus Christ and will be carried out fully in the prophecies and promises that remain to be fulfilled. As we hoped for Harry—or someone on the good side—to become the master, conqueror, vanquisher of death at the end of his story; now we can confidently hope and trust that Jesus Christ will do the same in our world and the one to come.

No Magic Can Raise the Dead, and That's That! Or Is It?

"All right, even if you want to kid yourself the Elder Wand's real, what about the Resurrection Stone?" Her fingers sketched quotation marks around the name, and her tone dripped sarcasm. *"No magic can raise the dead, and that's that!"*

—Hermione, to Harry and Ron, Book Seven, p. 427

> *Hermione would not like that idea, of course. . . . But then,*
> *she did not believe . . . Xenophilius had been right in a way*
> *. . . Limited. Narrow. Close-minded. The truth was that*
> *she was scared of the idea of the Deathly Hallows, espe-*
> *cially of the Resurrection Stone.*
>
> —Harry's musings, Book Seven, p. 434

*H*arry and Hermione took two different paths to believing in the Deathly Hallows. Harry was open-minded, pursuing the Deathly Hallows eagerly. Hermione was skeptical or—as Mr. Lovegood said—"Limited. Narrow. Close-minded, although not unintelligent." J. K. Rowling lets us watch both Harry—an eager, openminded seeker who was prone to becoming obsessed with the Hallows—and Hermione, a determined skeptic, struggle with their questions and their quest. As the story unfolds, both Harry and Hermione are amazed as what they discover exceeds their expectations. Harry learns from experience that the Deathly Hallows are real. Hermione comes to believe when she hears Harry's experience and trusts his testimony. Some people are more inclined to believe that which seems beyond belief; others have to overcome skepticism.

Hermione's skepticism is similar to the initial reaction of the disciples to Jesus' resurrection: "Later Jesus appeared to the eleven as they were eating; he rebuked them for their lack of faith and their stubborn refusal to believe those who had seen him after he had risen" (Mark 16:14 NIV). There were also other fantastic stories circulating around Jerusalem that week. The Bible says that at the time of the crucifixion of Jesus lots of strange things happened. Some of these were similar to that which was attributed to the Resurrection Stone.

At that moment [when Jesus died] the curtain of the temple was torn in two from top to bottom. The earth shook and the rocks split. The tombs broke open and the bodies of many holy people who had died were raised to life. They came out of the tombs, and after Jesus' resurrection they went into the holy city and appeared to many people. (Matt. 27:51–53 NIV)

Most people would find such stories hard to believe, but one of the disciples is attributed with being more Hermione-like than the others. We've come to know of him as "Doubting Thomas":

Now Thomas (called Didymus), one of the Twelve, was not with the disciples when Jesus came. So the other disciples told him, "We have seen the Lord!"

But he said to them, "Unless I see the nail marks in his hands and put my finger where the nails were, and put my hand into his side, I will not believe it."

A week later his disciples were in the house again, and Thomas was with them. Though the doors were locked, Jesus came and stood among them and said, "Peace be with you!" Then he said to Thomas, "Put your finger here; see my hands. Reach out your hand and put it into my side. Stop doubting and believe."

Thomas said to him, "My Lord and my God!"

Then Jesus told him, "Because you have seen me, you have believed; blessed are those who have not seen and yet have believed."

Jesus did many other miraculous signs in the presence of his disciples, which are not recorded in this book. But these are written that you may believe that Jesus is the Christ, the Son of God, and that by believing you may have life in his name. (John 20:24–31 NIV)

Jesus dealt with Thomas's need for physical proof by offering it. But he also gives more credit to those who are willing to believe without having to see for themselves. So whether we are more like Harry and inclined to believe and seek, or more like Thomas and Hermione, skeptically asking for proof, the Bible calls all of us to believe. These stories were recorded so that we can believe and discover the life after death that was of such interest to Harry and Hermione.

Friends . . . Friends . . . Friends

Luna had decorated her bedroom ceiling with five beauti-
fully painted faces: Harry, Ron, Hermione, Ginny, and
Neville. They were not moving as the portraits at Hog-
warts moved, but there was a certain charm about them
all the same: Harry thought they breathed. What appeared
to be fine golden chains wove around the pictures, linking
them together, but after examining them for a minute or so,
Harry realized that the chains were actually one word,
repeated a thousand times in golden ink: friends . . .
friends . . . friends . . .

—Book Seven, p. 417

*F*riendship is one of the best themes woven throughout all seven
of the Harry Potter stories. Seeing Luna Lovegood become a friend
of Harry and his group is particularly endearing because she had
not known friendship previously. We see each of these friends lay
down their lives for the others. Harry invited Luna to Slughorn's
party when many more popular girls wanted to go with him. Ron
was willing to let his knight be captured in the game of living chess
in order to let Harry and Hermione proceed. Harry rescued Ginny
from the Chamber of Secrets. Neville, Ginny, and Luna joined
Harry, Hermione, and Ron in their rescue mission to the Ministry
of Magic, which turned into a battle against the Death Eaters. Over
and over and over again they put themselves at risk socially and
physically for the sake of each other. In stark contrast, Voldemort
never knew a true friend.

The Bible says that Jesus—God come to earth in human flesh—
not only came as savior but, astoundingly, also as friend to those
who would follow him. He says in John's Gospel:

"Greater love has no one than this, that he lay down his life
for his friends. You are my friends if you do what I com-

mand. I no longer call you servants, because a servant does not know his master's business. Instead, I have called you friends, for everything that I learned from my Father I have made known to you. You did not choose me, but I chose you and appointed you to go and bear fruit—fruit that will last. Then the Father will give you whatever you ask in my name. This is my command: Love each other." (John 15:13–17 NIV)

Throughout the Harry Potter stories we see this kind of love repeatedly demonstrated in the relationships of this group of unlikely friends. As we consider how they love each other, and what it means to lay down our lives for our friends, we are considering one of the central themes of the New Testament as well as a central theme in the Harry Potter stories commemorated on Luna's ceiling: "*Friends . . . friends . . . friends . . .*" (Book Seven, p. 417).

Dobby Is a Free Elf— and a Christlike Character

"Dobby!" [Narcissa] screamed, and even Bellatrix froze. "You! You dropped the chandelier—?"

The tiny elf trotted into the room, his shaking finger pointing at his old mistress.

"You must not hurt Harry Potter," he squeaked.

"Kill him, Cissy!" shrieked Bellatrix, but there was another loud crack, and Narcissa's wand too flew into the air and landed on the other side of the room.

"You dirty little monkey!" bawled Bellatrix. "How dare you take a witch's wand, how dare you defy your masters?"

"Dobby has no master!" squealed the elf. "Dobby is a free elf, and Dobby has come to save Harry Potter and his friends!"

—Book Seven, p. 474

*D*uring the early stages of the anti–Harry Potter movement, Jack M. Roper, a guest on the Christian Broadcasting Network television program *The 700 Club* called Dobby a "dinky demon." He took an interesting route of illogic to arrive at that conclusion, noting that elves are defined in an occult dictionary as "unclean spirits" and applying this to Dobby. Anyone who takes the Harry Potter stories at face value and interprets them according to their internal logic would know that this critic could not have been more wrong about Dobby's character.

Dobby shows himself to be one of the most courageous, loving, self-sacrificing, and humble of all the characters in the series. Indeed, if there were a contest for who was the most Christlike in character among the Harry Potter characters, I would lean toward Dobby.

Dobby was a servant at heart. He began as a servant by force when he served the Malfoys, but he chose to be a servant even after Harry freed him.

Paul says in Philippians, "Do nothing out of selfish ambition or vain conceit, but in humility consider others better than yourselves. Each of you should look not only to your own interests, but also to the interests of others" (Phil. 2:2–4 NIV). Dobby epitomized this way of life. Paul goes on to show that this is the kind of attitude Jesus had and that we should follow suit:

> Your attitude should be the same as that of Christ Jesus:
> Who, being in very nature God,
>   did not consider equality with God something to be grasped,
> but made himself nothing,
>   taking the very nature of a servant,
>   being made in human likeness.
> And being found in appearance as a man,
>   he humbled himself
>   and became obedient to death—even death on a cross!
>   (2:5–8 NIV)

Dobby was a free elf, as his gravestone proclaimed by Harry's own hand. Yet he chose to make himself a bondservant to serve Harry, Dumbledore, and the cause of good. He chose to defy the evil his original masters were intent on doing. His attitude was one of humility and being willing to put himself in harm's way in order to save others. In the end he died seeking to save Harry and his friends, a final gift, a final act of service and self-sacrifice.

I found the gratitude shown to Dobby at his graveside a nice parallel to the kind of gratitude we should have for the one who saved us (if we trust in the Savior). As Harry looked down at the elf,

> he felt that Dobby deserved just as grand a funeral [as Dumbledore's], and yet here the elf lay between bushes in a roughly dug hole.
>
> "I think we ought to say something," piped up Luna. "I'll go first, shall I?"
>
> And as everybody looked at her, she addressed the dead elf at the bottom of the grave.
>
> "Thank you so much, Dobby, for rescuing me from that cellar. It's so unfair that you had to die, when you were so good and brave. I'll always remember what you did for us. I hope you're happy now."
>
> She turned and looked expectantly at Ron, who cleared his throat and said in a thick voice, "Yeah . . . thanks, Dobby."
>
> "Thanks," muttered Dean.
>
> Harry swallowed.
>
> "Good-bye, Dobby," he said. It was all he could manage, but Luna had said it all for him. (Book Seven, p. 480)

Since I see Dobby as a Christlike character, I appreciate that his funeral—not unlike Jesus' funeral—consisted of only a few devoted friends burying him while the world didn't even notice. Luna's sincere words of thanks for his rescue, echoed by the others, reminds me that all who have been saved by one who died for us should pause to give sincere thanks as well. Thanks, Dobby for that reminder.

Dobby's Clothes

Harry wrapped the elf more snugly in his jacket. Ron sat on the edge of the grave and stripped off his shoes and socks, which he placed upon the elf's bare feet. Dean produced a woolen hat, which Harry placed carefully upon Dobby's head, muffling the batlike ears.

—Book Seven, p. 479

*F*or much of his life, Dobby had no clothes of his own. The inadvertent gift by Lucius Malfoy of his first article of clothing, a sock, resulted in his freedom. Throughout his life, Dobby treasured the cast-off clothing that commemorated his freedom. I find it poignant that in death, Dobby was well clothed.

Isaiah depicts his audience as trying to clothe themselves with good works, but he declares, "All of us have become like one who is unclean, and all our righteous acts are like filthy rags" (Isa. 64:6 NIV). According to a story Jesus tells, the way we are clothed for eternity matters. He compares the kingdom of heaven to a wedding banquet where everyone is dressed appropriately except one man, who is thrown out (Matt. 22:1–14). So what is the appropriate attire for eternity? Nothing less than robes of righteousness that are given to us as a free gift. Isaiah describes it from the point of view of the one receiving the gift:

> I delight greatly in the LORD;
>   my soul rejoices in my God.
> For he has clothed me with garments of salvation
>   and arrayed me in a robe of righteousness,
> as a bridegroom adorns his head like a priest,
>   and as a bride adorns herself with her jewels.
>
> (Isa. 61:10 NIV)

When I think of how well clothed Dobby was in death, arrayed in the best clothes those who loved him could provide, it serves as a reminder that we all should hope to be well loved and well clothed in eternity.

Who amongst the Wand-Carriers Protests?

"It doesn't matter," said Harry, noting Griphook's rising color. "This isn't about wizards versus goblins or any other sort of magical creature—"
Griphook gave a nasty laugh.
"But it is, it is about precisely that! As the Dark Lord becomes ever more powerful, your race is set still more firmly above mine! Gringotts falls under Wizarding rule, house-elves are slaughtered, and who amongst the wand-carriers protests?"
"We do!" said Hermione. She had sat up straight, her eyes bright. "We protest! . . .
"Did you know that it was Harry who set Dobby free?" she asked. "Did you know that we've wanted elves to be freed for years?" (Ron fidgeted uncomfortably on the arm of Hermione's chair.)
—Book Seven, pp. 488–89

*I*t took Ron and Harry a while to catch on, but in the end Harry demonstrates his care for the downtrodden. This did not go unnoticed by Griphook, who noted that Harry rescued a goblin and gave a house-elf a decent burial, digging the grave with his own hands.

Justice for the oppressed, house-elves in particular, is one of Hermione's pet causes. Justice for the oppressed is also a major theme in the Bible:

> Cursed is the man who withholds justice from the alien, the fatherless or the widow. (Deut. 27:19 NIV)

> Righteousness and justice are the foundation of your throne. (Ps. 89:14 NIV)

> The LORD works righteousness and justice for all the oppressed. (Ps. 103:6 NIV)

Not only does the Bible state that God upholds justice, it also makes it a command for people to do likewise. The prophet Micah put it clearly: "He has showed you, O man, what is good. And what does the LORD require of you? To act justly and to love mercy and to walk humbly with your God" (Mic. 6:8 NIV).

So not only did Hermione's and Harry's demonstration of seeking justice for the oppressed impress Griphook—God would have been pleased as well.

Simply to Trust

> *Harry kept quiet. He did not want to express the doubts and uncertainties about Dumbledore that had riddled him for months now. He had made his choice while he dug Dobby's grave, he had decided to continue along the winding, dangerous path indicated for him by Albus Dumbledore, to accept that he had not been told everything that he wanted to know, but simply to trust. He had no desire to doubt again; he did not want to hear anything that would deflect him from his purpose.*
>
> —Book Seven, p. 563

*O*ne quality that makes Harry a great seeker—in the larger sense of the word—is his willingness to wrestle with doubts even when he doesn't fully believe. Harry faced his doubts time and time again, but he pressed on in the right direction, even when he didn't yet have a full understanding of the "bigger plan" that Dumbledore seemed to understand better than he did.

This willingness to trust even when our doubts assail us isn't quite flying blind, but is living by faith rather than by sight. In her 2007 interview with *Dateline*, J. K. Rowling said that the books reflect her religious beliefs but also her struggle to keep believing. Who cannot relate to that at some point in life?

This reminds me of a man who had heard that Jesus had the power to cast out demon spirits and heal the sick. The man's son was mute and possessed by an evil spirit that continually put his life at risk. The man had enough faith to bring his son to Jesus, but he still had his doubts. Jesus' disciples tried to help the boy but failed. Thankfully, Jesus showed up and addressed the boy's father:

"How long has he been like this?"

"From childhood," he answered. "It has often thrown him into fire or water to kill him. But if you can do anything, take pity on us and help us."

"'If you can'?" said Jesus. "Everything is possible for him who believes."

Immediately the boy's father exclaimed, "I do believe; help me overcome my unbelief!" (Mark 9:21–24 NIV)

This man too was a seeker; he was seeking help for his son. He was seeking God's help, which led him to listen to the stories he was hearing about Jesus. He couldn't truly be called a confirmed believer, but he pushed past his doubts. His persistence in doing so led him to Jesus. Once there, confessing his desire to believe— simply to trust—preceded Jesus' casting the spirit out of his son and healing him completely. Most people who are honest about their faith will have to admit times when they doubt. But those who choose to continue along the winding, dangerous path despite not having all the answers will experience the moment of triumph that comes to those who determine simply to trust. So it was with Harry and with the man in this story who brought his ailing son to Jesus.

You're Going to Leave Us
in This Mess?

"We all thought that if you came back, it would mean revolution. That we were going to overthrow Snape and the Carrows."

"Of course that's what it means," said Luna brightly. "Isn't it, Harry? We're going to fight them out of Hogwarts?"

"Listen," said Harry with a rising sense of panic, "I'm sorry, but that's not what we came back for. There's something we've got to do, and then—"

"You're going to leave us in this mess?" demanded Michael Corner.

"No!" said Ron. "What we're doing will benefit everyone in the end, it's all about trying to get rid of You-Know-Who—"

—Book Seven, p. 581

After Dumbledore's death, Neville and the remaining students from the D.A. at Hogwarts opposed the oppressive regime in hopes that Harry would return to help them overthrow it. They didn't understand that Harry's aim was to overthrow the power behind the oppressive regime—Voldemort himself. Therefore, they were understandably confused and discouraged when Harry showed up and revealed that his plans were different from their expectations.

This is similar to the reception Jesus had after his resurrection. Those who had been following him for three years thought of him as the Messiah, but their idea of the Messiah was of one who would come to overthrow the oppressive regime the Romans exerted over the Jews. That is why the crucifixion made little sense to them. When Jesus rose from the dead, his aim was to deliver the entire world and many generations from the dominant fear of death exerted by the devil. His aim was to offer eternal life to as many as would trust him for salvation. But, when he appeared alive from the dead, all his disciples wanted to know was how soon the Romans would be expelled:

> When they met together, they asked him, "Lord, are you at this time going to restore the kingdom to Israel?"
>
> He said to them: "It is not for you to know the times or dates the Father has set by his own authority. But you will receive power when the Holy Spirit comes on you; and you will be my witnesses in Jerusalem, and in all Judea and Samaria, and to the ends of the earth."
>
> After he said this, he was taken up before their very eyes, and a cloud hid him from their sight. (Acts 1:6–9 NIV)

In essence, Jesus' followers were asking, "You're going to leave us in this mess?" And the answer, like Harry's to his fellow students at Hogwarts, was yes. They were left to fight the battle. In the case of Jesus' followers, they were given supernatural power, the Holy Spirit with them, to carry on the battle until all was well. Likewise, Neville and friends would come to see that the battle was greater than the one they thought they were fighting. However, by fighting the larger battle against Voldemort, everyone benefited in the end, just as Ron had assured them.

Penitence or Repentance: The Bloody Baron and Percy Weasley

"The Baron? You mean—"

"The Bloody Baron, yes," said the Gray Lady, and she lifted aside the cloak she wore to reveal a single dark wound in her white chest. "When he saw what he had done, he was overcome with remorse. He took the weapon that had claimed my life, and used it to kill himself. All

these centuries later, he wears his chains as an act of pen-
itence . . . as he should," she added bitterly.
—Book Seven, p. 616

*T*here is an interesting contrast between the way the Bloody
Baron and Percy Weasley deal with their recognition of wrongdoing. The Baron, upon realizing that he had killed the Gray Lady,
committed suicide and went through eternity carrying the weight
of his own sin. He is left as a sad symbol of one trying to work off
his sins through an act of penitence. He has known no forgiveness,
as we see from the comments of the Gray Lady, her bitterness
unabated, who thinks that his suffering in the afterlife is what he
deserves.

Percy Weasley was a traitor to his family and the cause of good.
He came to realize this late in the story, but instead of destroying
himself, he truly repented. He made a change of mind and heart
that resulted in a change in his life's direction. He found a way to
go to those he had wronged, admit his wrongdoing, receive forgiveness, and rejoin the battle on the right side.

> "I was a fool," Percy roared, so loudly that Lupin nearly
> dropped his photograph. "I was an idiot, I was a pompous
> prat, I was a—a—"
> "Ministry-loving, family-disowning, power-hungry moron,"
> said Fred.
> Percy swallowed.
> "Yes, I was!"
> "Well, you can't say fairer than that," said Fred, holding
> out his hand to Percy.
> Mrs. Weasley burst into tears. She ran forward, pushed
> Fred aside, and pulled Percy into a strangling hug, while he
> patted her on the back, his eyes on his father.
> "I'm sorry, Dad," Percy said.
> Mr. Weasley blinked rather rapidly, then he too hurried to
> hug his son. (Book Seven, pp. 605–6)

Percy's approach to his own wrongdoing was best. Perhaps the
love of his family helped Percy make his dramatic turnaround.
Percy knew Mr. Weasley was the kind of father who would receive

him with open arms regardless of the offenses against him at the Ministry or the slights to their family.

Jesus told a story of a son who denied and disgraced his family, then finally came to himself and realized that he would be better off back at home: "So he got up and went to his father. But while he was still a long way off, his father saw him and was filled with compassion for him; he ran to his son, threw his arms around him and kissed him" (Luke 15:20–21 NIV).

So Percy Weasley is a model of the repentant prodigal son who receives a warm welcome home, while the Bloody Baron is left to wander the halls of Hogwarts carrying the chains he forged in life, a sad example of one who took his own life rather than repent.

Harry Potter Is No Saint

> *"It's not a case of what* you'll *permit, Minerva McGonagall. Your time's over. It's us what's in charge here now, and you'll back me up or you'll pay the price."*
>
> *And he spat in her face. Harry pulled the Cloak off himself, raised his wand, and said, "You shouldn't have done that."*
>
> *As Amycus spun around, Harry shouted, "Crucio!" . . .*
>
> *"I see what Bellatrix meant," said Harry, the blood thundering through his brain, "you need to really mean it."*
>
> —Book Seven, p. 593

*W*hen asked about Harry's use of unforgivable curses, J. K. Rowling noted that Harry is no saint. This is borne out by his misdeeds throughout the series. If the foes of the Harry Potter series had a problem with Harry's lying and breaking rules during his first year, they would be appalled to see that he went on to attempted murder (using Sectum Sempra on Draco), using the Imperius Curse to help him break into Gringotts Bank to rob a vault, using the Cruciatis Curse on Amycus Carrow, and "having things to hide" in his time. Yes, Harry was a confirmed sinner. Yet he was also a great seeker, one who went on to fight on the side of good and ended up sacrificing his own life for the cause as well as being saved by his mother's sacrifice of her life, which was an undeserved gift of grace.

Those who are willing to engage in more than a simplistic, moralistic view of life in order to consider the beauty of the Christian gospel will see similarities between Harry's record of wrongdoing and some of the Bible's greatest heroes. The apostle Paul, who was party to the killing of Stephen, the first Christian martyr, wrote:

> Here is a trustworthy saying that deserves full acceptance: Christ Jesus came into the world to save sinners—of whom I am the worst. But for that very reason I was shown mercy so that in me, the worst of sinners, Christ Jesus might display his unlimited patience as an example for those who would believe on him and receive eternal life. (1 Tim. 1:15–16 NIV)

Others who ended up as heroes in the Bible began as confirmed sinners, adulterers, murderers, and cheats. In the case of King David, his adultery and murder took place after he had devoted his life to God. While sin is never condoned, there is always hope for those willing to admit their sins. Those who doubt this should read the full stories of Noah, Abraham, Sarai/Sarah, Moses, Rahab (a one-time prostitute turned great-great-grandmother of the Messiah), David, Saul/Paul, and many other Bible heroes. They, like Harry Potter, had things to hide in their time.

Cursed Fire: It's a Hell of a Way to Die

They soared up into the air, missing by feet the horned beak of a flaming raptor that snapped its jaws at them. The smoke and heat were becoming overwhelming: Below them the cursed fire was consuming the contraband of generations of hunted students, the guilty outcomes of a thousand banned experiments, the secrets of the countless souls who had sought refuge in the room. Harry could not see a trace of Malfoy, Crabbe, and Goyle anywhere: He swooped as low as he dared over the marauding monsters of flame to try to find them, but there was nothing but fire: What a terrible way to die. . . . He had never wanted this.

—Book Seven, p. 632

*E*ven though Crabbe set the cursed fire himself, it was terrible to know that he would die that way. You wouldn't wish that on your worst enemy. In the fire were all manner of flaming creatures, among them a snake, which seems fitting because it is a symbol of Satan.

The Bible speaks of hell, a fiery place of eternal punishment, in many places. However, Jesus is careful to point out that it was never intended for people. In one story, Jesus told about separating people like sheep and goats, with those on the right going into eternal life and rewards, and those on the left going to hell:

> Then he will say to those on his left, "Depart from me, you who are cursed, into the eternal fire *prepared for the devil and his angels.* For I was hungry and you gave me nothing to eat, I was thirsty and you gave me nothing to drink, I was a stranger and you did not invite me in, I needed clothes and you did not clothe me, I was sick and in prison and you did not look after me."

They also will answer, "Lord, when did we see you hungry or thirsty or a stranger or needing clothes or sick or in prison, and did not help you?"

He will reply, "I tell you the truth, whatever you did not do for one of the least of these, you did not do for me."

Then they will go away to eternal punishment, but the righteous to eternal life. (Matt. 25:41–46 NIV)

As Harry had not wanted anyone to die in the cursed fire, God never wants any human being to go to hell. The Bible also speaks of the earth being consumed in fire to make way for new heavens and a new earth. In response to some who were complaining that God was taking too long, the apostle Peter wrote:

But you must not forget, dear friends, that a day is like a thousand years to the Lord, and a thousand years is like a day. The Lord isn't really being slow about his promise to return, as some people think. No, he is being patient for your sake. He does not want anyone to perish, so he is giving more time for everyone to repent. But the day of the Lord will come as unexpectedly as a thief. Then the heavens will pass away with a terrible noise, and everything in them will disappear in fire, and the earth and everything on it will be exposed to judgment.

Since everything around us is going to melt away, what holy, godly lives you should be living! (2 Pet. 3:8–11 NLT)

Cursed fire is a hell of a way to die. Harry, Ron, and Hermione swooped down into the cursed flames to rescue their enemies and were sobered by Crabbe's death. They wouldn't have wished that kind of end for anyone. God does not wish anyone to perish in the cursed fires of hell. Therefore, God warns everyone in hopes that we will take the way of escape offered us through Jesus Christ, who came down into our world to rescue us.

Harry the Horcrux

"Then explain . . . more," said Harry, and Dumbledore smiled.

"You were the seventh Horcrux, Harry, the Horcrux he never meant to make. He had rendered his soul so unstable that it broke apart when he committed those acts of unspeakable evil, the murder of your parents, the attempted killing of a child. But what escaped from that room was even less than he knew. He left more than his body behind. He left part of himself latched to you, the would-be victim who had survived."

—Book Seven, p. 709

After Book Five, when the occlumency lessons did not work, I guessed that the strange connection between Harry and Voldemort was a result of a part of Voldemort's soul being in Harry (I thought Harry's scar was the last Horcrux). Given that I saw New Testament themes throughout the stories, I concluded this would mean that Harry would have to willingly die but that only the part of Voldemort's soul within him would die and Harry would be able to go on to live his life free of Voldemort's previous hold on him. If Snape had understood this, he would not have been so surprised when Dumbledore revealed this to him:

"So the boy . . . the boy must die?" asked Snape quite calmly.

"And Voldemort himself must do it, Severus. That is essential."

Another long silence. Then Snape said, "I thought . . . all these years . . . that we were protecting him for her. For Lily."

"We have protected him because it has been essential to teach him, to raise him, to let him try his strength," said Dumbledore, his eyes still tight shut. "Meanwhile, the connection between them grows ever stronger, a parasitic growth: Sometimes I have thought he suspects it himself. If I know him, he will have arranged matters so that when he does set out to meet his death, it will truly mean the end of Voldemort." (Book Seven, pp. 686–87)

Dumbledore trusted that Harry would destroy the Horcruxes and then be willing to face his own death without defending himself if he understood that this meant Voldemort's destruction.

This was a familiar concept to me since a willingness to put to death the sinful nature within us is an essential of the Christian life. We do not become free of evil through a program of self-improvement. It requires death and resurrection.

The Bible says that we all have a sinful nature resident within us. As with Harry, we received this sin nature through the curse of the evil one in our world. That sinful nature could be likened to Harry's having a little bit of Voldemort resident within him even though he wants to do good. The only way Harry could be free of Voldemort was to allow himself to be hit with the curse of death; similarly, the only way we can have power over our sin nature is for it to die. That happens when we acknowledge our sinfulness and need of a savior. When we trust the work of Jesus Christ and his death on the cross as payment for our sins, it's like we are willingly dying with him. Then our trust in him carries over to grant us the chance of a new life, likened to his resurrection.

Therefore, Paul says in the Letter to the Galatians:

> I have been crucified with Christ and I no longer live, but Christ lives in me. The life I live in the body, I live by faith in the Son of God, who loved me and gave himself for me. I do not set aside the grace of God, for if righteousness could be gained through the law, Christ died for nothing! (Gal. 2:20–21 NIV)

And he says in the Letter to the Romans:

> If we have been united with him like this in his death, we will certainly also be united with him in his resurrection. For we know that our old self was crucified with him so that the body of sin might be done away with, that we should no longer be slaves to sin—because anyone who has died has been freed from sin. (Rom. 6:5–7 NIV)

Dumbledore was right in his estimation of Harry. Perhaps he surmised that since Harry was the descendant of Ignotus Peverell, the third brother who greeted death like an old friend, Harry would do likewise. Harry's realization that the only way to destroy Voldemort was to die, and his willingness to do so, made it possible for him to live free of that evil influence.

But You're Dead

Harry fell into the other [seat], staring at his old head-master's face. Dumbledore's long silver hair and beard, the piercingly blue eyes behind half-moon spectacles, the crooked nose: Everything was as he had remembered it. And yet . . .
    "But you're dead," said Harry.
    "Oh yes," said Dumbledore matter-of-factly.
                         —Book Seven, p. 707

*H*arry had many questions about death. He asked them of Nearly Headless Nick after Sirius fell through the veil in the Death Chamber, but he got few answers. As he stood at his parents' grave, puzzling over the quotation inscribed there, Hermione had to explain to him that "The last enemy that shall be destroyed is death" meant that there would be life after death. Harry's thoughts at the graveside revealed his lack of understanding at that point:

> But they were not living, thought Harry: They were gone. The empty words could not disguise the fact that his parents' moldering remains lay beneath snow and stone, indifferent, unknowing. And tears came before he could stop them, boiling hot then instantly freezing on his face, and what was the point in wiping them off or pretending? He let them fall, his lips pressed hard together, looking down at the thick snow hiding from his eyes the place where the last of Lily and James lay, bones now, surely, or dust, not

knowing or caring that their living son stood so near, his heart still beating, alive because of their sacrifice and close to wishing, at this moment, that he was sleeping with them. (Book Seven, p. 329)

Dumbledore had given Harry a hint about life after death while trying to console him earlier, asking, "Do you think the dead we love ever truly leave us?" But it was only after Harry had been in the forest again, after turning the Resurrection Stone three times in his hand, that Harry came to realize that his parents had never truly left him. Seeing his parents, Sirius, and Lupin again in the afterlife, and hearing their encouragement, revealed that they did know and care all about everything that had been going on in his life. They had never truly left him. Harry was able to see that which is unseen after Voldemort hit him with the Killing Curse. He seemed to have died, but survived to see beyond death and realize his previous understanding of death had been lacking. Although the physical remains of Harry's dearly departed were decaying, their true selves, their souls, were fully alive, appearing better than they had in their earthly life (Sirius and Lupin both appeared younger, and Lupin less shabby; all were wearing "the same loving smile," Book Seven, p. 699).

The Bible speaks of this contrast between the physical body being subject to decay but the true self being glorious in eternity:

> Therefore we do not lose heart. Though outwardly we are wasting away, yet inwardly we are being renewed day by day. For our light and momentary troubles are achieving for us an eternal glory that far outweighs them all. So we fix our eyes not on what is seen, but on what is unseen. For what is seen is temporary, but what is unseen is eternal. (2 Cor. 4:16–18 NIV)

Standing at his parents' grave, Harry fixed his eyes on what he could see, not realizing that what he could see with his eyes is temporary. When he saw Lily, James, Sirius, and Lupin by the power of the Resurrection Stone and saw Dumbledore alive again at King's Cross, he was seeing that which is unseen and eternal. In so doing, Harry realized that he had been wrong about his parents' deaths and about death itself. Thus, he gained the courage to face life with all its pain and difficulties; we too can do likewise if we view our physical life and momentary troubles in the larger scale of eternal life and eternal rewards (see 2 Cor. 4:16–5:10).

Much More than Ghosts Walking beside Him

Less substantial than living bodies, but much more than ghosts, [Lily, James, Sirius, and Lupin] moved toward him, and on each face, there was the same loving smile. . . .

Lily's smile was widest of all. She pushed her long hair back as she drew close to him, and her green eyes, so like his, searched his face hungrily, as though she would never be able to look at him enough.

"You've been so brave."

He could not speak. His eyes feasted on her, and he thought that he would like to stand and look at her forever, and that would be enough.

"You are nearly there," said James. "Very close. We are . . . so proud of you."

—Book Seven, p. 699

*H*arry's was strengthened and encouraged by the earthly appearance of those who had preceded him in death.

This has its counterpart in the Bible's account of Jesus' approach to his death (similarly a willing self-sacrifice to save others from the evil foe). Jesus was trying to prepare his disciples for what he knew was about to happen when he arrived in Jerusalem. Jesus knew the prophecies of his impending death and spelled that out plainly for them. But Jesus also said and did things they found hard to understand:

> [Jesus told them] "I tell you the truth, some who are standing here will not taste death before they see the kingdom of God."
>
> About eight days after Jesus said this, he took Peter, John and James with him and went up onto a mountain to pray. As he was praying, the appearance of his face changed, and his clothes became as bright as a flash of lightning. Two men, Moses and Elijah, appeared in glorious splendor, talking with Jesus. They spoke about his departure, which he was about to bring to fulfillment at Jerusalem. (Luke 9:27–31 NIV)

The purpose of the conversation between Moses, Elijah, and Jesus sometimes gets lost in the wonder of Jesus' being transfigured in heavenly glory on that mountain near Jerusalem and the voice from heaven telling the disciples to listen rather than talk. But if we stop to focus on the appearance of Moses and Elijah, we can see a clear similarity to what happened when Harry saw and spoke with his dearly departed.

Moses is the great lawgiver and liberator; Elijah, the great prophet. Together they represented the law and the prophets, both of which had to be appeased and fulfilled through the death Jesus was about to accomplish. By his death the law's requirement of death for sin would be paid; by his death the prophecies throughout the Old Testament about the Messiah would be fulfilled. So the identity of these two people sent to Jesus makes sense. But what were they talking about? "They spoke about his departure, which he was about to bring to fulfillment at Jerusalem." His "departure" was his death on the cross. Jesus, too, found that it was not so easy to die. Moses and Elijah showed up in Jesus' world to encourage Jesus as he was about to take his last determined steps toward the predestined death that he would have to choose to carry through. Isn't this very similar to what Harry had to do and the role that those called by the Resurrection Stone played for him?

> Beside him, making scarcely a sound, walked James, Sirius, Lupin, and Lily, and their presence was his courage, the rea-

son he was able to keep putting one foot in front of the other. (Book Seven, p. 700)

He glanced sideways, and his mother smiled at him, and his father nodded encouragement. (p. 701)

Here again the Harry Potter stories echo the gospel story, where we see one willingly facing death being encouraged by those who have already gone before.

It Was Not, After All, So Easy to Die

He had no strength left for a Patronus. He could no longer control his own trembling. It was not, after all, so easy to die. Every second he breathed, the smell of the grass, the cool air on his face, was so precious: To think that people had years and years, time to waste, so much time it dragged, and he was clinging to each second. At the same time he thought that he would not be able to go on, and knew that he must.

—Book Seven, p. 697–98

Although a wizard, Harry Potter is fully human. Though he is brave, self-sacrificing, loving, and kind, Harry experiences tremendous fear as he moves toward his impending death. I found myself feeling very close to Harry as he faced the reality that he must choose to die as it was prophesied. With each step Harry took away from the castle, away from his loved ones, away from his friends, away from the smell of the grass and the cool air on his face, my heart raced with his. As he realized that his "cold-blooded walk to his own destruction would require a different kind of bravery" (p. 692), I came to appreciate one aspect of my Christian faith as never before.

I have been a Christian for many years and have read and heard the story of Christ's struggles in the garden of Gethsemane numerous times. However, I had not felt it so keenly as when I read it immediately after walking with Harry as he chose to allow Voldemort to kill him. Although Harry was certainly not sinless, as Jesus was, there are many similarities to their respective death marches.

Although Jesus was fully God, he was also fully human (which is hard to grasp, so we may minimize the agony he experienced as the time for his death arrived). Jesus came to earth knowing the plan, but being in human flesh, he found that it was not, after all, so easy to die.

Once Harry made up his mind that his death was the only way "to end it," he set his face toward the Forbidden Forest, where Voldemort was waiting. As the appointed time for his death approached, Jesus set his face to go to Jerusalem, even though he knew betrayal, arrest, and crucifixion awaited him there. Both were dying to save those they loved and to stop an evil foe. Both feared death and felt deep trepidation as the actual time of death approached. Here is Matthew's account of Jesus' approach to death:

> Jesus went with his disciples to a place called Gethsemane, and he said to them, "Sit here while I go over there and pray." He took Peter and the two sons of Zebedee along with him, and he began to be sorrowful and troubled. Then he said to them, "My soul is overwhelmed with sorrow to the point of death. Stay here and keep watch with me."
> Going a little farther, he fell with his face to the ground and prayed, "My Father, if it is possible, may this cup be taken from me. Yet not as I will, but as you will." (Matt. 26:36–39 NIV)

Luke's Gospel records even more details of the tremendous suffering Christ experienced as he faced death:

> Jesus went out as usual to the Mount of Olives, and his disciples followed him. On reaching the place, he said to them, "Pray that you will not fall into temptation." He withdrew about a stone's throw beyond them, knelt down and prayed, "Father, if you are willing, take this cup from me; yet not my will, but yours be done." An angel from heaven appeared to him and strengthened him. And being in anguish, he prayed

more earnestly, and his sweat was like drops of blood falling
to the ground. (Luke 22:39–44 NIV)

Anyone who loves Harry and has experienced his walk to his
appointed death knows something of the poignancy of Jesus' time
in the garden of Gethsemane preceding his death even if they have
not yet read the account in the Gospels.

I Didn't Defend Myself!
I Meant to Let Him Kill Me!

"Then . . . I'm dead too?"

*"Ah," said Dumbledore, smiling still more broadly.
"That is the question, isn't it? On the whole, dear boy, I
think not."*

They looked at each other, the old man still beaming.

"Not?" repeated Harry.

"Not," said Dumbledore.

*"But . . ." Harry raised his hand instinctively toward
the lightning scar. It did not seem to be there. "But I
should have died—I didn't defend myself! I meant to let
him kill me!"*

*"And that," said Dumbledore, "will, I think, have made
all the difference."*

*Happiness seemed to radiate from Dumbledore like
light, like fire: Harry had never seen the man so utterly, so
palpably content.*

—Book Seven, pp. 707–8

*H*arry understood that in order for the Horcrux within him to be
destroyed, thus enabling Voldemort's destruction, he would have
to die willingly and without putting up a fight. That's why he put
his wand beneath his robes where he could not reach it. This was
essential.

Likewise, in order for the death of Jesus of Nazareth to have qual-
ified as substitutionary, he would have had to go without argument
and without putting up a fight. His disciples didn't understand this,
though, and Peter drew his sword to fight:

> "Put your sword back in its place," Jesus said to him, "for all
> who draw the sword will die by the sword. Do you think I
> cannot call on my Father, and he will at once put at my dis-
> posal more than twelve legions of angels? But how then
> would the Scriptures be fulfilled that say it must happen in
> this way?" (Matt. 26:52–54 NIV)

Harry had his wand, with which he might have attempted to fight
back; Jesus had access to legions of angelic warriors. Neither chose
to use the power available to them. Jesus explained that this was necessary to fulfill the Scriptures. One of these prophecies had been
penned by Isaiah hundreds of years before his birth. This aspect of
the story was used to convert an Ethiopian official shortly after
Jesus' death. Philip, one of Jesus' disciples, was led by the Spirit of
God to go to a particular street where he would be shown what to do.
Philip went there and heard a man reading aloud from Isaiah while
in his chariot. Philip ran up to the man and struck up a conversation:

> "Do you understand what you are reading?" Philip asked.
>   "How can I," he said, "unless someone explains it to me?"
> So he invited Philip to come up and sit with him.
>   The eunuch was reading this passage of Scripture:
>   "He was led like a sheep to the slaughter,
>   and as a lamb before the shearer is silent,
>   so he did not open his mouth.
>   In his humiliation he was deprived of justice.
>   Who can speak of his descendants?
>   For his life was taken from the earth."
>   The eunuch asked Philip, "Tell me, please, who is the
> prophet talking about, himself or someone else?" Then Philip
> began with that very passage of Scripture and told him the
> good news about Jesus. (Acts 8:30–35 NIV)

In order for the prophecies to be fulfilled, Jesus had to go to his death willingly, without complaint, without putting up a fight, without opening his mouth. He was the human-divine embodiment of the Passover Lamb. The good news Philip shared with the man in the chariot that day is that because Jesus didn't defend himself and meant to let the Roman authorities kill him, his death could be reversed with resurrection and that same death held in account to pay for the sins of those who would place their trust in him as their Savior, thus netting them eternal life too. In Harry's story, because he meant to let Voldemort kill him, because he chose to lay down his life for his friends and did not defend himself, the death curse was reversed in his case too. Once again, Harry became the Boy Who Lived!

The Power in the Blood

He took your blood believing it would strengthen him. He took into his body a tiny part of the enchantment your mother laid upon you when she died for you. His body keeps her sacrifice alive, and while that enchantment survives, so do you and so does Voldemort's one last hope for himself.
—Book Seven, Dumbledore to Harry, p. 710

*T*here were hints about the power of Harry's blood going back to Book Six when he and Dumbledore were in the cave that required blood as payment. After Harry offered his blood,

Dumbledore merely smiled. There was a flash of silver and a spurt of scarlet; the rock face was peppered with dark glistening drops.
"You are very kind Harry. . . . But your blood is worth more than mine." (Book Six, p. 560).

As it turns out, Harry's blood wasn't the source of the value. The value came from Lily's sacrifice. Much later, at King's Cross,

Dumbledore explained the power and value of Harry's blood when Harry questioned him further:

> "But if Voldemort used the Killing Curse," Harry started again, "and nobody died for me this time—how can I be alive?"
>
> "I think you know," said Dumbledore. "Think back. Remember what he did, in his ignorance, in his greed and his cruelty."
>
> Harry thought. He let his gaze drift. . . .
>
> "He took my blood," said Harry.
>
> "Precisely!" said Dumbledore. "He took your blood and rebuilt his living body with it! Your blood is in his veins, Harry, Lily's protection inside both of you! He tethered you to life while he lives!" (Book Seven, pp. 708–9)

The blood that ran in Harry's veins, which was stolen by Voldemort to rebuild his body at the end of Book Four, tethered him to life because it held the power of life granted back when Lily died in Harry's place.

The Bible stresses the importance of blood throughout the Old and New Testaments. Humanity had a problem; all had sinned and fallen short of God's commands for righteousness. In the Old Testament, people were allowed to use the blood of animals to cover their sins temporarily, shielding them from God's wrath against sin from year to year through animal sacrifices. The New Testament states that "the wages of sin is death" (Rom. 6:23) and that "without the shedding of blood there is no forgiveness" (Heb. 9:22). So the power in the blood of Jesus was twofold: it provided forgiveness through paying for our sins, and it tethered us to eternal life, for when our sins are forgiven the death sentence that should be carried out against us when we die is lifted, because Jesus shed his blood on the cross to die in our place.

The blood of Lily Potter had power to protect Harry from death, but she had to stay dead. However, since Jesus was perfect and sinless, the death sentence could not hold against him, so death could not hold him; that is why he rose from the dead. The blood of Jesus Christ was accepted as payment for the sins of any who would believe in Jesus' blood and its power. Those who believe receive imparted righteousness and therefore the forgiveness of sins that leads to eternal life after death:

> This righteousness from God comes through faith in Jesus Christ to all who believe. There is no difference, for all have sinned and fall short of the glory of God, and are justified freely by his grace through the redemption that came by Christ Jesus. God presented him as a sacrifice of atonement, through faith in his blood. (Rom. 3:22–25 NIV)

Harry was tethered to life because the blood of the one who gave her life for him continued to flow in a living person. Those who believe in Jesus and the power of his blood are tethered to life eternally because Jesus rose from the dead never to die again. As long as he lives we will live also, and he will live forever because he never sinned. We will live forever because his blood was shed for the forgiveness of our sins, and because his life goes on eternally. That is power in the blood.

Going Back or Going On

The realization of what would happen next settled gradually over Harry in the long minutes, like softly falling snow.

"I've got to go back, haven't I?"

"That is up to you."

"I've got a choice?"

"Oh yes." Dumbledore smiled at him. "We are in King's Cross, you say? I think that if you decided not to go back, you would be able to . . . let's say . . . board a train."

"And where would it take me?"

"On," said Dumbledore simply.

> *Silence again.*
> *"Voldemort's got the Elder Wand."*
> *"True. Voldemort has the Elder Wand."*
> *"But you want me to go back?"*
> *"I think," said Dumbledore, "that if you choose to return, there is a chance that he may be finished for good. I cannot promise it. But I know this, Harry, that you have less to fear from returning here than he does."*
> —Book Seven, p. 722

*T*his episode, with Harry hanging between life and death after Voldemort tried to execute him, presented Harry with a choice. He could have gone back to continue the fight against evil, or he could have gone on. He was persuaded to go back because he had a chance of putting an end to Voldemort for good.

There is a similar situation alluded to in the New Testament. After Saul of Tarsus had been actively persecuting the early followers of Jesus, he experienced a dramatic conversion and began preaching that Jesus was the true Messiah. This brought the fury of Christ's opponents down on him. He was stoned—apparently to death— dragged outside the city of Lystra and left for dead (see Acts 14:8–18). However, something was going on that was not immediately apparent to those who stood around his body. It bears striking similarities to what happened with Harry after he was hit with Voldemort's killing curse in the forest.

Saul, who became known as the apostle Paul wrote about this in a letter to the Corinthian church in which he mentions "a man in Christ" who is actually Paul himself:

> I must go on boasting. Although there is nothing to be gained, I will go on to visions and revelations from the Lord. I know a man in Christ who fourteen years ago was caught up to the third heaven. Whether it was in the body or out of the body I do not know—God knows. And I know that this man— whether in the body or apart from the body I do not know, but

God knows—was caught up to paradise. He heard inexpress-
ible things, things that man is not permitted to tell. (2 Cor.
12:1–5 NIV)

Like Harry, Paul wasn't sure whether this was "in his head" or
not, but he knew it was real. Since Paul can't tell us about what he
heard during his episode, we look elsewhere to see what may have
motivated his continued fight against evil after he came back,
apparently, from the dead. Paul got up after being stoned in Lystra
and continued his ministry, living to be executed on account of his
faith in Jesus many years later in Rome. While facing execution at
that time, Paul was not afraid of death. Rather, he anticipated that
he had longer to live because his work was not finished. To the
church in Philippi, Paul wrote:

I eagerly expect and hope that I will in no way be ashamed,
but will have sufficient courage so that now as always Christ
will be exalted in my body, whether by life or by death. For
to me, to live is Christ and to die is gain. If I am to go on living in the body, this will mean fruitful labor for me. Yet what
shall I choose? I do not know! I am torn between the two: I
desire to depart and be with Christ, which is better by far; but
it is more necessary for you that I remain in the body. Convinced of this, I know that I will remain, and I will continue
with all of you for your progress and joy in the faith. (Phil.
1:20–25 NIV)

Harry was persuaded by Dumbledore to return to the battle
because by returning he might ensure that fewer souls would be
maimed, fewer families torn apart (see p. 722). That seemed to him
a worthy goal. The apostle Paul was also given a choice; because
he found it necessary for the living that he remain with them, that
was the choice he made as well. When the time did come for Paul
to "go on" he faced that with courage and anticipation of life after
death.

I'll Join You When Hell Freezes Over

*"You show spirit and bravery, and you come of noble
stock. You will make a very valuable Death Eater. We need
your kind, Neville Longbottom."*

*"I'll join you when hell freezes over," said Neville.
"Dumbledore's Army!" he shouted, and there was an
answering cheer from the crowd, whom Voldemort's
Silencing Charms seemed unable to hold.*

—Book Seven, p. 731

*N*eville didn't start out as the bravest kid in Gryffindor, but he
grew in courage. After being trained in Dumbledore's Army and
determined to resist Voldemort at all costs, Neville ended up defy-
ing the opposition and leading the charge after it appeared Harry
was dead.

The New Testament Letter of James says, "Submit yourselves,
then, to God. Resist the devil, and he will flee from you" (Jas. 4:7
NIV). Neville's stance is a great example of resisting evil. As he had
explained earlier, "It helps to stand up to them."

Neville's transformation from one who was easily intimidated
to one who dared to lead the opposition against Voldemort could
be likened easily to the transformation that took place in Simon
Peter, who denied Christ on the night of his arrest but, after Jesus'
death and resurrection, boldly led the disciples against Jesus'
opponents. Shortly after Christ's resurrection and ascension back
into heaven, Peter and John took the lead among the Christ-fol-
lowers. God empowered them to heal a man who had been unable
to walk from birth. They proclaimed that their power had come
from the risen Jesus, so they were arrested and taken before the
authorities:

When [the authorities] saw the courage of Peter and John and
realized that they were unschooled, ordinary men, they were

astonished and they took note that these men had been with Jesus. But since they could see the man who had been healed standing there with them, there was nothing they could say. So they ordered them to withdraw from the Sanhedrin and then conferred together. "What are we going to do with these men?" they asked. "Everybody living in Jerusalem knows they have done an outstanding miracle, and we cannot deny it. But to stop this thing from spreading any further among the people, we must warn these men to speak no longer to anyone in this name."

Then they called them in again and commanded them not to speak or teach at all in the name of Jesus. But Peter and John replied, "Judge for yourselves whether it is right in God's sight to obey you rather than God. For we cannot help speaking about what we have seen and heard."

After further threats they let them go. (Acts 4:13–21 NIV)

The authorities who had fought against Jesus and his disciples were beginning to lose their power. The tide had turned; those who were previously running scared were now standing their ground. The least likely became the most courageous leaders. Likewise, in the Harry Potter stories it was the least likely members of the D.A.—Neville, Luna, and Ginny—who ended up standing their ground in the face of evil.

Neville Aflame and the Power of Pentecost

He pointed his wand at Neville, who grew rigid and still, then forced the hat onto Neville's head, so that it slipped down below his eyes. There were movements from the watching crowd in front of the castle, and as one, the Death Eaters raised their wands, holding the fighters of Hogwarts at bay.

"Neville here is now going to demonstrate what happens

pens to anyone foolish enough to continue to oppose me,"
said Voldemort, and with a flick of his wand, he caused the
Sorting Hat to burst into flames.

Screams split the dawn, and Neville was aflame, rooted
to the spot, unable to move, and Harry could not bear it:
He must act—

And then many things happened at the same moment.

—Book Seven, p. 732

*J*ust a few weeks after *Harry Potter and the Deathly Hallows* was released, I spoke at *Prophecy 2007,* a Harry Potter symposium that was held in Toronto. I also moderated a group discussion on *The Gospel according to Harry Potter and the Deathly Hallows.* One of the participants in that discussion suggested this parallel.[10] After Harry had been hit with the Killing Curse and had returned from King's Cross, this scene occurred in which Neville had flames atop his head but was not burned. This became a turning point in the story when Harry revealed himself as risen and the power of the opposition was shaken.

The appearance of fire above someone's head holds significant meaning in the New Testament. When John the Baptist had come preparing the way for Jesus' ministry he told people, "I baptize you with water for repentance. But after me will come one who is more powerful than I, whose sandals I am not fit to carry. He will baptize you with the Holy Spirit and with fire" (Matt. 3:11 NIV).

After Jesus had risen from the dead, he told his disciples, "Do not leave Jerusalem, but wait for the gift my Father promised, which you have heard me speak about. For John baptized with water, but in a few days you will be baptized with the Holy Spirit" (Acts 1:4–5). After saying this, Jesus ascended into heaven and the disciples waited.

When the day of Pentecost came, they were all together in one place. Suddenly a sound like the blowing of a violent wind came from heaven and filled the whole house where they were sitting. They saw what seemed to be tongues of fire that separated and came to rest on each of them. All of them were filled with the Holy Spirit and began to speak in other tongues as the Spirit enabled them. (Acts 2:1–4 NIV)

This moment when fire appeared above the heads of the disciples signaled the coming of the power God had promised those who stood with Jesus. The disciples were enabled to speak in languages they had not learned, drawing a multiethnic crowd of people of many tongues who were visiting Jerusalem for a major religious holiday. When that crowd assembled, it was Peter (the former coward) who stood up after the fire had appeared above his head to forcefully challenge those who had crucified Jesus and continued to oppose him. Peter's standing up to the opposition, empowered after his baptism of fire, marked the moment when the battle turned in favor of Jesus' disciples. That day Peter boldly proclaimed the power of Jesus, and about three thousand people believed and joined the disciples.

So when Neville stood up to Voldemort with fire above his head, this marked a "Pentecostal moment" when the battle turned in favor of those on the good side. That was also when Neville was able to pull the sword of Gryffindor out of the hat and Harry revealed himself. At that moment the fighters were greatly encouraged. The balance of power had turned, and they were set for the final battle.

The Sword of Gryffindor Destroys the Snake

Harry pulled the Invisibility Cloak from inside his robes, swung it over himself, and sprang to his feet, as Neville moved too.

In one swift, fluid motion, Neville broke free of the Body-Bind Curse upon him; the flaming hat fell off him and he drew from its depths something silver, with a glittering, rubied handle—

The slash of the silver blade could not be heard over the roar of the oncoming crowd or the sounds of the clashing giants or of the stampeding centaurs, and yet it seemed to draw every eye. With a single stroke Neville sliced off the great snake's head, which spun high into the air, gleaming in the light flooding from the entrance hall, and Voldemort's mouth was open in a scream of fury that nobody could hear, and the snake's body thudded to the ground at his feet—

Hidden beneath the Invisibility Cloak, Harry cast a Shield Charm between Neville and Voldemort before the latter could raise his wand.

—Book Seven, p. 733

*T*he Sorting Hat, which Voldemort had set aflame on Neville's head, did not destroy him. Instead, Neville—who had proved to be a true Gryffindor—pulled the sword of Godric Gryffindor out of the hat. Just as Harry used the sword of Gryffindor to slay the basilisk in the Chamber of Secrets, Neville used it to behead Nagini and destroy the final Horcrux. So that which had appeared as a "great silver cross" when hidden in the forest pool destroyed the snake that embodied Voldemort's final protection.

Likewise, the cross on which Jesus died was not the death of him, but the means of destroying Satan's plan to rule and oppress the world. Look how Peter used the cross as he stood up to his opposition on that day of Pentecost:

"Everyone who calls on the name of the Lord will be saved.

Men of Israel, listen to this: Jesus of Nazareth was a man accredited by God to you by miracles, wonders and signs, which God did among you through him, as you yourselves know. This man was handed over to you by God's set purpose and foreknowledge; and you, with the help of wicked men, put him to death by nailing him to the cross. But God raised him from the dead, freeing him from the agony of death, because it was impossible for death to keep its hold on him." (Acts 2:21–25 NIV)

All it took was a transformed coward with the power of the cross—someone like a Neville Longbottom or a Simon Peter—who dared to wield the cross and declare its power to turn the tables in favor of the good side. In the Harry Potter stories, once Neville had destroyed the final Horcrux, it was time for Harry to finally take care of Voldemort.

He's Alive!

> "Protego!" roared Harry, and the Shield Charm expanded in the middle of the Hall, and Voldemort stared around for the source as Harry pulled off the Invisibility Cloak at last.
> The yell of shock, the cheers, the screams on every side of "Harry!" "HE'S ALIVE!" were stifled at once. The crowd was afraid, and silence fell abruptly and completely as Voldemort and Harry looked at each other, and began at the same moment to circle each other.
> —Book Seven, p. 737

Harry Potter was famous for being "the Boy Who Lived" since the first page of the series; in Book Seven he became the boy who lived again. The excitement of the joyous moment when Harry returned alive after everyone thought he was dead was captured in the shouts of his friends and admirers.

The parallel to the story of Jesus Christ's dying and rising from the dead to the joyous amazement of his friends and disciples is obvious. The difference is that Jesus was confirmed dead with more than the kind of unsubstantiated check Narcissa Malfoy made of

Harry's body, even though her nails pierced him (which might remind some of very different nails that pierced Jesus). As with Harry, Jesus' slayers wanted to make sure he was dead. Since the executioners were in a hurry to get done early since it was the Passover holiday, they were about to break the legs of all three men being crucified on the hill that day to hasten their deaths. They broke the legs of both men on either side of Jesus, but when they came to Jesus he appeared dead. To make sure, one of the Roman soldiers pierced his heart with a long spear. Out of the wound flowed a substance that appeared as blood and water. This showed that the blood had separated and that Jesus was truly dead. So they didn't break his legs (they were unaware that this fulfilled a prophecy that said the Messiah would have no bones broken – see Ps. 34:20 and John 19:36). After he was proven to be dead, Jesus was buried. The tomb was sealed with a heavy stone and the official seal of Rome, which threatened prosecution of anyone who tried to steal the body or pretend Jesus had risen from the dead, as he predicted before his death. If that weren't enough, a group of soldiers was stationed outside the tomb to make sure Jesus' body did not get away.

After all of that, it's little wonder that even Jesus' disciples didn't expect him to appear alive from the dead. Mary Magdalene reported seeing Jesus outside the tomb, but the disciples didn't believe her. Then two disciples who had given up and were leaving Jerusalem for their hometown of Emmaus spent a long walk talking with a man they didn't recognize who turned out to be Jesus. J. K. Rowling has said Caravaggio's Supper at Emmaus, a painting of the moment Jesus was recognized by these two disciples is perhaps her favorite.[11] Here is that moment, as described by Luke:

> When he was at the table with them, he took bread, gave thanks, broke it and began to give it to them. Then their eyes were opened and they recognized him, and he disappeared from their sight. They asked each other, "Were not our hearts burning within us while he talked with us on the road and opened the Scriptures to us?"
> They got up and returned at once to Jerusalem. There they

found the Eleven and those with them, assembled together and saying, "It is true! The Lord has risen and has appeared to Simon." Then the two told what had happened on the way, and how Jesus was recognized by them when he broke the bread.

While they were still talking about this, Jesus himself stood among them and said to them, "Peace be with you."

They were startled and frightened, thinking they saw a ghost. He said to them, "Why are you troubled, and why do doubts rise in your minds? Look at my hands and my feet. It is I myself! Touch me and see; a ghost does not have flesh and bones, as you see I have."

When he had said this, he showed them his hands and feet. And while they still did not believe it because of joy and amazement, he asked them, "Do you have anything here to eat?" They gave him a piece of broiled fish, and he took it and ate it in their presence.

He said to them, "This is what I told you while I was still with you: Everything must be fulfilled that is written about me in the Law of Moses, the Prophets and the Psalms."

Then he opened their minds so they could understand the Scriptures. He told them, "This is what is written: The Christ will suffer and rise from the dead on the third day, and repentance and forgiveness of sins will be preached in his name to all nations, beginning at Jerusalem. You are witnesses of these things. I am going to send you what my Father has promised; but stay in the city until you have been clothed with power from on high."

When he had led them out to the vicinity of Bethany, he lifted up his hands and blessed them. While he was blessing them, he left them and was taken up into heaven. Then they worshiped him and returned to Jerusalem with great joy. And they stayed continually at the temple, praising God. (Luke 24:30–49 NIV)

The similarities between Harry's return from "King's Cross" after being hit with the Killing Curse and Jesus' resurrection, along with the joy and amazement of startled friends, are clear enough to make this a very "Christian" ending to the story. Even though Harry is not the perfect sinless sacrifice for all humanity that Jesus was, the Christian influence in the climactic moment of the final book is unmistakable. And from the way Jesus appeared and disappeared at will, the idea of an Invisibility Cloak doesn't seem so farfetched either.

Try for a Little Remorse

"Before you try to kill me, I'd advise you to think about what you've done. . . . Think, and try for some remorse, Riddle. . . ."

Of all the things Harry had said to him, beyond any revelation or taunt, nothing had shocked Voldemort like this. . . .

"It's your one last chance," said Harry, "it's all you've got left. . . . I've seen what you'll be otherwise. . . . Be a man . . . try . . . Try for some remorse."

—Book Seven, p. 741

*H*arry understood that the only possible remedy for Voldemort to undo the damage he had done to his soul through making Horcruxes was remorse. This is in keeping with the teaching from 2 Corinthians that "godly sorrow brings repentance that leads to salvation and leaves no regret, but worldly sorrow brings death" (7:10 NIV).

Harry and Ron didn't learn this from the Bible, but from Hermione as she explained the only remedy for a Horcrux:

"Isn't there any way of putting yourself back together?" Ron asked.

"Yes," said Hermione with a hollow smile, "but it would be excruciatingly painful."

"Why? How do you do it?" asked Harry.

"Remorse," said Hermione. "You've got to really feel what you've done. There's a footnote. Apparently the pain of it can destroy you. I can't see Voldemort attempting it some-how, can you?" (Book Seven, p. 103)

Voldemort's refusal to try for some remorse stands in stark con-trast to Dumbledore. Albus Dumbledore showed remorse for his youthful error of putting his selfish dreams above the needs of his family, an error that had deadly results. He wept over having been a partner in evil plans to force Muggles into subservience with Grindelwald, and he demonstrated his remorse by spending his adult life working to protect the rights of Muggles and others who were in danger of oppression. Dumbledore felt the pain, and Harry was allowed to see it when he met up with him at King's Cross.

At first, I found Dumbledore's remorse a bit troubling, given that it was expressed in the afterlife. The book of Revelation says that the afterlife will be marked by an absence of tears and pain: "They will be his people, and God himself will be with them and be their God. He will wipe every tear from their eyes. There will be no more death or mourning or crying or pain, for the old order of things has passed away" (Rev. 21:3–4 NIV).

On October 15, 2007, I had the privilege of attending a press conference with J. K. Rowling in Los Angeles. Given the oppor-tunity to ask only one question, mine addressed this issue. I wanted to know if this display of remorse after his death indi-cated that Dumbledore was not going to rest in peace during eter-nity. She assured me—and anyone else troubled by this—that Dumbledore's emotional display of grief was not meant to indi-cate the quality of Dumbledore's experience in the afterlife. Rather, it was important for Harry to see his mentor's admissions of human frailty attended with remorse. Harry had put Dumble-dore on a pedestal; in order to become a man, Harry had to under-stand Dumbledore as someone who made mistakes but who—unlike Voldemort—was man enough to feel and express remorse.

What Became of Voldemort's Soul?

[Harry] recoiled. He had spotted the thing that was mak-
ing the noise. It had the form of a small, naked child,
curled on the ground, its skin raw and rough, flayed-
looking, and it lay shuddering under a seat where it had
been left, unwanted, stuffed out of sight, struggling for
breath.

He was afraid of it. Small and fragile and wounded
though it was, he did not want to approach it. . . .

Harry glanced over his shoulder to where the small,
maimed creature trembled under the chair.

"What is that, Professor?"

"Something that is beyond either of our help," said
Dumbledore. . . .

He was distracted by the whimpering and thumping of
the agonized creature behind them and glanced back at it
yet again.

"Are you sure we can't do anything?"

"There is no help possible."

—Book Seven, pp. 706–9

*W*hen Harry said he had seen what Riddle would become otherwise, he was referring to the condition in which he had seen the
fragment of Voldemort's soul, which he and Dumbledore were
unable to rescue at King's Cross after Harry had been hit with the
Killing Curse.

Harry tried to help even his greatest enemy. Harry showed
pity. Perhaps he had taken Dumbledore's words to heart: "Do not
pity the dead, Harry. Pity the living, and, above all, those who
live without love. By returning you may ensure that fewer souls
are maimed, fewer families are torn apart. If that seems to you a
worthy goal, then we say good-bye for the present" (Book Seven,
p. 722).

As long as Tom Riddle was alive, Harry had pity for him. Harry
knew that Voldemort lived without love. Because Voldemort had
no love, he felt no remorse for the terrible suffering he had caused

or would cause to others. Surely few readers were surprised when Voldemort refused his last chance.

Those who know the Bible could have predicted that Voldemort would lose both his life and his own soul in the end on the basis of a teaching of Jesus: "For whoever wants to save his life will lose it, but whoever loses his life for me and for the gospel will save it. What good is it for a man to gain the whole world, yet forfeit his soul? Or what can a man give in exchange for his soul?" (Mark 8:35–37 NIV)

From the start of the series, the story has been driven by Voldemort's self-centered attempt to save his own life at the expense of the lives of others. He had exchanged his soul for his own attempt at immortality. It was clear that if the story line followed a biblical pattern, Voldemort would end up losing his own life and his soul.

In contrast, we see that both Dumbledore and Harry valued their souls more than their lives. Both of them were willing to lose their lives to save others, so it is also not surprising that they did not lose their lives or their souls. We see Dumbledore alive after his death in another dimension (although it's only in Harry's head—but why should we think that isn't real?) and carrying on his influence through his portrait at Hogwarts. We see Harry alive in this world. So Voldemort, who sought to save his life, did lose it, and those who lost their lives for others ended up saving them, in keeping with the Bible's teaching.

So, It All Comes Down to This

"So it all comes down to this, doesn't it?" whispered Harry. "Does the wand in your hand know its last master was Disarmed? Because if it does . . . I am the true master of the Elder Wand."

—Book Seven, p. 743

*I*n the final battle between Harry and Voldemort, the outcome was determined by a matter of whose authority trumped the other's. Voldemort thought he had authority over the Elder Wand because he had killed Snape, who had killed the wand's previous owner, Dumbledore. Actually the wand's allegiance was transferred to the one who *disarmed* the previous owner. So, since Draco Malfoy—not Snape—disarmed Dumbledore against his will, Draco unwittingly became the master of the Elder Wand. But Draco never realized this authority, and never used it. When Harry disarmed Draco of his wand against his will by triumphing over him, Draco's wand turned its allegiance to Harry. In the final battle Harry ended up holding Draco's wand, which had been used to disarm Dumbledore of the Elder Wand, so the authority over the Elder Wand transferred to Harry. When it came time to cast the spells that would decide the battle,

> a red-gold glow burst suddenly across the enchanted sky about them as an edge of the dazzling sun appeared over the sill of the nearest window. The light hit both of their faces at the same time, so that Voldemort's was suddenly a flaming blur. Harry heard the high voice shriek as he too yelled his best hope to the heavens, pointing Draco's wand:
> "Avada Kedavra!"
> "Expelliarmus!"
> The bang was like a cannon blast, and the golden flames that erupted between them, at the dead center of the circle they had been treading, marked the point where the spells collided. Harry saw Voldemort's green jet meet his own spell, saw the Elder Wand fly high, dark against the sunrise, spinning across the enchanted ceiling like the head of Nagini, spinning through the air toward the master it would not kill, who had come to take full possession of it at last. (pp. 743–44)

The author is careful to affiliate Voldemort with the snake in this final scene, which links him one more time to the character of Satan in the Bible. Harry did not use the Killing Curse; he trusted in the authority he had through the wand lore he had learned, trusted that because he had disarmed Draco he had in effect disarmed the powers and authority Voldemort thought he had with the Elder Wand. Harry was right; because of his authority over Voldemort's wand, Voldemort's spell rebounded on him once again, only this time he had no more Horcruxes to protect him.

This understanding of authority is central to the work of Jesus Christ and his disciples. Jesus had authority over demonic spirits, and he conveyed his power to cast out demons and heal the sick to seventy-two of his disciples, who were then able to exercise that authority miraculously as they went out to spread Jesus' message that the kingdom of God had come near. Upon returning,

> The seventy-two returned with joy and said, "Lord, even the demons submit to us in your name."
> He replied, "I saw Satan fall like lightning from heaven. I have given you authority to trample on snakes and scorpions and to overcome all the power of the enemy; nothing will harm you. However, do not rejoice that the spirits submit to you, but rejoice that your names are written in heaven." (Luke 10:17–20 NIV)

So Jesus started out with significant authority over the evil one. His mission at the cross was to disarm him. When Jesus died on the cross, Satan probably thought he had defeated him, not realizing that if Jesus died as a sinless man and as a voluntary self-sacrifice, his death would be available for transfer to anyone who trusted in him for salvation. Since death is the rightful wages of sin (Rom. 6:23), by taking away the sins of the world, Jesus effectively removed the power Satan had over the human race. The Letter to the Colossians describes what Jesus did: "And having disarmed the powers and authorities, he made a public spectacle of them, triumphing over them by the cross" (Col. 2:15).

Jesus himself spoke of the centrality of his authority to his victory at the cross:

> "The reason my Father loves me is that I lay down my life—only to take it up again. No one takes it from me, but I lay it

down of my own accord. I have authority to lay it down and authority to take it up again. This command I received from my Father." (John 10:17–18 NIV)

In a prayer Jesus prayed shortly before his death, he was already trusting in his authority to accomplish the purpose of the cross: to defeat the one who comes only to kill, steal, and destroy, and to offer eternal life to all those the evil one would have killed if he had had the authority:

> "Father, the time has come. Glorify your Son, that your Son may glorify you. For you granted him authority over all people that he might give eternal life to all those you have given him. Now this is eternal life: that they may know you, the only true God, and Jesus Christ, whom you have sent. I have brought you glory on earth by completing the work you gave me to do. And now, Father, glorify me in your presence with the glory I had with you before the world began." (John 17:1–5 NIV)

When Harry faced his climactic battle with Voldemort, he put his confidence in the authority he had as the true master of the Elder Wand. When Jesus faced his showdown with the devil at the cross, he trusted in the authority his Father in heaven had given him. Just as Harry's triumph over Voldemort was glorious (with the sun bursting through at the appropriate moment), even more so Jesus' triumph over Satan and death was glorious when he rose from the dead as the sun rose on the third day. This proved that Jesus truly had the rightful authority to defeat the devil; thus he won the victory over death (the last enemy to be defeated).

It Is Finished

One shivering second of silence, the shock of the moment suspended: and then the tumult broke around Harry as the screams and the cheers and the roars of watchers rent the air. The fierce new sun dazzled the windows. . . . Harry could not hear a word that anyone was shouting, nor tell whose hands were seizing him, pulling him, trying to hug some part of him, hundreds of them pressing in, all of them determined to touch the Boy Who Lived, the reason it was over at last—

. . . They wanted him there with them, their leader and symbol, their savior and their guide. . . . He must speak to the bereaved, clasp their hands, witness their tears, receive their thanks, hear the news now creeping in from every quarter as the morning drew on; that the Imperiused up and down the country had come back to themselves, that Death Eaters were fleeing or else being captured, that the innocent of Azkaban were being released at that very moment, and that Kingsley Shacklebolt had been named temporary Minister of Magic.

—Book Seven, pp. 744–45

*T*he battle is over at last. It is finished. All the schemes of the evil one have been thwarted. Love has conquered death. Self-sacrifice has triumphed over selfish cruelty. As a result of Harry's triumph over Voldemort, the power of darkness has lost its hold. That's why justice had come to Azkaban, the captives were being released, and those who had been in darkness while under the Imperius Curse were coming back to the light of reason—all of this as the sun broke through the darkness.

When Jesus first began his ministry, he announced that he was the fulfillment of a prophecy from Isaiah penned hundreds of years before:

> The Spirit of the Sovereign LORD is on me,
>   because the LORD has anointed me
>   to preach good news to the poor.
> He has sent me to bind up the brokenhearted,
>   to proclaim freedom for the captives
>   and release from darkness for the prisoners,
> to proclaim the year of the LORD's favor

> and the day of vengeance of our God,
> to comfort all who mourn,
>   and provide for those who grieve in Zion—
> to bestow on them a crown of beauty
>   instead of ashes,
> the oil of gladness
>   instead of mourning,
> and a garment of praise
>   instead of a spirit of despair.
> They will be called oaks of righteousness,
>   a planting of the LORD
>   for the display of his splendor.
>
>   (Isa. 61:1–3 NIV)

During his earthly life, Jesus sought to bring good news to the poor, comfort the brokenhearted, offer freedom to those held captive by sin and disease, and to bring light to the blind (whether physically or spiritually). He came to upset the oppression of evil tyrants and to free those who were overwhelmed by life's suffering. When Jesus completed his life's mission by sacrificing himself on the cross, he said, "It is finished." He had done what he had come to do. At the end of the Harry Potter stories, after Voldemort has been defeated, we see a similar effect. The end of the reign of evil makes way for a new day where there is freedom for the captives, justice for the oppressed, praise, and celebration.

Applause from Above

But it was applause. All around the walls, the headmasters and headmistresses of Hogwarts were giving him a standing ovation; they waved their hats and in some cases their wigs, they reached through their frames to grip each other's hands; they danced up and down on the chairs in which they

had been painted; Dilys Derwent sobbed unashamedly;
Dexter Fortescue was waving his ear-trumpet. . . .

—Book Seven, p. 747

*H*arry and his friends always had an audience made up of those who had gone before them. The former headmasters of Hogwarts, whose portraits gave them a window into the living world, were a reminder that those who had lived before them were watching, bearing witness to the heritage from which Hogwarts, and all that was taught there, had grown. Harry had also discovered another tier to that audience when he realized that his mother, father, Sirius, and Lupin—though dead—were aware of what was happening in his life. Their encouragement had strengthened him for the final battle against Voldemort.

The Bible indicates that we too have an audience from history and heaven. The entire eleventh chapter of the Letter to the Hebrews recounts the triumphs of those who have gone before us, whose faith in God brought about heroic feats. Then it says, "Therefore, since we are surrounded by such a great cloud of witnesses, let us throw off everything that hinders and the sin that so easily entangles, and let us run with perseverance the race marked out for us" (Heb. 12:1 NIV).

Those who trust God can take strength from those whose faith carried them through all manner of difficulties. They have "gone on," but they are not gone from us entirely. The imagery used in this verse from Hebrews evokes the idea of a stadium full of people assembled to watch a contest or race. Those in the audience are the people of faith who have lived before us. Therefore, as a runner in the Olympics would take off his outer garments so that he might run his race without hindrance, we who are living today are to get rid of every sinful habit that might slow us down in completing our race of life. Knowing that our life's races, our life's battles, take place before an interested audience of those who have gone before should encourage us. Surely Harry felt encouraged by the reception he received from his circle of cheering witnesses in the headmaster's office, "but Harry had eyes only for the man who stood in the largest portrait directly behind the headmaster's chair. Tears were sliding down from behind the half-moon spectacles into the long silver beard, and the pride and the gratitude emanating from him filled Harry with the same balm as phoenix song (p. 747).

Likewise, Hebrews says that those who put their faith in Jesus are encouraged by all who have preceded us, but we should "only have eyes" for the one who stands above the rest. The passage goes on to say, "Let us fix our eyes on Jesus, the author and perfecter of our faith, who for the joy set before him endured the cross, scorning its shame, and sat down at the right hand of the throne of God. Consider him who endured such opposition from sinful men, so that you will not grow weary and lose heart" (Heb. 12:2–3 NIV).

Just as Harry and his friends found inspiration and strength to overcome their weariness from the battle by looking up to the portraits—with Harry fixing his eyes on Dumbledore, who was so proud of him—we can find strength by remembering that we too have a "great cloud of witnesses" watching us, from whom we can gain strength to go on to the final victory.

Let the Contribution of Slytherin House Not Be Forgotten

Phineas Nigellus called, in his high, reedy voice, "And let it be noted that Slytherin House played its part! Let our contribution not be forgotten."

—Book Seven, p. 747

Slytherin House helped significantly in the battle to defeat Voldemort. Professor Slughorn contributed the accurate memory of Tom Riddle's pursuit of the multiple Horcruxes. Regulus Black (R.A.B) came to his senses and gave his life in his attempt to destroy the Horcrux in the locket. Phineas Nigellus acted as messenger and reporter back and forth between his Hogwarts portrait and the one Hermione took with her while she, Harry, and Ron were on their quest to find the remaining Horcruxes. His reports back to Headmaster Snape allowed Snape to send his doe Patronus and the sword of Godric Gryffindor to Harry in the forest. Dobby had started out as a servant of a Slytherin family—albeit unwillingly—before he risked his life to warn Harry of the dangers that awaited him during his second year at Hogwarts. Kreacher also turned from his allegiance to those devoted to Slytherin to lead the charge of house-elves fighting against the Death Eaters and Voldemort at the Battle of Hogwarts. Let us not forget Severus Snape, head of Slytherin House, who subjugated his own loathing of Harry to the power of the love he held for Lily. Snape was essential to the final victory over Voldemort. So Phineas Nigellus was right: we should not forget the contribution of Slytherin House to the final victory.

This too has its parallel in the Bible. Many who end up on the list of the Bible's heroes spent much of their lives on the list of foes. For example, Paul the apostle, who penned most of the New Testament, had been Saul the proud Pharisee who opposed Jesus, persecuted the first believers in Jesus' resurrection, and acquired legal documents that allowed him to haul them off to prison, which he did with enthusiasm. After a dramatic conversion when the risen Jesus appeared to Saul on his way to arrest Jesus' followers, Saul became Paul the apostle.

A woman named Rahab had been a prostitute living in the walls of the ancient city of Jericho when spies from the army of the Hebrews came to scope out the city. She changed sides, helping the Hebrew spies evade capture. In return, she was granted her life and the lives of all who came under her protection. This same Rahab—former prostitute—was honored in the Gospel of Matthew as one of four women listed by name in the genealogy of the Messiah.

Finally, there were two men crucified on crosses next to Jesus, thieves deserving of death under Roman law. Yet when one thief began mocking Jesus, the other responded in surprising fashion:

> "Don't you fear God, . . . since you are under the same sentence? We are punished justly, for we are getting what our deeds deserve. But this man has done nothing wrong."
>
> Then he said, "Jesus, remember me when you come into your kingdom."
>
> Jesus answered him, "I tell you the truth, today you will be with me in paradise." (Luke 23:40–43 NIV)

As we reflect on those in Slytherin House who fought on the side of good, and on the lives of biblical heroes who were once opposed to God, we see that people can change and that the story isn't over until it's over. People can change sides and change the course of their lives. They can even change in character over the course of their lives. Phineas Nigellus gives us good advice: "Let us not forget that Slytherin House played its part." As we remember that some of those who were once on the side of Voldemort and the Death Eaters helped overthrow them, we are given hope for anyone and everyone, that they might change and become useful on the side of good.

Family Trumps All

Now he could move through the Hall without interference. He spotted Ginny two tables away; she was sitting with her head on her mother's shoulder: There would be time to talk later, hours and days and maybe years in which to talk. . . . Along the aisle between the tables he walked, and he spotted the three Malfoys, huddled together as though unsure whether or not they were supposed to be there, but nobody was paying them any attention. Everywhere he looked he saw families reunited, and finally he saw the two whose company he craved most.

—Book Seven, pp. 745–46

*A*s the Harry Potter series comes to its conclusion, family takes precedence over almost everything else. There was the showdown between Bellatrix Lestrange, who had said she wished she had sons so she could sacrifice them to Voldemort, and Molly Weasley, who epitomized the loving mother. When Molly Weasley triumphed over Bellatrix Lestrange, it was a triumph for motherhood and family. Scenes of families being reunited—even the Malfoys—put the battle into the larger context of protecting one's family. Finally, there is the epilogue, "Nineteen Years Later," in which we don't learn about anyone's careers or financial standing (although there is the note pointing out that Rose Weasley was wearing *new* robes, unlike her father before her). All that earned a place in the epilogue relates to families carrying on.

The final verse of the Old Testament relates these words of the prophet Malachi: "See, I will send you the prophet Elijah before that great and dreadful day of the LORD comes. He will turn the hearts of the fathers to their children, and the hearts of the children to their fathers; or else I will come and strike the land with a curse" (Mal. 4:5–6 NIV). With this conclusion also came a word of hope for the family. Family would be central to the work of God being lived out on earth. The Harry Potter series began with a curse, but it ended with families breaking free of the curse. It ended with Harry, the orphan boy who grew up to marry Ginny and have children who were part of the Weasley family. It ended with Harry, who had never had the benefit of his godfather's care while he was growing up, being a good godfather to the orphaned boy, Teddy Lupin, who "came around for dinner four or five times a week." It ended with friends becoming family: Ron and Hermione raising their children alongside Harry and Ginny's children, even with an acknowledgment of Draco Malfoy's family. And the hearts of the fathers—Harry, Ron, and even Draco— turned toward their children.

The Sorting Hat Takes Your Choice into Account

"What if I'm in Slytherin?"

The whisper was for his father alone, and Harry knew that only the moment of departure could have forced Albus to reveal how great and sincere that fear was.

Harry crouched down so that Albus's face was slightly above his own. Alone of Harry's three children, Albus had inherited Lily's eyes.

"Albus Severus," Harry said quietly, so that nobody but Ginny could hear, and she was tactful enough to pretend to be waving to Rose, who was now on the train, "you were named after two headmasters of Hogwarts. One of them was a Slytherin and he was probably the bravest man I ever knew."

"But just say—"

"—then Slytherin House will have gained an excellent student, won't it? It doesn't matter to us, Al. But if it matters to you, you'll be able to choose Gryffindor over Slytherin. The Sorting Hat takes your choice into account."

"Really?"

"It did for me," said Harry.

He had never told any of his children that before, but he saw the wonder in Albus's face when he said it.

—Book Seven, p. 758

*T*hroughout the Harry Potter series there is an emphasis on the power of free will. "It's our choices, Harry, that show what we truly are," as Dumbledore so aptly put it. So it is no wonder that Rowling returns to this theme as the series wraps up. When eleven-year-old Harry sat on the stool as the Sorting Hat was placed on his head, he wished, "Not Slytherin, not Slytherin!" His heart longed to stay away from what he perceived as a tendency toward evil. Although Harry prefaced his advice to his own eleven-year-old son, Albus Severus Potter, with an acknowledgment of Severus Snape's Slytherin connection and his bravery, Harry also affirmed his son's aversion of perceived evil, telling him that the Sorting Hat would take his choice into account.

Both the Harry Potter stories and the Bible maintain a tension between free will and predestination. Harry was prophesied as the one who would have the power to defeat the Dark Lord, but he still had to choose to do it. The Bible speaks of predestination and free will. It says that God already knows those who are his. But Jesus also said:

> "If anyone is thirsty, let him come to me and drink. Whoever believes in me, as the Scripture has said, streams of living water will flow from within him." By this he meant the Spirit, whom those who believed in him were later to receive. Up to that time the Spirit had not been given, since Jesus had not yet been glorified. (John 7:37–39 NIV)

And the final chapter of the final book of the New Testament includes this: "The Spirit and the bride say, 'Come!' And let him who hears say, 'Come!' Whoever is thirsty, let him come; and whoever wishes, let him take the free gift of the water of life" (Rev. 22:17 NIV).

As Harry confided to his son, Albus, that the Sorting Hat would take his choice into account, I confide to you that God takes our hearts' desires and our choices into account. Even though God knows those who are his, even though he knows the end of our story better than we know the end of Harry's story, he still calls us to choose to come to him. So if you are thirsty, come to God; if you wish, come to God and take his free gift of the water of life. He takes our choices into account.

All Was Well

"He'll be all right," murmured Ginny.
As Harry looked at her, he raised his hand absentmind-
edly and touched the lightning scar on his forehead.
"I know he will."
The scar had not pained Harry for nineteen years. All
was well.

—Book Seven, p. 759

As Harry and Ginny say farewell to their boys, James and Albus, watching the Hogwarts Express round the bend, the story has come full circle. The Boy Who Lived, who survived the Killing Curse only to find a bit of the cursed one in himself, who questioned and yet followed his quest, was hit with the Killing Curse again only to find that it did not destroy him, but the evil residing in him. Harry had come to a place where he was rid of the curse. The scar that once connected him to the soul of evil had been loosed from the power of the evil one. All was well. Truly, all was well.

This is God's hope for all. It is the hope shared in the good news of God's story told in the New Testament, that we too will conquer the curse of death through the sacrifice of one who loved us so much that he willingly died in our place. This was told so that, at the end of our story, all will be well. That hope for a day when all will be well is captured in a final scene from Revelation:

> And I heard a loud voice from the throne saying, "Now the dwelling of God is with men, and he will live with them. They will be his people, and God himself will be with them and be their God. He will wipe every tear from their eyes. There will be no more death or mourning or crying or pain, for the old order of things has passed away." (Rev. 21:3–4 NIV)

I hope you have found this look at Christian and biblical themes in the Harry Potter stories rewarding. It was my privilege and enrichment to look for these themes and share those I found with you. All along I have kept my fingers crossed that Harry's story would end with good triumphing over evil, and thus my assertion of Christian themes upheld. I also hoped this approach to both Harry Potter and the Bible would spark further discussion among those who may have been prejudiced against either. Many who hold the Bible dear have been warned against the "evils" of Harry Potter. I pray that in some small way this volume will be of use to those who want to dispel such views. So please pass this book along to someone who has not yet seen the good in the Harry Potter stories. My other hope in writing this book was that those who may have been prejudiced against the Bible—perhaps from the misbehavior of some who tout it—might rethink that as well. So, as an ambassador for both the Harry Potter stories and the Bible, my wish for all of us is that we will treat each other with the kind of love and respect upheld by Albus Dumbledore and championed by the Apostle Paul in the New Testament. In closing, my hope for you and yours is that all will be well. Amen.

Notes

1. C. S. Lewis, *Reflections on the Psalms* (New York: Harcourt, Brace, Jovanovich, 1958), 99–100.

2. Nancy Gibbs, "J. K. Rowling: Harry's Done but the Best-selling Author in History Still Has Some Secrets She Can Finally Share," *Time*, December 31, 2007–January 7, 2008, 102.

3. Kurt Bruner and Jim Ware, *Finding God in Lord of the Rings* (Wheaton, IL: Tyndale House Publishers, 2001), 110.

4. From Thomas L. Martin, "Lewis: A Critical Perspective," in *Reading the Classics with C .S. Lewis,* ed. Thomas L. Martin (Grand Rapids: Baker Academic, 2000), 277. "By the year 1931, Lewis came from the idea of myth as a mere falsehood to the belief that Christianity is a 'true myth' verified by a historical 'fact,' whereas Pagan myths chiefly remain products of human imagination. Their origins are vague and mixed: 'in the huge mass of mythology which has come down to us a good many different sources are mixed—true history, allegory, ritual, the human delight in story-telling, etc. But among these sources I include the supernatural, both diabolical and divine'" ("Religion Without Dogma?" in *Undeceptions: Essays on Theology and Ethics.* [London: Geoffrey Books, 1971], 99–114). Thus, Lewis came to believe that "at its best" myth is "a real though unfocused gleam of divine truth falling on human imagination" (*Miracles: A Preliminary Study* [London: Collins, 1966]).

5. Josh McDowell, *The New Evidence That Demands a Verdict* (Nashville: Thomas Nelson, 1999); Lee Strobel, *The Case for Christ* (Grand Rapids: Zondervan, 1998); William Lane Craig, *Reasonable Faith* (Wheaton, IL: Crossway Books, 1994); J. P. Moreland, *Scaling the Secular City* (Grand Rapids: Baker Book House, 1987).

6. C. S. Lewis, *Mere Christianity* (San Francisco: HarperSanFrancisco, 2001), 52.

7. *Matthew Henry's Commentary on the Whole Bible*, new modern ed., electronic database (Peabody, MA: Hendrickson Publishers, 1991).

8. Max Wyman of the *Vancouver Sun,* October 26, 2000

9. As stated 8/4/2007 at *Prophecy 2007: From Hero to Legend Harry*

Potter Symposium in Toronto, Canada, by James W. Thomas, PhD, Professor of English at Pepperdine University, Seaver College.

10. The idea for the flames atop Neville being like pentecostal tongues of fire came from Barbara Purdom during our discussion group at Prophecy 2007 on *The Gospel according to Harry Potter and the Deathly Hallows*. Others in that discussion group offered contributions that may have influenced my writing, among them Mary Hansen and Lynsay McCaully. Thanks to all who took part.

11. Lindsay Fraser, *Conversations with J. K. Rowling* (New York: Scholastic, 2001), 30–31.

Acknowledgments

*M*y sincere appreciation goes to the following people:

Mark I. Pinsky, author of *The Gospel according to The Simpons,* sparked the idea of addressing Harry Potter in this context while interviewing me for the *Orlando Sentinel.* Thanks, Mark! Not all of my interactions with the media are as fruitful.

David Dobson, senior editor, had enthusiasm for this book from the beginning, which blossomed into a very positive collaborative effort.

John W. Morehead of Watchman Fellowship reviewed the manuscript with an eye toward any theological statements that might be perceived to fall outside the bounds of biblical orthodoxy. Hopefully his expertise, careful theological review, and the excellent reputation of the Watchman Fellowship will help some who might otherwise hesitate to fully enjoy this book.

Julie Tonini and the production team at Westminster John Knox Press did a fine job of editing. The creative process employed in this kind of writing requires the balance of good editing. Their careful work clarified my intentions and made the book far more enjoyable to read.

Dr. David George, pastor, and the community at Valley Springs Presbyterian Church provided the spiritual base our family needs to grow in our love for God as well as an appreciation for literature and the arts. The fun, enthusiastic spiritual discussions we had in our "Harry Potter Book Club and Bible Study" showed me how much there was to develop from these stories. My special thanks to **the James family (especially Charlotte, Beth, and Martha) and my daughter, Haley,** for their continued participation and encouragement.

About the Author

*C*onnie Neal is a popular author, speaker, and Bible teacher. She is sought by secular and Christian media as an expert on the intersection of Christianity and pop culture and has spoken at dozens of workshops, conferences, Christian colleges, churches, and library and literacy events. She was also a keynoter at a worldwide Harry Potter symposium.

Her books have been featured in a variety of media, including *Entertainment Weekly*, *Time Magazine*, *Newsweek*, *Christian Parenting Today*, *Christianity Today*, *USA Today*, *U.S. Catholic*, *The New York Times* (Religion Page), MSNBC.com, and *Publisher's Weekly*, among others.

Speaking inquiries: Contact Susan Yates at (714) 285-9540 or see Connie Neal's Web site: www.ConnieNeal.com

Other Books by Connie Neal Related to Harry Potter

What's a Christian to Do with Harry Potter? (Colorado Springs, CO: WaterBrook Press, 2001).

Wizards, Wardrobe, and Wookiees: Navigating Good and Evil in Harry Potter, Narnia and Star Wars (Downers Grove, IL: InterVarsity Press, 2007).